SUMMER BEFORE GRADE 3

Summer Link

MATH plus READING

American Education Publishing™
An imprint of Carson-Dellosa Publishing LLC
Greensboro, North Carolina

American Education Publishing™
An imprint of Carson-Dellosa Publishing LLC
P.O. Box 35665
Greensboro, NC 27425 USA

ISBN 978-1-60996-193-0

1 2 3 4 5 6 7 8 WCR 15 14 13 12 11

030118454

Table of Contents
by Section

Summer Link Math
Table of Contents

Summer Link Reading
Table of Contents

This page intentionally left blank.

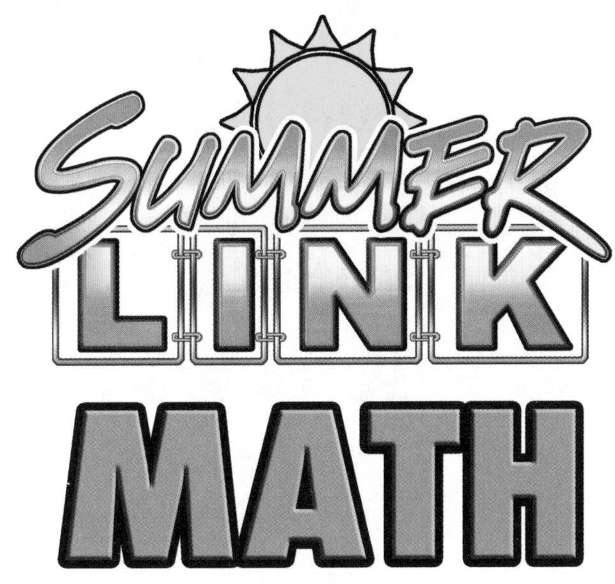
SUMMER
LINK
MATH

Name ____________________

Counting

Directions: Write the numbers that are:

next in order	one less	one greater
22, 23, ____, ____	____, 16	6, ____
674, ____, ____	____, 247	125, ____
227, ____, ____	____, 550	499, ____
199, ____, ____	____, 333	750, ____
329, ____, ____	____, 862	933, ____

Directions: Write the missing numbers.

Counting by 2's

Directions: Each basket the players make is worth 2 points. Help your team win by counting by 2's to beat the other team's score.

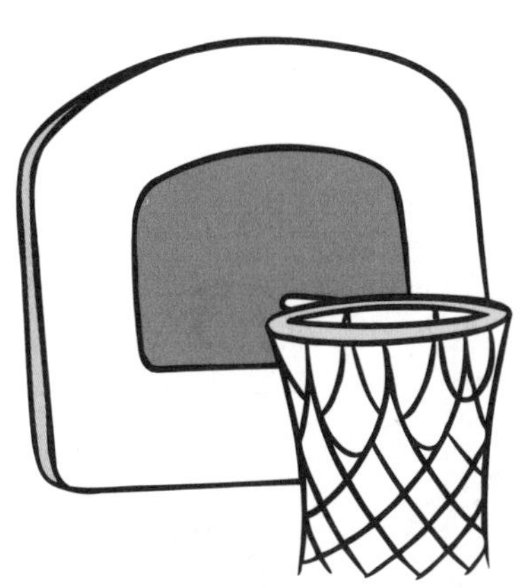

Final Score

Home	Visitor
☐	**30**

Name ____________________

Counting by 5's

Directions: Count by 5's. Color the correct number of nickels for each bag. Begin at the star.

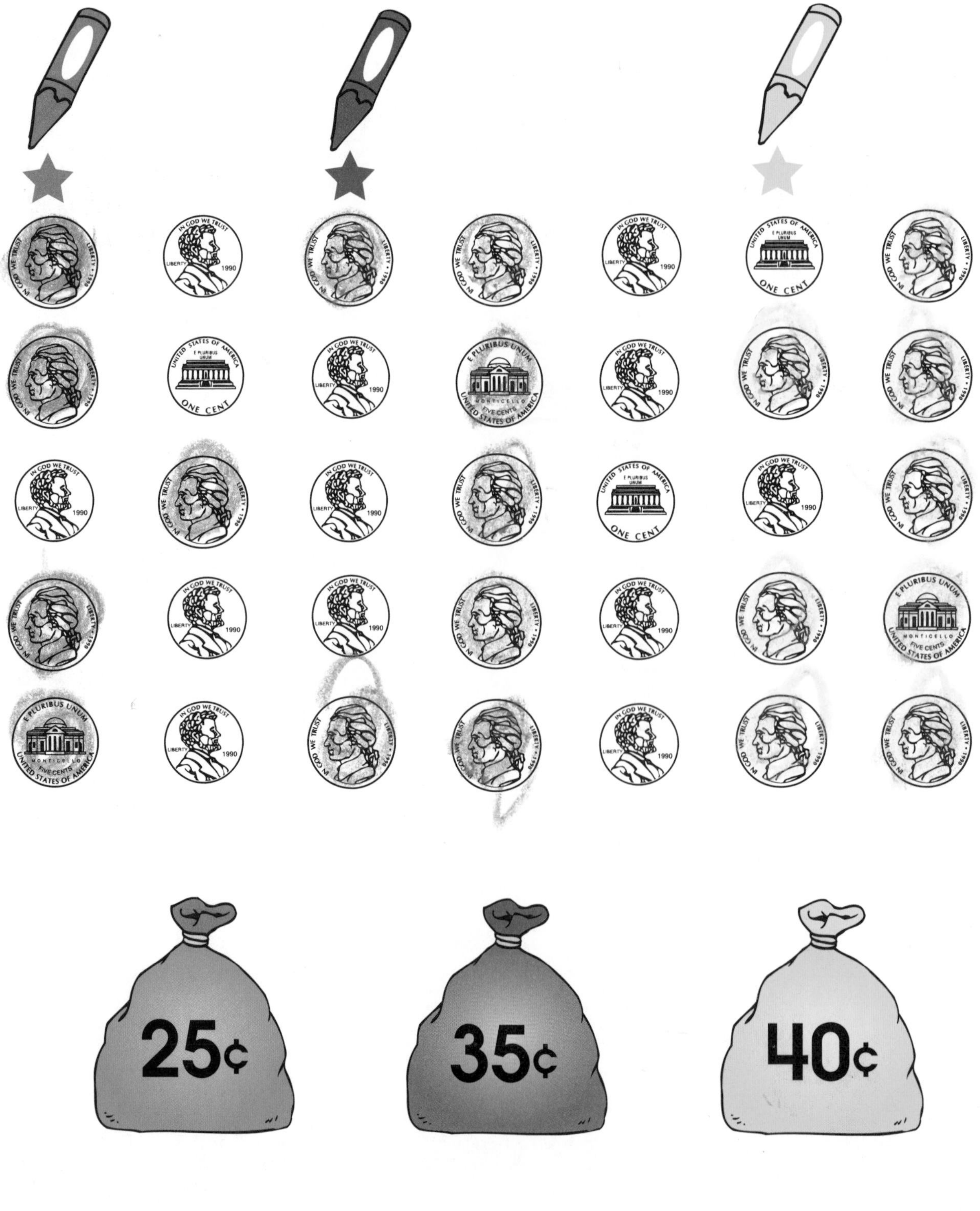

Name ______________________

Counting by 10's

Directions: Count by 10's to complete each row.

20	30	40	50	60
 50	60	70	80	90
 40	50	60	70	80
 30	40	50	60	70

Name ______________________________

Patterns

Directions: Connect the dots in each row to continue the pattern.

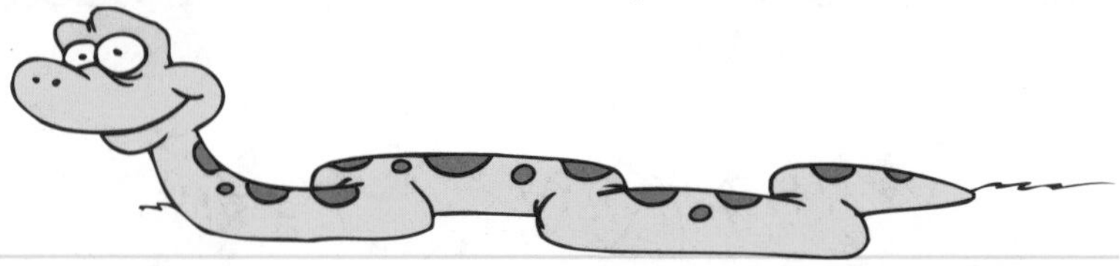

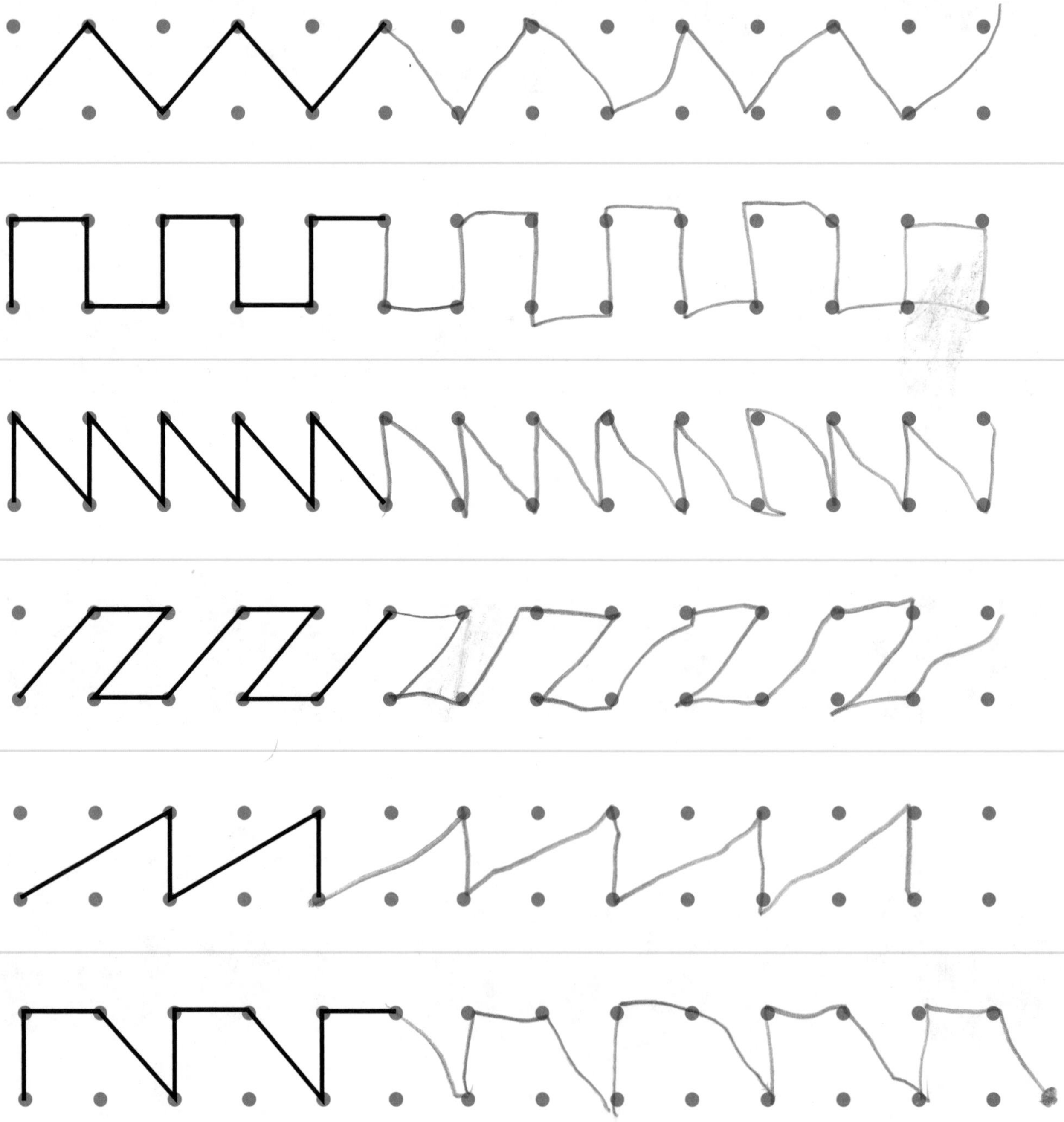

Name ____________________

Patterns

Directions: Write or draw what comes next in the pattern.

Example: 1, 2, 3, 4, 5

A, 1, B, 2, C, 3, D 4

2, 4, 6, 8, 10, 12

A, C, E, G, I, K

5, 10, 15, 20, 25, 30

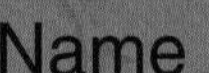

Name ______________________

Patterns

Directions: Write the one that would come next in each pattern.

0 2 0 4 0 6 ________

1 3 5 7 9 11 ________

5 10 20 40 80 ________

▽ □ ▷ ▭ ▽ □ ________

◇ □ ▽ ◇ □ ▽ ________

○ ◯ • ● ○ ◯ ________

1 A 2 B 3 C ________

A B C 1 2 3 ________

⊞ ⊞ ⊞ ⊞ ⊞ ⊞ ________

Name ______________________________

Patterns: Shapes

Directions: Complete each row by drawing the correct shape.

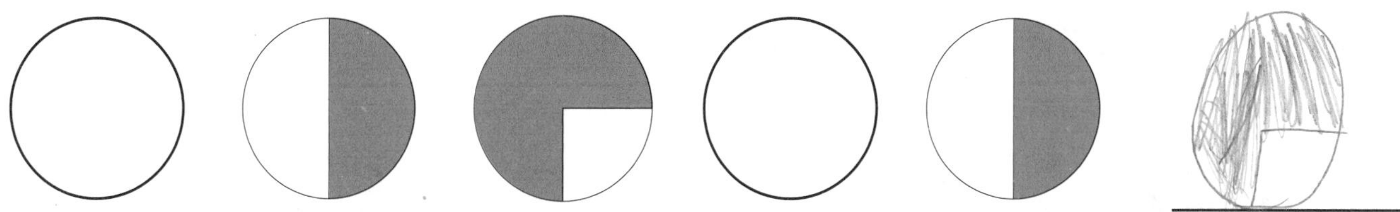

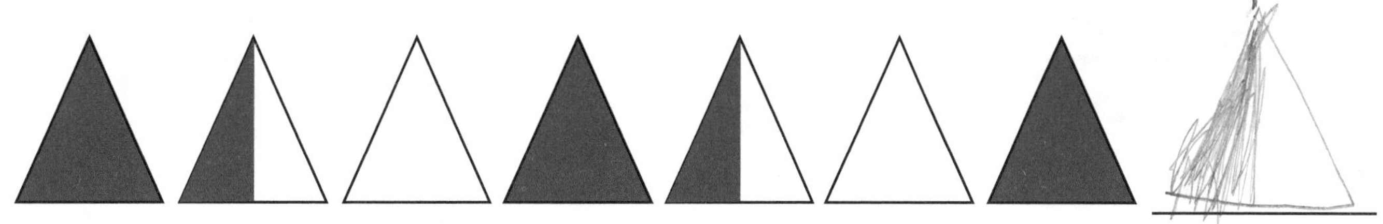

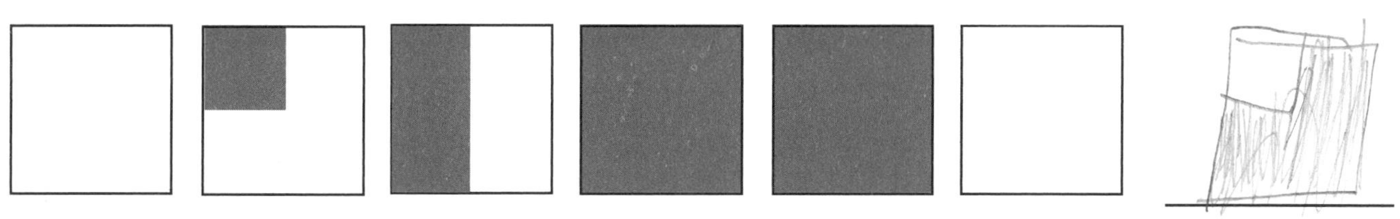

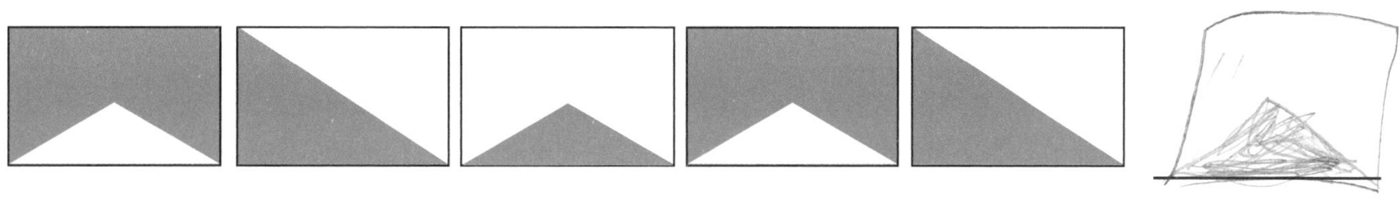

Name ____________________

Place Value: Hundreds, Tens, and Ones

The place value of a digit or numeral is shown by where it is in the number. For example, in the number **123**, **1** has the place value of **hundreds, 2** is **tens** and **3** is **ones.**

Directions: Study the examples. Then write the missing numbers in the blanks.

Examples:

  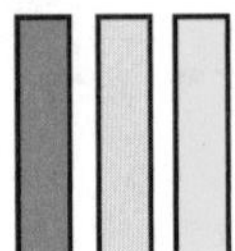 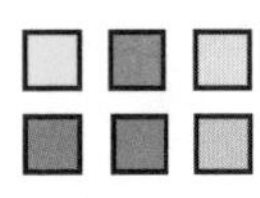

2 hundreds + 3 tens + 6 ones =

hundreds	tens	ones	
2	**3**	**6**	= 236

 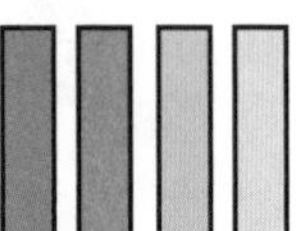 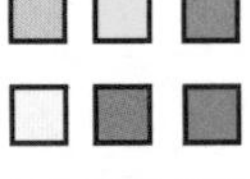

1 hundreds + 4 tens + 9 ones =

hundreds	tens	ones	
1	4	9	= 149

	hundreds	tens	ones	total
3 hundreds + 4 tens + 8 ones =	3	4	8	= 348
2 hundreds + 1 ten + 7 ones =	2	1	7	= 217
6 hundreds + 3 tens + 5 ones =	6	3	5	= 635
4 hundreds + 7 tens + 9 ones =	4	7	9	= 479
2 hundreds + 9 tens + 4 ones =	2	9	4	= 294
4 hundreds + 5 tens + 6 ones =	4	5	6	= 456
3 hundreds + 1 ten + 3 ones =	3	1	3	= 313
3 hundreds + 5 tens + 7 ones =	3	5	7	= 357
6 hundreds + 2 tens + 8 ones =	6	2	8	= 628

Name ________________________________

Addition: 2-Digit

Directions: Study the example. Follow the steps to add.

Example: 33
+41

Step 1: Add the ones.

tens	ones
3	3
+4	1
	4

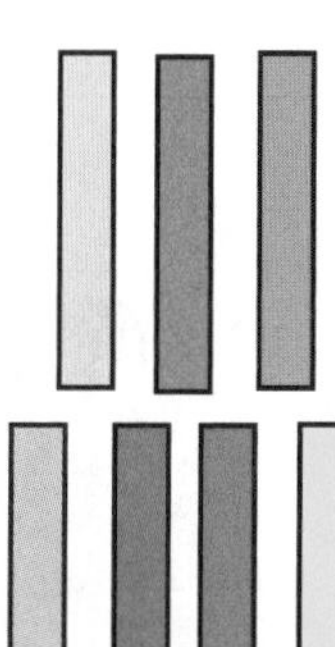

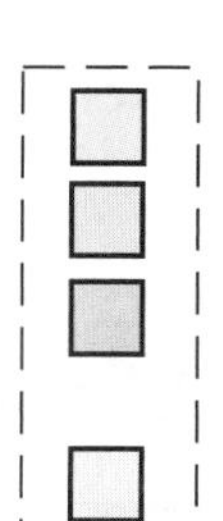

Step 2: Add the tens.

tens	ones
3	3
+4	1
7	4

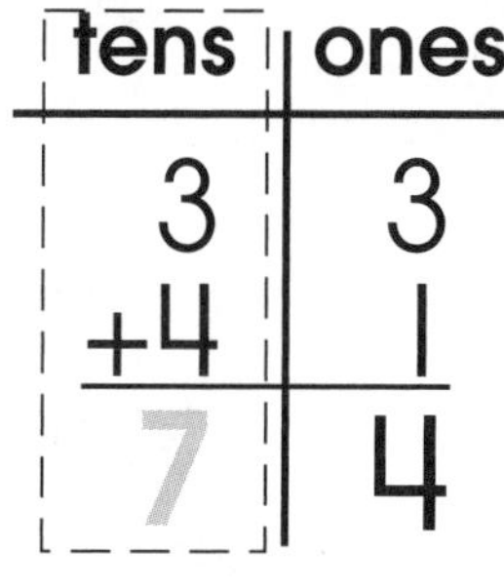

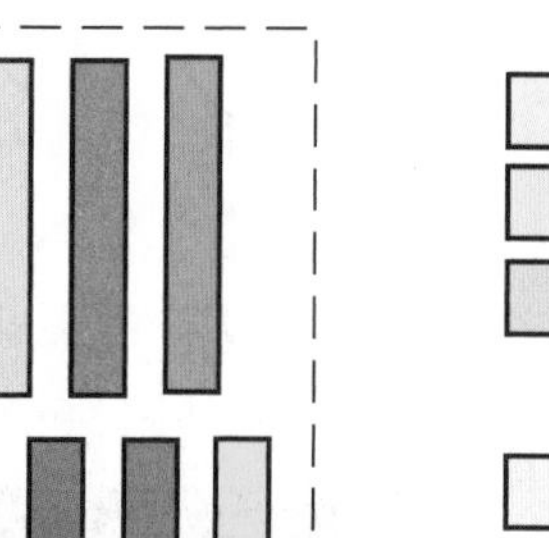

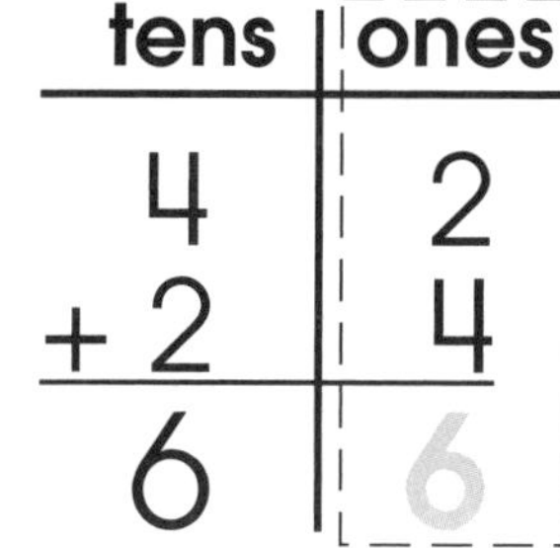

tens	ones
4	2
+2	4
6	6

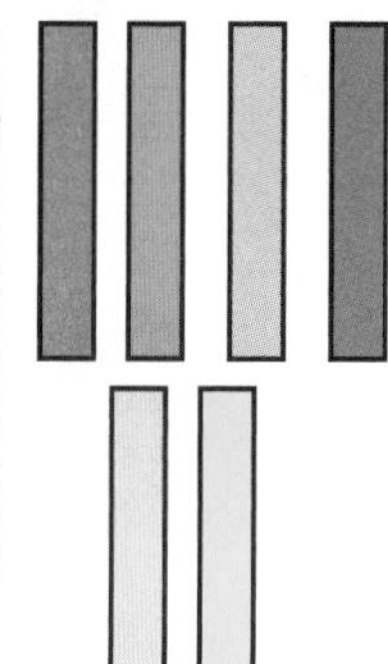

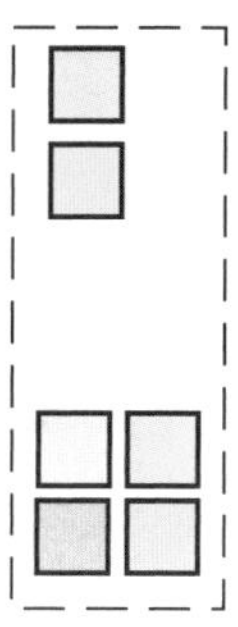

tens	ones
5	0
+4	7
9	7

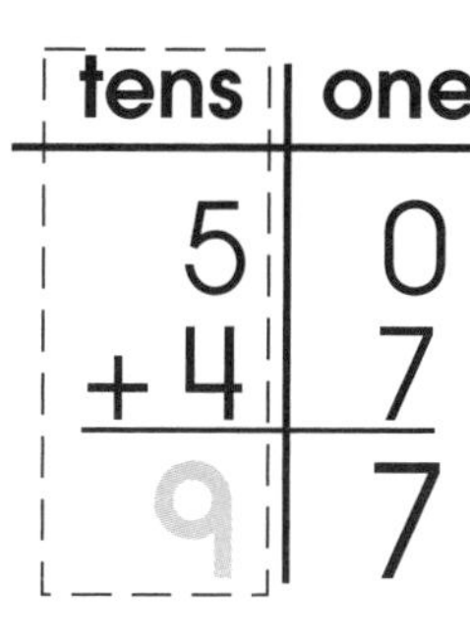

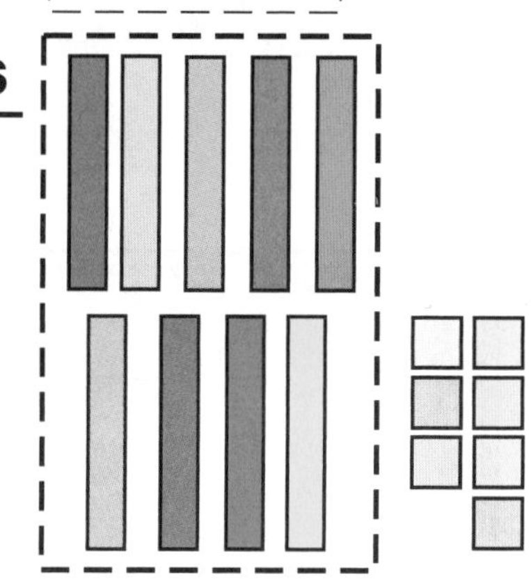

24	15	38	11	37	72	33	10
+62	+23	+61	+26	+42	+11	+51	+30

25	62	32	25	82	91	16	55
+42	+14	+44	+13	+ 6	+ 5	+71	+ 3

Addition: 2-Digit

Directions: Add the total points scored in each game. Remember to add **ones** first and **tens** second.

Example:

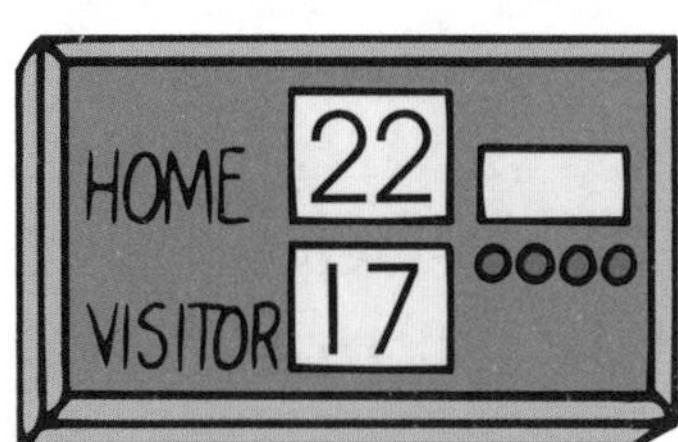

Total 39

Total 58

Total 76

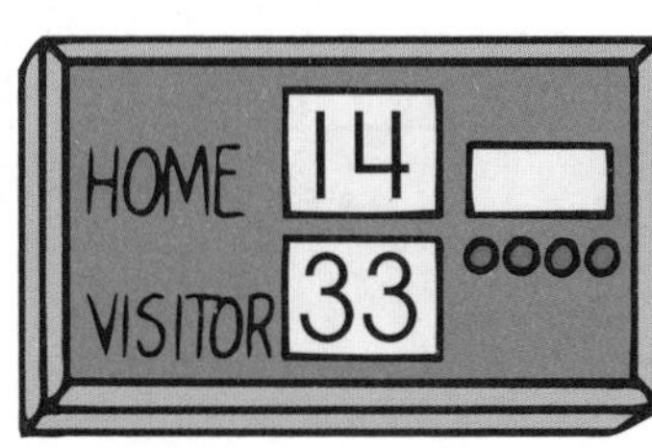

Total 47

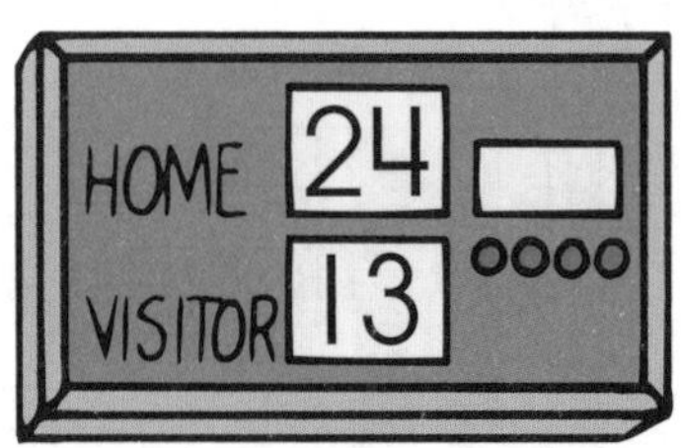

Total 37

Total 78

Total 89

Total 50

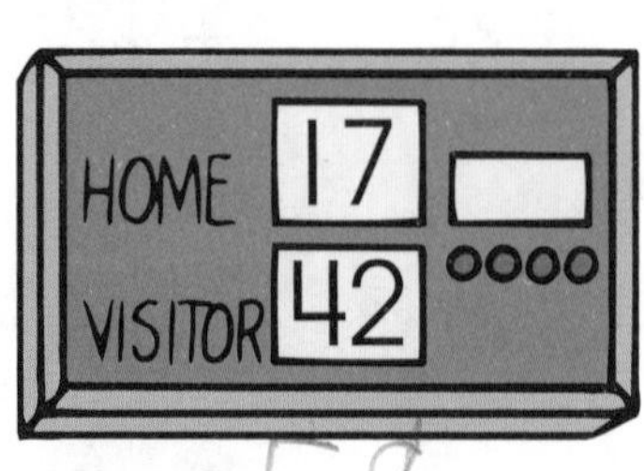

Total 59

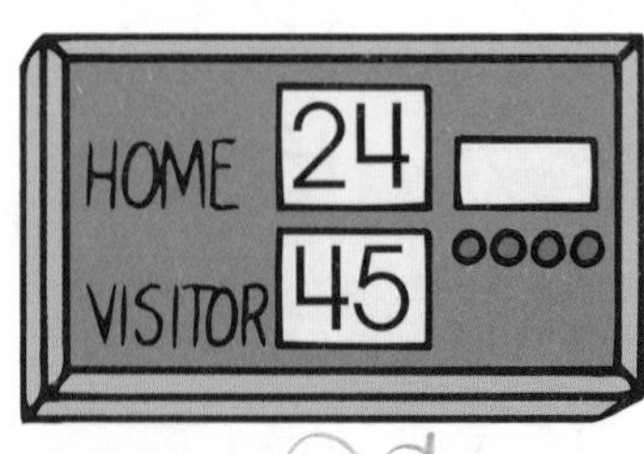

Total 69

Name ____________________________

Addition: Raccoon Roundup

Directions: Solve the addition problems. Write your answers inside the ropes.

$$\begin{array}{r} 26 \\ +\,43 \\ \hline 69 \end{array}$$

$$\begin{array}{r} 43 \\ +\,31 \\ \hline 74 \end{array}$$

$$\begin{array}{r} 34 \\ +\,10 \\ \hline 44 \end{array}$$

$$\begin{array}{r} 48 \\ +\,20 \\ \hline 68 \end{array}$$

$$\begin{array}{r} 57 \\ +\,20 \\ \hline 77 \end{array}$$

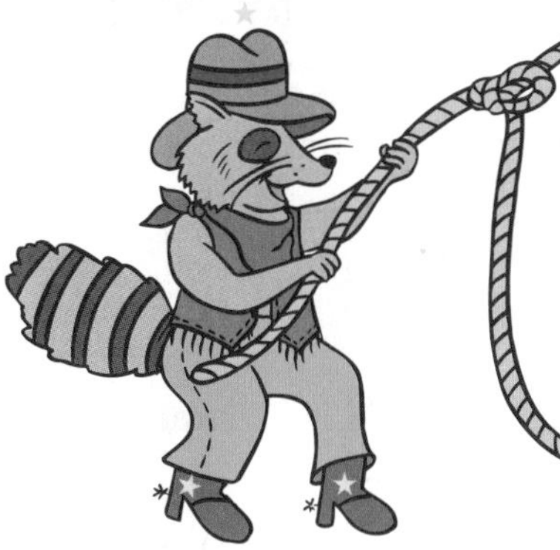

$$\begin{array}{r} 52 \\ +\,34 \\ \hline 86 \end{array}$$

$$\begin{array}{r} 43 \\ +\,55 \\ \hline 98 \end{array}$$

$$\begin{array}{r} 67 \\ +\,22 \\ \hline 89 \end{array}$$

Name ______________________________

2-Digit Addition: Regrouping

Addition is "putting together" or adding two or more numbers to find the sum. Regrouping is using **ten ones** to form **one ten, ten tens** to form **one 100, fifteen ones** to form **one ten** and **five ones** and so on.

Directions: Study the examples. Follow the steps to add.

Example:

$$\begin{array}{r} 14 \\ +\ 8 \\ \hline \end{array}$$

Step 1: Add the ones.

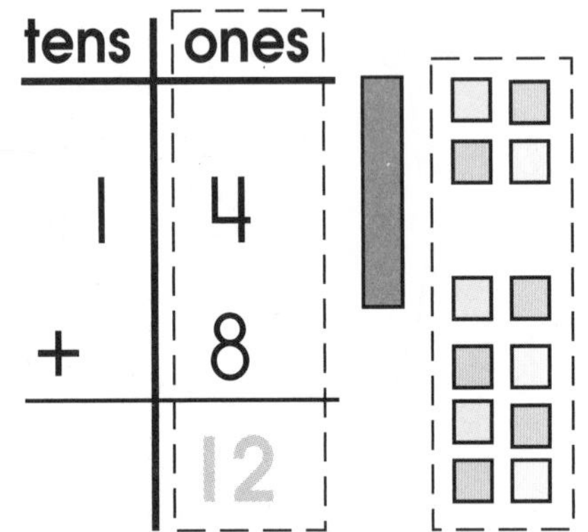

Step 2: Regroup the tens.

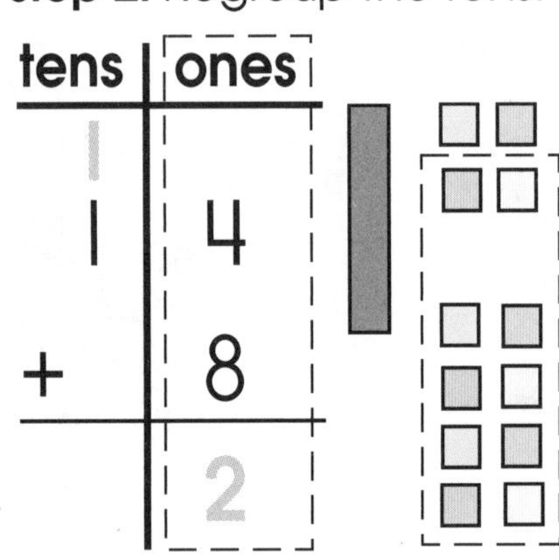

Step 3: Add the tens.

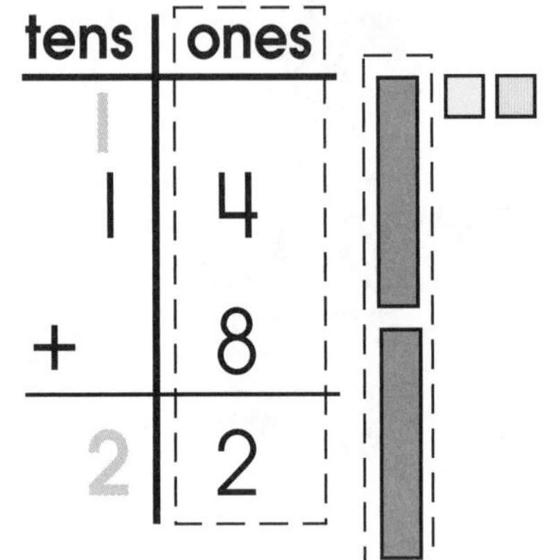

tens	ones
1	
1	6
+3	7
5	3

tens	ones
1	
3	8
+5	3
9	1

tens	ones
1	
2	4
+4	7
7	1

28	32	54	19	44	25	29	79
+17	+38	+25	+55	+48	+64	+33	+15
45	70	79	74	92	89	62	94

Name ____________________

Addition: Just Like Magic

Directions:
Add.

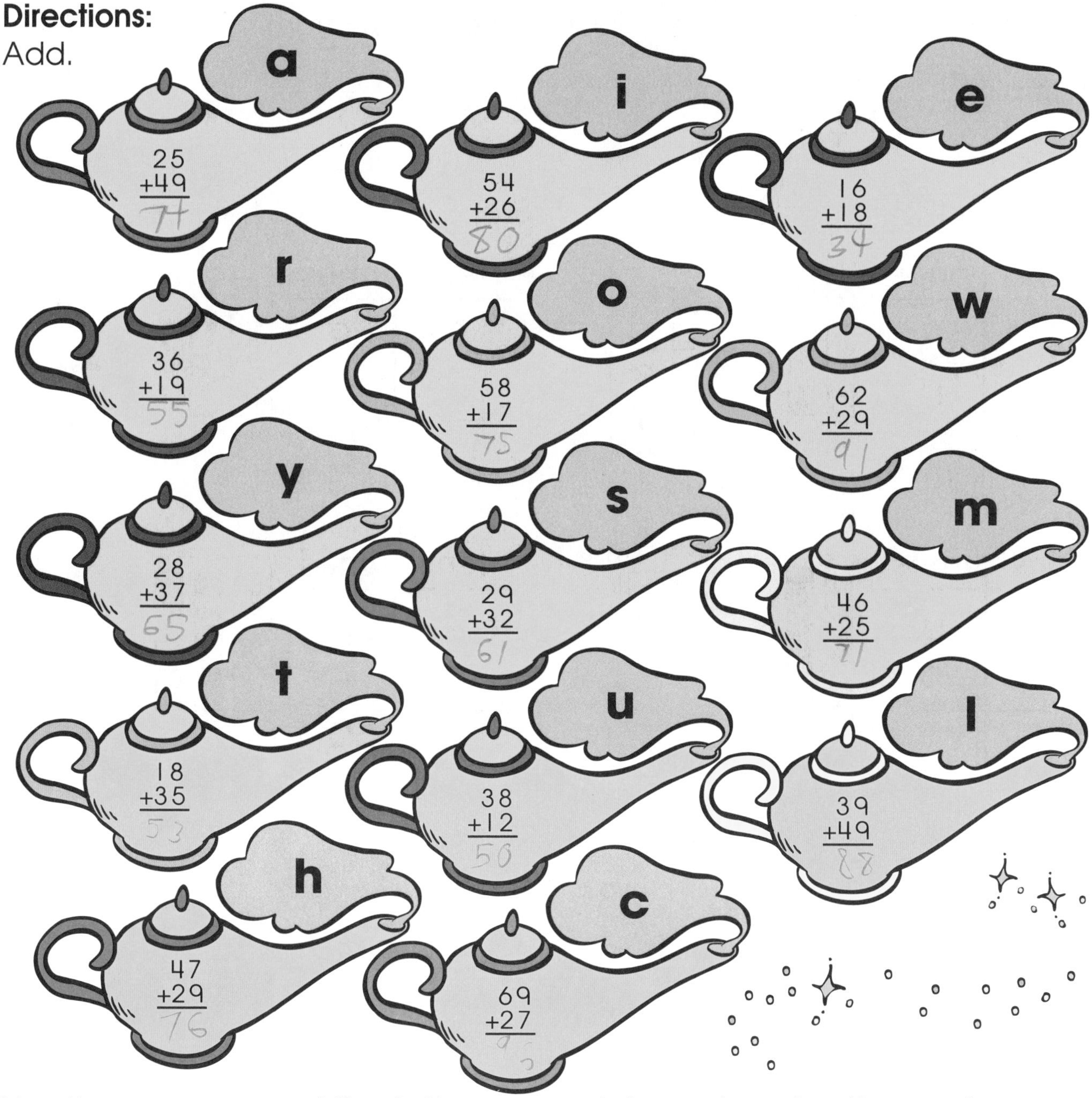

a	25 + 49
i	54 + 26
e	16 + 18
r	36 + 19
o	58 + 17
w	62 + 29
y	28 + 37
s	29 + 32
m	46 + 25
t	18 + 35
u	38 + 12
l	39 + 49
h	47 + 29
c	69 + 27

Use the answers and the letter on each lamp to solve the code.

___ ___ ___   ___ ___ ___   ___ ___ ___ ___
71 74 65   74 88 88   65 75 50 55

___ ___ ___ ___ ___ ___   ___ ___ ___ ___   ___ ___ ___ ___!
91 80 61 76 34 61   96 75 71 34   53 55 50 34

Name ____________________

Subtraction: 2-Digit

Directions: Study the example. Follow the steps to subtract.

Example:

$$\begin{array}{r} 28 \\ -14 \\ \hline \end{array}$$

Step 1: Subtract the ones.

tens	ones
2	8
-1	4
	4

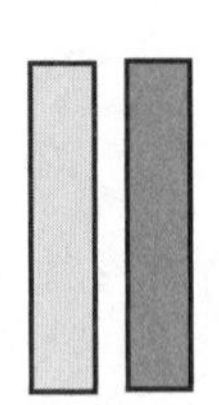

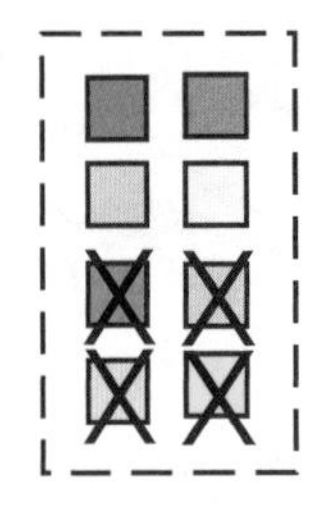

tens	ones
2	4
-1	2
1	2

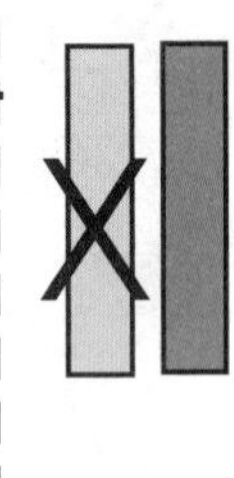

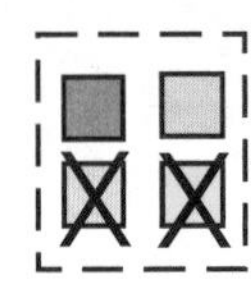

Step 2: Subtract the tens.

tens	ones
2	8
-1	4
1	4

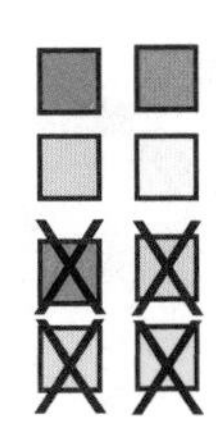

tens	ones
3	8
-1	5
2	3

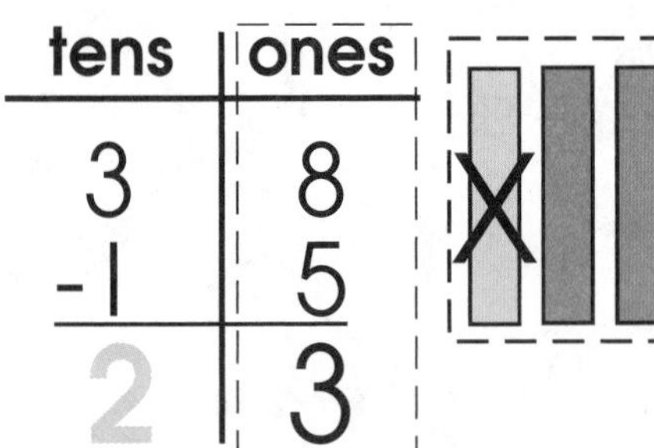

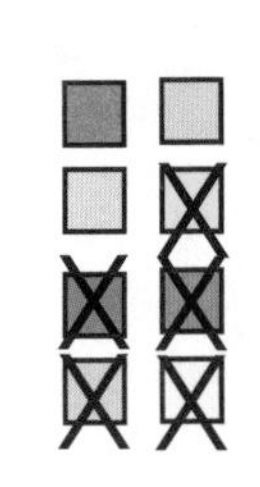

24	61	77	85	57	87	59	96
− 12	− 30	− 44	− 24	− 23	− 33	− 34	− 16
12	31	33	61	34	54	25	80

29	74	46	69	95	33	78	22
− 15	− 51	− 32	− 35	− 32	− 33	− 26	− 11
14	23	14	34	63	0	52	11

Name ____________________

Subtraction: Cookie Craze!

Subtract to solve the problems. Circle the answers. Color the cookies with answers greater than 30.

$$\begin{array}{r} 49 \\ -\ 23 \\ \hline \end{array}$$

16 26 25

$$\begin{array}{r} 67 \\ -\ 41 \\ \hline \end{array}$$

26 15 62

$$\begin{array}{r} 58 \\ -\ 37 \\ \hline \end{array}$$

81 11 21

$$\begin{array}{r} 75 \\ -\ 50 \\ \hline \end{array}$$

20 25 35

$$\begin{array}{r} 86 \\ -\ 21 \\ \hline \end{array}$$

67 86 65

$$\begin{array}{r} 64 \\ -\ 52 \\ \hline \end{array}$$

12 26 16

$$\begin{array}{r} 97 \\ -\ 65 \\ \hline \end{array}$$

31 33 32

$$\begin{array}{r} 77 \\ -\ 43 \\ \hline \end{array}$$

34 43 39

$$\begin{array}{r} 49 \\ -\ 13 \\ \hline \end{array}$$

56 36 37

Name ______________________________

Subtraction: Prehistoric Problems

Directions: Solve the subtraction problems. Use the code to color the picture.

Code:

25 — blue	57 — green
31 — yellow	14 — orange
21 — brown	11 — red

52
− 21

47
− 22

25
− 11

62
− 31

77
− 20

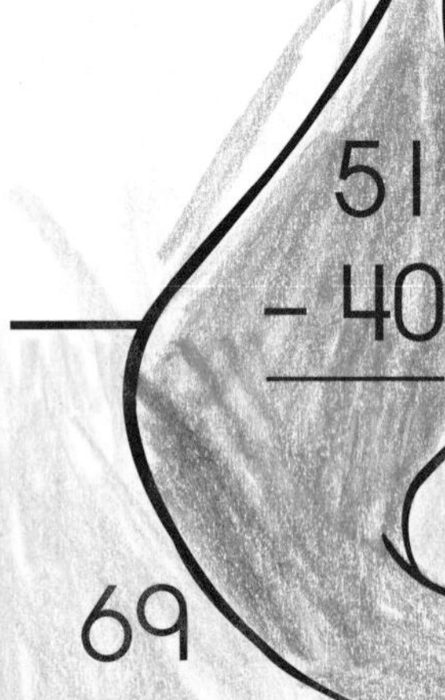

51
− 40

55
− 34

69
− 12

98
− 41

Subtraction

Subtraction means "taking away" or subtracting one number from another t find the difference. For example, 10 – 3 = 7.

Directions: Subtract.

Example:

Subtract the ones.	Subtract the tens.
39 -24 5	39 -24 15

48 -35	95 -22	87 -16	55 -43
37 -14	69 -57	44 -23	99 -78

66 - 44 = ______

57 - 33 = ______

The yellow car traveled 87 miles per hour. The orange car traveled 66 miles per hour.
How much faster was the yellow car traveling? ______

Name ______________________________

2-Digit Subtraction: Regrouping

Subtraction is "taking away" or subtracting one number from another to find the difference. Regrouping is using **one ten** to form **ten ones, one 100** to form **ten tens** and so on.

Directions: Study the examples. Follow the steps to subtract.

Example:

$$\begin{array}{r} 37 \\ -19 \\ \hline \end{array}$$

Step 1: Regroup.

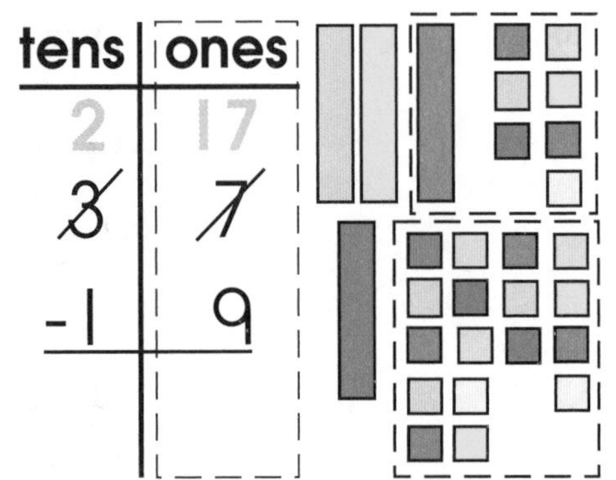

Step 2: Subtract the ones.

tens	ones
2	17
~~3~~	~~7~~
-1	9
	8

Step 3: Subtract the tens

tens	ones
2	17
~~3~~	~~7~~
-1	9
1	8

tens	ones
0	12
~~1~~	~~2~~
-	9
	3

tens	ones
2	14
~~3~~	~~4~~
-1	6
1	8

tens	ones
3	15
~~4~~	~~5~~
-2	9
1	6

28	46	12	30	52	47	21	45
− 19	− 18	− 8	− 12	− 25	− 35	− 13	− 25
9	28	4	18	27	12	8	20

Name ______________________

Subtraction: Just Like Magic...Again

Directions:
Subtract.

- **i**: 90 − 24
- **a**: 52 − 15
- **r**: 52 − 19
- **o**: 98 − 59
- **w**: 43 − 29
- **y**: 95 − 37
- **s**: 80 − 8
- **m**: 73 − 26
- **n**: 82 − 28
- **u**: 93 − 48
- **d**: 52 − 26
- **h**: 57 − 29
- **c**: 81 − 38

Use the answers and the letter on each lamp to solve the code.

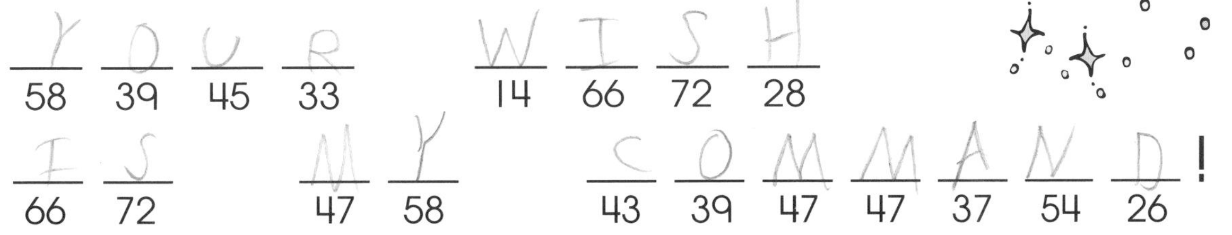

__ __ __ __   __ __ __ __
58 39 45 33   14 66 72 28

__ __   __ __   __ __ __ __ __ __ __ !
66 72   47 58   43 39 47 47 37 54 26

Name ______________________

Subtraction on the Beach

Directions: Subtract to find the difference. Regroup as needed. Color the spaces with differences of:

10 — 19 red	20 — 29 blue	30 — 39 green
40 — 49 yellow	50 — 59 brown	60 — 69 orange

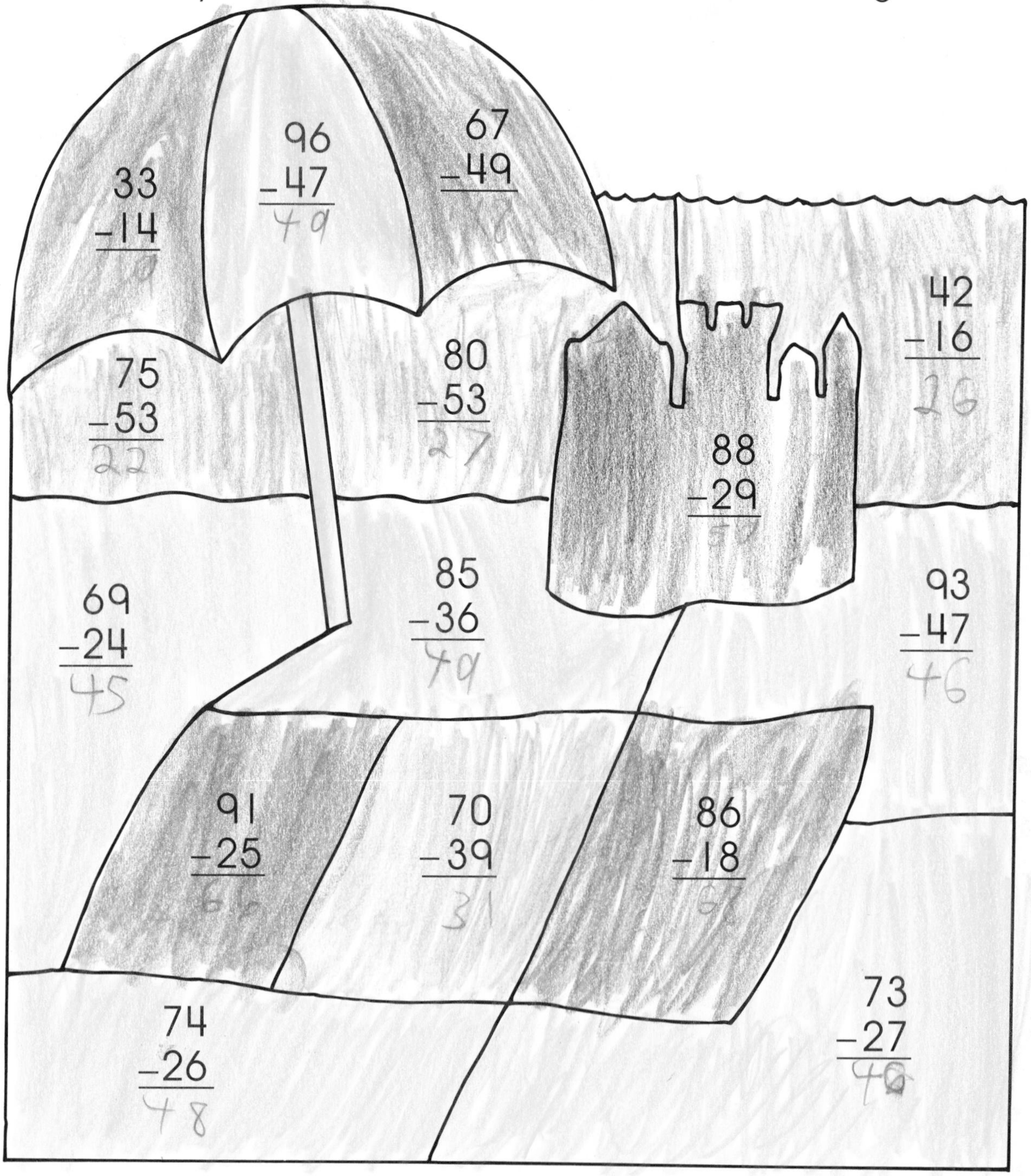

33 − 14

96 − 47

67 − 49

75 − 53

80 − 53

42 − 16

88 − 29

69 − 24

85 − 36

93 − 47

91 − 25

70 − 39

86 − 18

74 − 26

73 − 27

Monster Math

Directions: Add or subtract using regrouping.

84
− 56
28

41
− 17
24

52
− 28
24

84
− 27
57

57
− 39
28

72
− 19
53

33
− 15
18

64
+ 17
81

36
− 19
17

65
− 28
37

48
− 30
18

33
+ 18
51

25
+ 35
60

Name ____________________

2-Digit Addition and Subtraction

Addition is "putting together" or adding two or more numbers to find the sum. Subtraction is "taking away" or subtracting one number from another to find the difference. Regrouping is using **one ten** to form **ten ones**, **one** 100 to form **ten tens**, and so on.

Directions: Add or subtract using regrouping.

Example:

tens	ones
2	15
~~3~~	5
-2	7
	8

56	40	35	42	53	97	44	93
− 27	− 16	+ 27	− 14	+38	− 48	+ 27	− 39
29	24	62	28	91	49	71	54

56	44	68	73	33	49	77	27
− 17	+ 28	− 49	− 24	+ 18	+ 32	− 68	+ 19
39	72	19	49	51	81	9	46

Name ____________________

2-Digit Addition and Subtraction

Directions: Add or subtract using regrouping.

23 +48 71	84 –56 28	69 +29 98	41 –17 24
52 –28 24	73 +18 91	84 –27 57	57 –39 18
33 –15 18	64 +17 81	37 +58 95	36 –19 17
65 –28 37	48 –30 18	33 +18 51	25 +35 60

Name ___________________________

Addition: 3-Digit

Directions: Solve the addition problems. Use the code to color the picture.

Code: 456 — brown 645 — yellow
564 — blue 654 — purple

233 + 223 =

345 + 111 =

$$\begin{array}{r} 332 \\ +\ 232 \\ \hline \end{array}$$

$$\begin{array}{r} 464 \\ +\ 100 \\ \hline \end{array}$$

$$\begin{array}{r} 323 \\ +\ 322 \\ \hline \end{array}$$

$$\begin{array}{r} 444 \\ +\ 201 \\ \hline \end{array}$$

600 + 54 =

322 + 332 =

411 + 243 =

541 + 113 =

$$\begin{array}{r} 510 \\ +\ 135 \\ \hline \end{array}$$

$$\begin{array}{r} 635 \\ +\ 10 \\ \hline \end{array}$$

$$\begin{array}{r} 524 \\ +\ 40 \\ \hline \end{array}$$

$$\begin{array}{r} 243 \\ +\ 321 \\ \hline \end{array}$$

444 + 12 =

326 + 130 =

Name ____________________

3-Digit Addition: Regrouping

Directions: Study the example. Follow the steps to add. Regroup when needed.

Step 1: Add the ones.
Step 2: Add the tens.
Step 3: Add the hundreds.

hundreds	tens	ones
1	1	
3	4	8
+4	5	4
8	0	2

348	172	575	623	369	733
+214	+418	+329	+268	+533	+229

411	423	639	624	272	393
+299	+169	+177	+368	+469	+418

Name ______________________

3-Digit Subtraction: Regrouping

Directions: Subtract. Circle the 7's that appear in the **tens** place.

7 14
1~~8~~4
−129
55

358 −238	765 −326	584 −435	693 −314	921 −362
128 −109	744 −674	835 −217	248 −199	635 −428

Name ______________________

Problem-Solving: Addition, Subtraction

Directions: Read and solve each problem. The first one is done for you.

The clown started the day with 200 balloons. He gave away 128 of them. Some broke. At the end of the day, he had 18 balloons left. How many of the balloons broke? 54

On Monday, there were 925 tickets sold to adults and 1,412 tickets sold to children. How many more children attended the fair than adults? ________

At one game booth, prizes were given out for scoring 500 points in three attempts. Sally scored 178 points on her first attempt, 149 points on her second attempt, and 233 points on her third attempt. Did Sally win a prize? ________

The prize-winning steer weighed 2,348 pounds. The runner-up steer weighed 2,179 pounds. How much more did the prize steer weigh? ________

There were 3,418 people at the fair on Tuesday, and 2,294 people on Wednesday. What was the total number of people there for the two days? ________

Ordinal Numbers

Ordinal numbers indicate order in a series, such as **first**, **second**, or **third**.

Directions: Follow the instructions to color the train cars. The first car is the engine.

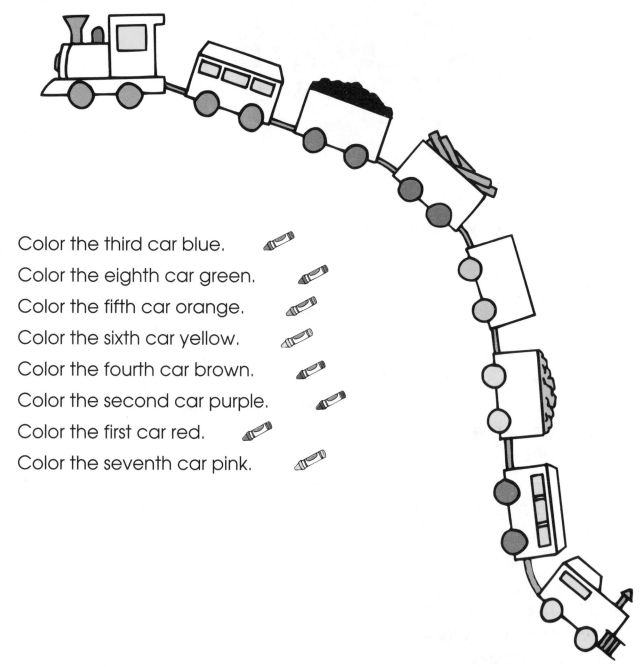

Color the third car blue.

Color the eighth car green.

Color the fifth car orange.

Color the sixth car yellow.

Color the fourth car brown.

Color the second car purple.

Color the first car red.

Color the seventh car pink.

Graphs

A graph is a chart that shows information about numbers.

Directions: Count the bananas in each row. Color the boxes to show how many have been eaten by the monkeys.

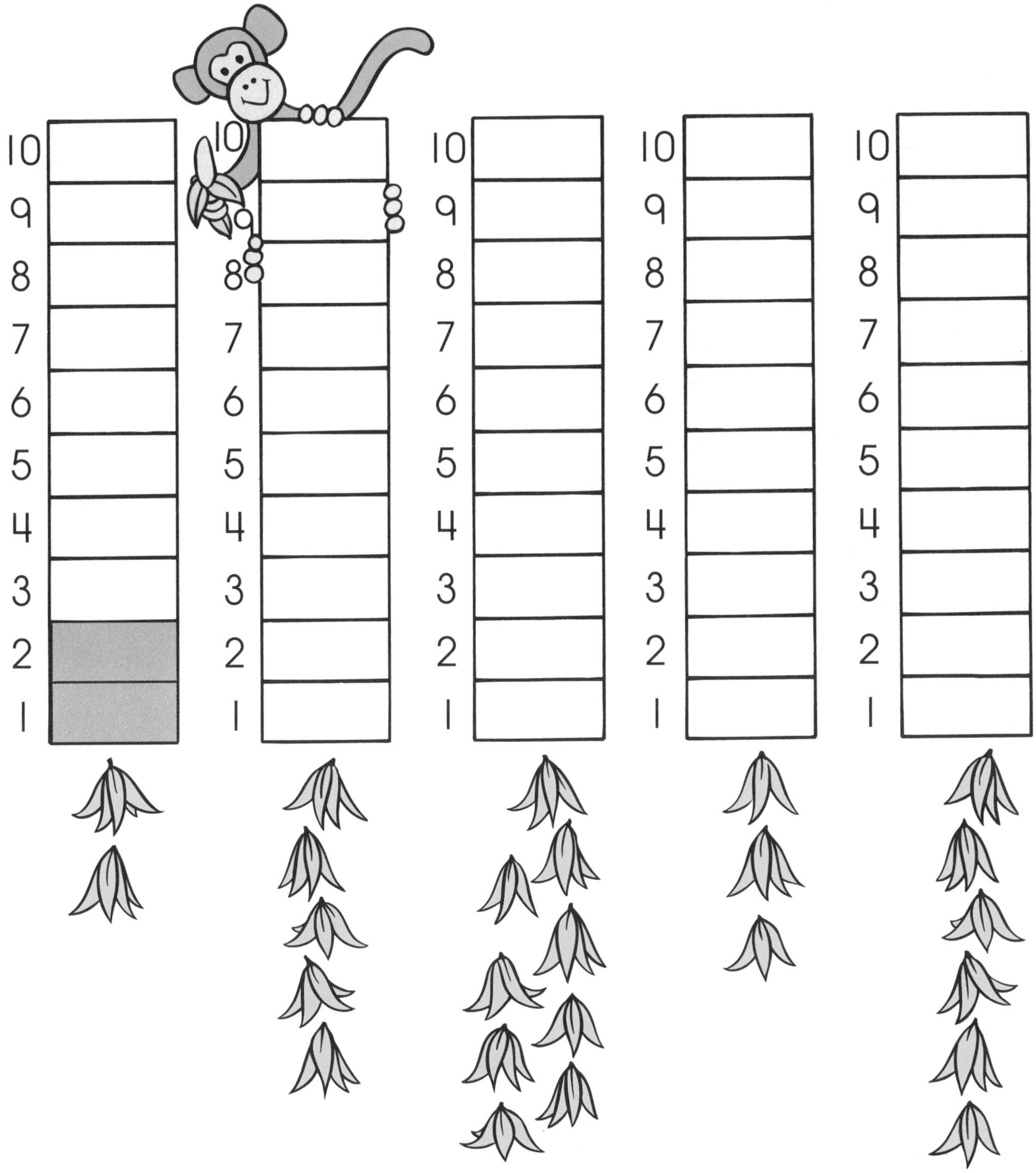

10	10	10	10	10
9	9	9	9	9
8	8	8	8	8
7	7	7	7	7
6	6	6	6	6
5	5	5	5	5
4	4	4	4	4
3	3	3	3	3
2	2	2	2	2
1	1	1	1	1

Name ____________________

Graphs

Directions: Answer the questions.

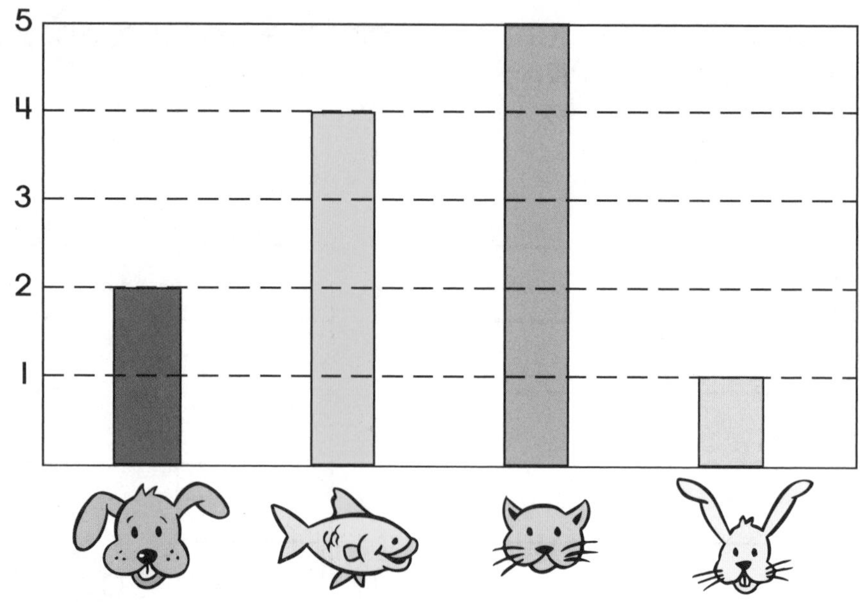

Which animal is there the most of? ____________

Which animal is there the fewest of? ____________

How many animals altogether? ____________

Measurements

Directions: Answer the questions.
What unit of measure would you use to measure...

Example: ...a cow? pound

...a mouse? ____________

...length of a pencil? ____________

...length of a semi-truck? ____________

...length of a river? ____________

...width of a river? ____________

...height of a flag pole? ____________

Name ____________________

Graphs

Directions: Use the chart to help you answer the questions below. Then, graph your results by coloring in the circles for each ball.

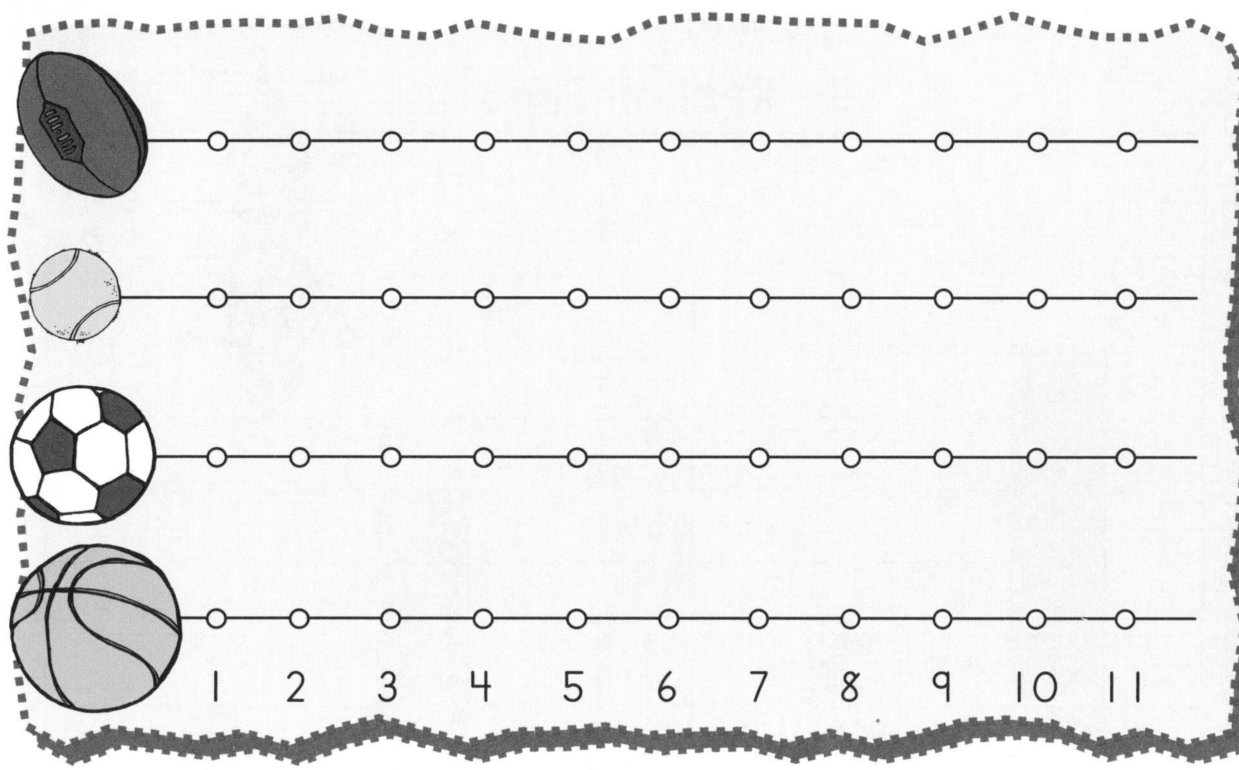

How many did you find?

_____ footballs _____ soccer balls _____ tennis balls _____ basketballs

Name ______________________

Graphs

Directions: Answer the questions about the graph.

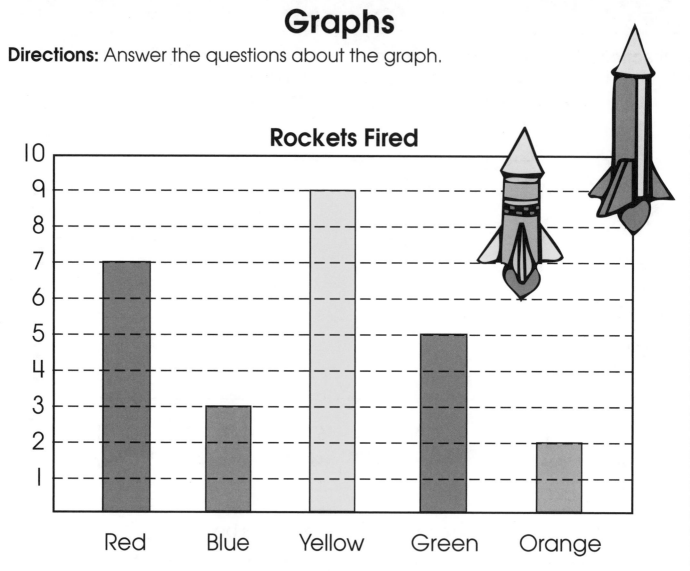

Rockets Fired

Club	Rockets Fired
Red	7
Blue	3
Yellow	9
Green	5
Orange	2

How many rockets did the Red Club fire? ____________

How many rockets did the Green Club fire? ____________

The Yellow Club fired 9 rockets. How many more rockets did it fire than the Blue Club? ____________

How many rockets were fired in all? ____________

Name ______________________________

Graphs

Directions: A very simple type of code is called a **grid**. Simply use the coordinates of the letters to solve the riddle. For example, the letter **A** would be **A1**, and **B** would be **A2**. Use the coordinates to discover what baseball great, Yogi Berra, said about the game.

	1	2	3	4	5
A	A	B	C	D	E
B	F	G	H	I	K
C	L	M	N	O	P
D	Q	R	S	T	U
E	V	W	X	Y	Z

___ ___   ___ ___ ___ ___,   ___ ___ ___ ___,
B4 D4   A1 B4 C3 D4   C4 E1 A5 D2

___' ___ ___ ___   ___ ___' ___   ___ ___ ___ ___.
D4 B4 C1 C1   B4 D4 D3   C4 E1 A5 D2

Name ______________________________

Graphs

Directions: Use the pictograph of the World Cup champions to answer the questions below.

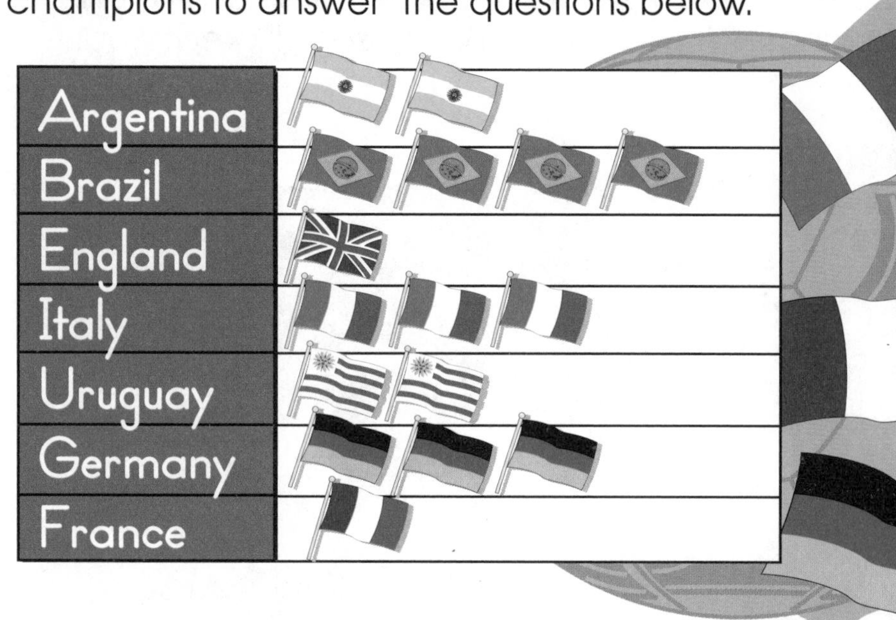

1. Which country won the most World Cups? ______________________

2. Which countries won the fewest? ______________________________

3. How many more World Cups did Brazil win than England? __________

4. Which two teams are tied for second place in number of championships? ______________________________________

5. What is the total number of World Cup championships played? ______

6. Brazil won the 1994 World Cup Championship. Before 1994, which three teams were tied for the most championships? __________________

____

7. Which teams are from South America? ________________________

____

8. How many championships were won by South American teams? _____

Name ____________________

Greater Than, Less Than

Directions: Write < or > in each circle. Make sure the "mouth" is open toward the greater number!

36 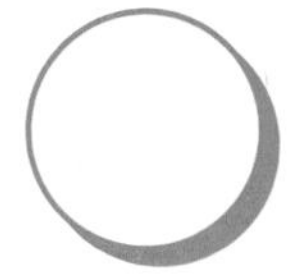 49

35  53

20  18

74  21

53  76

68  80

29  26

45  19

90  89

70  67

Greater Than, Less Than

Directions: Circle the numbers in each line that make the sentence correct.

3	<	0	1	2	3	4	5	6	7	8	9	10
7	>	0	1	2	3	4	5	6	7	8	9	10
4	=	0	1	2	3	4	5	6	7	8	9	10
8	<	0	1	2	3	4	5	6	7	8	9	10
2	>	0	1	2	3	4	5	6	7	8	9	10
5	<	0	1	2	3	4	5	6	7	8	9	10
10	>	9	5	4								
1	>	9	4	0								
0	<	2	7	10								
9	=	4	8	9								

Name ______________________________

Multiplication

Multiplication is a short way to find the sum of adding the same number a certain amount of times. For example, 7 x 4 = 28 instead of 7 + 7 + 7 + 7 = 28.

Directions: Study the example. Solve the problems.

Example:

3 + 3 + 3 = 9
3 threes = 9
3 x 3 = 9

7 + 7 = 14
2 sevens = 14
2 x 7 = 14

4 + 4 + 4 + 4 = ____
4 fours = ____
4 x ____ = ____

5 + 5 = ____
2 fives = ____
2 x ____ = ____

2 + 2 + 2 + 2 = ____
4 twos = ____
4 x ____ = ____

6 + 6 = ____
2 sixes = ____
2 x ____ = ____

Name ______________________

Multiplication

Multiplication is repeated addition.

Directions: Draw a picture for each problem. Then write the missing numbers.

Example: Draw 2 groups of three apples. 3 + 3 = 6

or 2 x 3 = 6

Draw 3 groups of four hearts.

4 + 4 + 4 = ______

or 3 x ______ = ______

Draw 2 groups of five boxes.

5 + ______ = ______

or 2 x ______ = ______

Draw 6 groups of two circles.

2 + ____ + ____ + ____ + ____ + ____ = ____

or 6 x ____ = ____

Draw 7 groups of three triangles.

3 + ____ + ____ + ____ + ____ + ____ + ____ = ____

or ____ x ____ = ____

SUMMER
LINK

Name ______________________

Multiplication

Directions: Solve the problems.

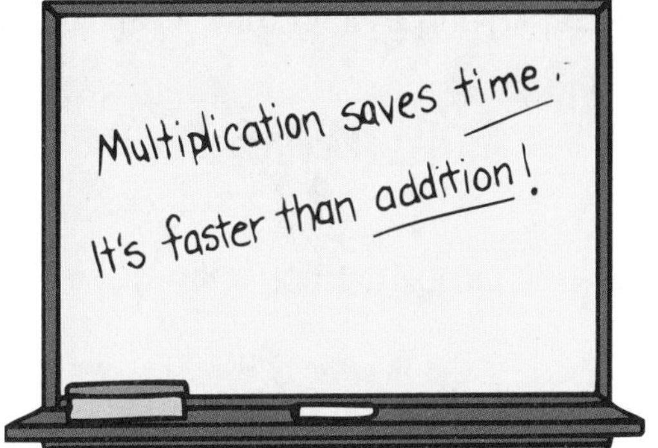
Multiplication saves time.
It's faster than addition!

9 + 9 = 18   7 + 7 = ______

2 nines = ______   2 sevens = ______

2 x 9 = ______   2 x 7 = ______

4 + 4 + 4 + 4 = ______   8 + 8 + 8 + 8 + 8 = ______

4 fours = ______   ______ eights = ______

______ x 4 = ______   ______ x 8 = ______

5 + 5 + 5 = ______   9 + 9 = ______   6 + 6 + 6 = ______

______ fives = ______   ______ nines = ______   ______ sixes = ______

______ x 5 = ______   ______ x 9 = ______   ______ x 6 = ______

3 + 3 = ______   7 + 7 + 7 + 7 = ______   2 + 2 = ______

______ threes = ______   ______ sevens = ______   ______ twos = ______

______ x 3 = ______   ______ x 7 = ______   ______ x 2 = ______

Name ____________________

Multiplying by 2 to 5

When multiplying, the first factor tells how many groups there are.

<u>5</u> x 3 = ___ There are 5 groups.

The second factor tells how many there are in each group.

5 x <u>3</u> = ___ There are 3 in each group.

3 + 3 + 3 + 3 + 3 = ____

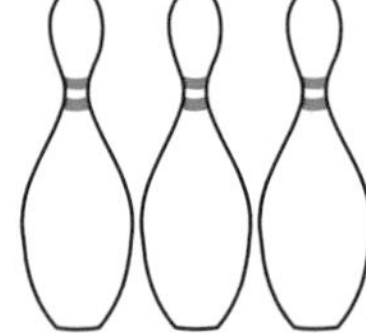 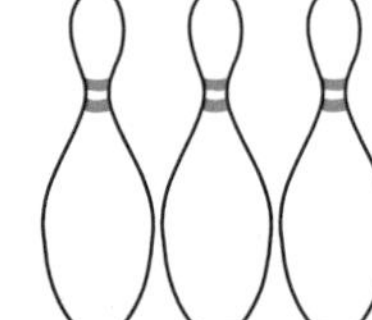 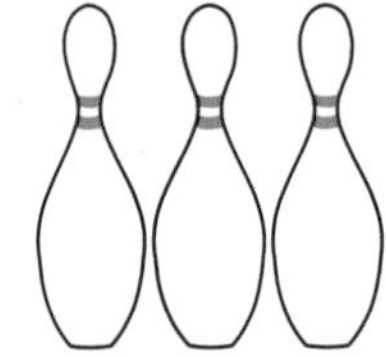  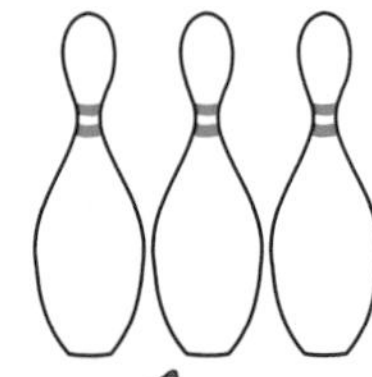

5 groups of 3 equal **<u>15</u>**.

Mark, David, and Bill met at the park to launch rockets. They each launched their rocket 4 times! How many rocket launches were there altogether?

3 x 4 = ____

Directions: Multiply.

5	3	2	3	8	4
x 2	x 6	x 7	x 9	x 2	x 5

4 x 9 = _____ 4 x 8 = _____ 5 x 7 = _____

6 x 2 = _____ 5 x 3 = _____ 5 x 5 = _____

Name ____________________

A Hole in One

Directions: Multiply. Score a "hole in one" for each multiplication fact you have learned.

5 x 3	7 x 3	6 x 1	9 x 2	7 x 7	1 x 2	9 x 9	2 x 6
9 x 4	4 x 8	1 x 2	7 x 9	6 x 8	3 x 2	7 x 5	1 x 9
4 x 7	6 x 4	5 x 4	0 x 4	2 x 9	2 x 2	6 x 2	3 x 3
8 x 1	5 x 9	1 x 1	1 x 3	6 x 6		0 x 7	1 x 6
3 x 4	6 x 3	7 x 4	9 x 6	5 x 6		9 x 9	
1 x 4	5 x 7	0 x 6	7 x 6	3 x 5	1 x 7	4 x 4	
4 x 6	6 x 9	8 x 7	1 x 5	5 x 8			

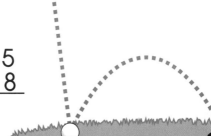

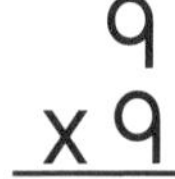

Name ______________________________

Slam Dunk Multiplication

Directions: Solve each multiplication problem. If the product ends in an odd number, color the net yellow. If the product ends in an even number, color the net orange.

7 x 8 =

7 x 5 =

8 x 8 =

3 x 3 =

9 x 7 =

3 x 7 =

7 x 6 =

5 x 3 =

4 x 3 =

2 x 4 =

6 x 4 =

5 x 4 =

3 x 9 =

6 x 5 =

6 x 6 =

6 x 8 =

7 x 7 =

8 x 4 =

9 x 9 =

Name ____________________

Problem-Solving: Addition, Subtraction, Multiplication

Directions: Tell if you add, subtract, or multiply. Then write the answer.

Example:

There were 12 frogs sitting on a log by a pond, but 3 frogs hopped away. How many frogs are left?

Subtract ____ 9 ____ frogs

There are 9 flowers growing by the pond. Each flower has 2 leaves. How many leaves are there? ____________ ______ leaves

A tree had 7 squirrels playing in it. Then 8 more came along. How many squirrels are there in all? ____________ ______ squirrels

There were 27 birds living in the trees around the pond, but 9 flew away. How many birds are left? ____________ ______ birds

Name ______________________________

Fractions

Directions: A fraction is a number that names part of a whole, such as $\frac{1}{2}$ or $\frac{1}{3}$. Write the fraction that tells what part of each figure is colored. The first one is done for you.

Example: 2 parts shaded
5 parts in the whole figure $\frac{2}{5}$

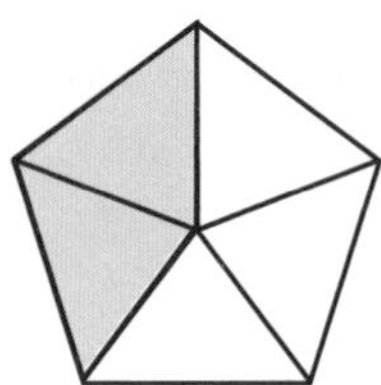

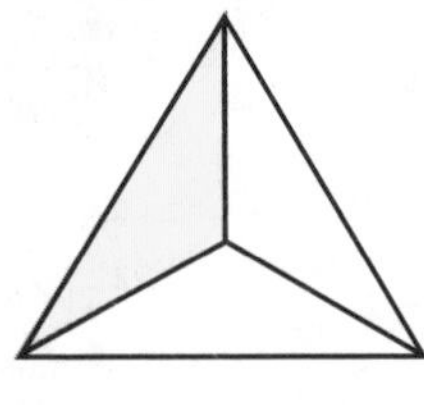

$\frac{1}{3}$ ____________

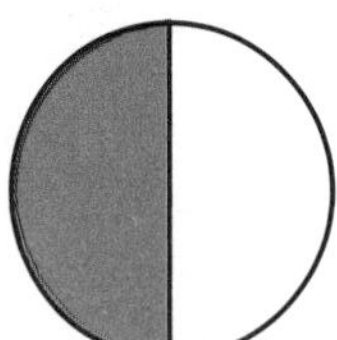

____

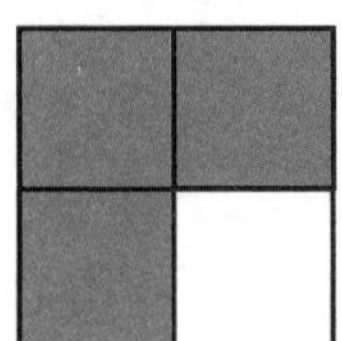

____

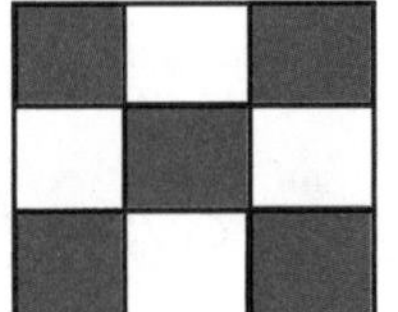

____

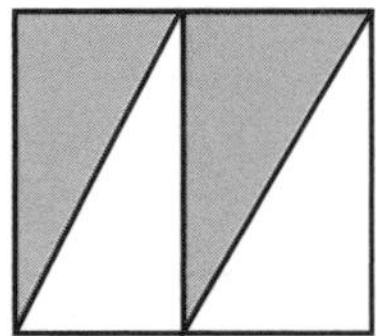

____

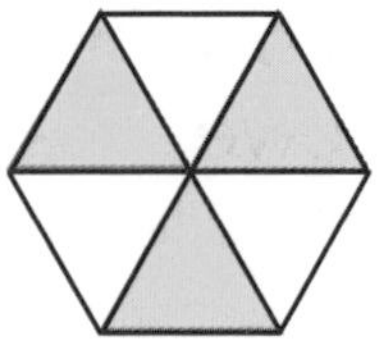

Figure 6 (hexagon): ____________

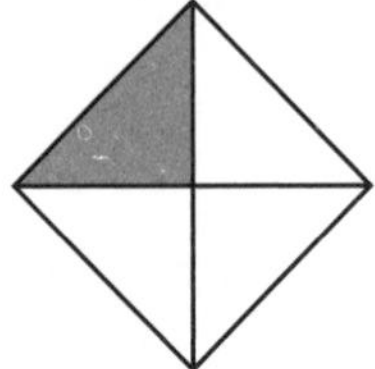

____

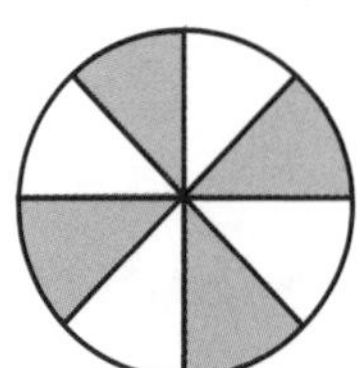

____

____

Name ______________________________

Fraction Food

Directions: Count the equal parts. Circle the fraction that names one of the parts.

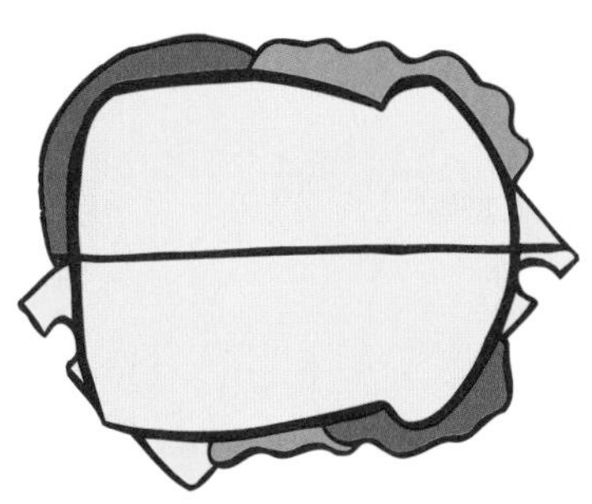

$\frac{1}{2}$ $\frac{1}{3}$ $\frac{1}{4}$

$\frac{1}{2}$ $\frac{1}{3}$ $\frac{1}{4}$

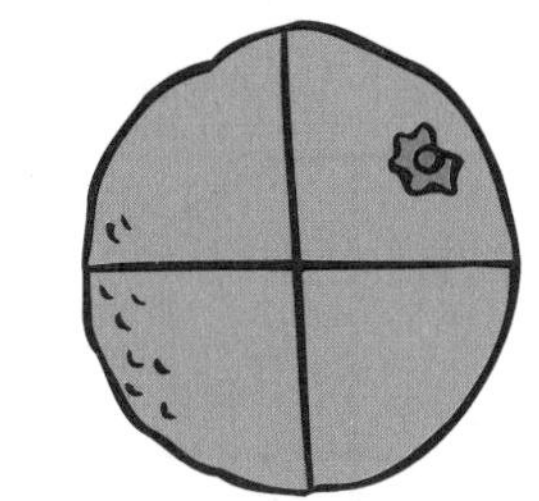

$\frac{1}{2}$ $\frac{1}{3}$ $\frac{1}{4}$

$\frac{1}{2}$ $\frac{1}{3}$ $\frac{1}{4}$

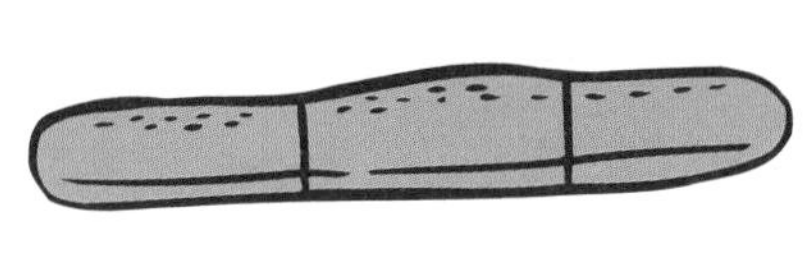

$\frac{1}{2}$ $\frac{1}{3}$ $\frac{1}{4}$

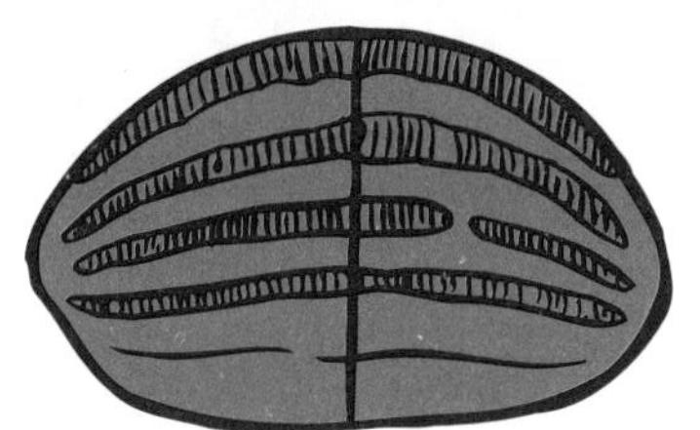

$\frac{1}{2}$ $\frac{1}{3}$ $\frac{1}{4}$

$\frac{1}{2}$ $\frac{1}{3}$ $\frac{1}{4}$

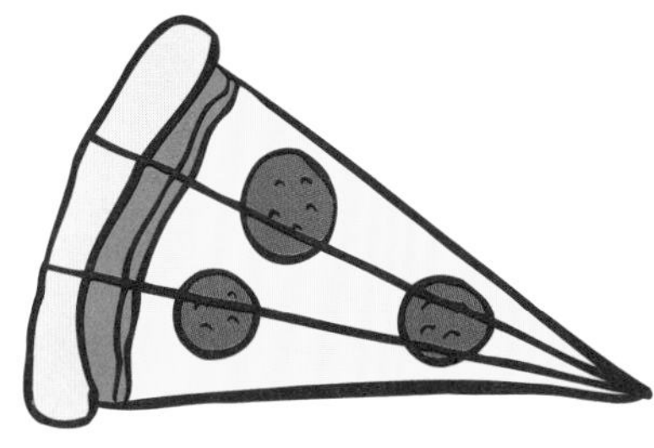

$\frac{1}{2}$ $\frac{1}{3}$ $\frac{1}{4}$

$\frac{1}{2}$ $\frac{1}{3}$ $\frac{1}{4}$

Name ______________________

Fraction: A Part of the Whole

Directions: A member is part of the whole team. A fraction is part of a whole object. Color the fractional part for each object.

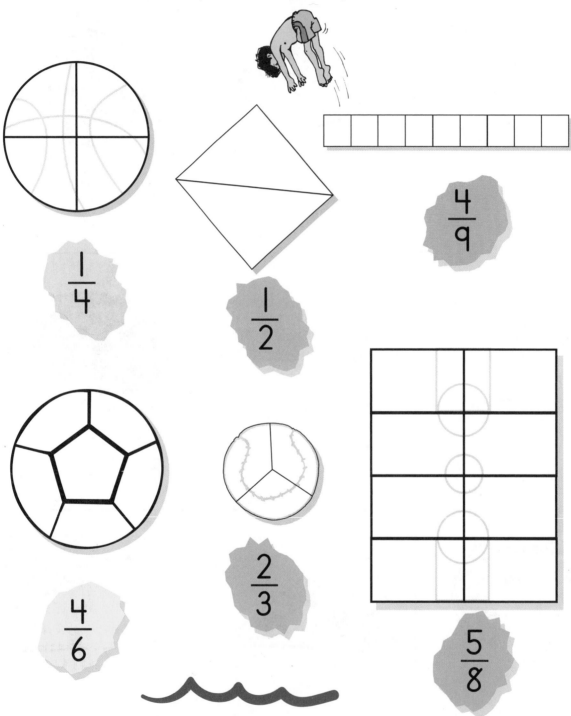

$\frac{1}{4}$

$\frac{1}{2}$

$\frac{4}{9}$

$\frac{4}{6}$

$\frac{2}{3}$

$\frac{5}{8}$

Name ____________________

Fractions: Comparing

Directions: Circle the fraction in each pair that is larger.

Example:

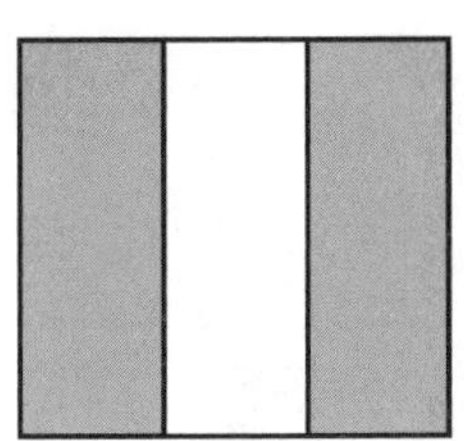

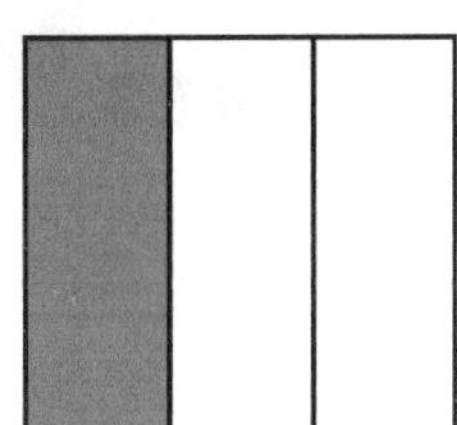

$\frac{2}{3}$ (circled) $\frac{1}{3}$

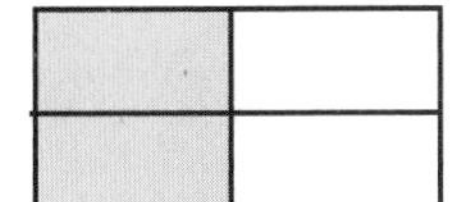

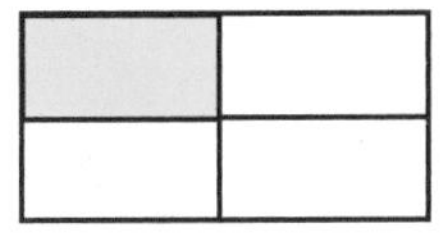

$\frac{2}{4}$ $\frac{1}{4}$

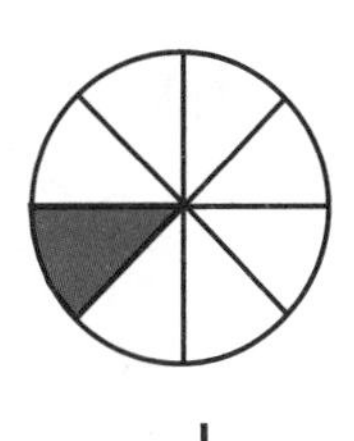

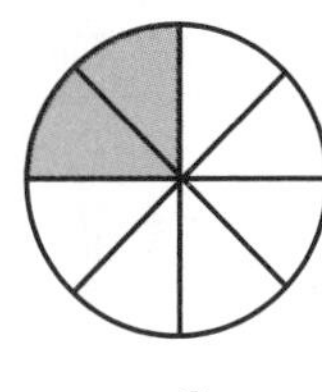

$\frac{1}{8}$ $\frac{2}{8}$

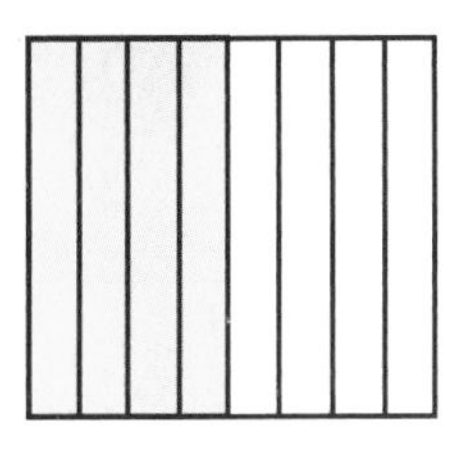

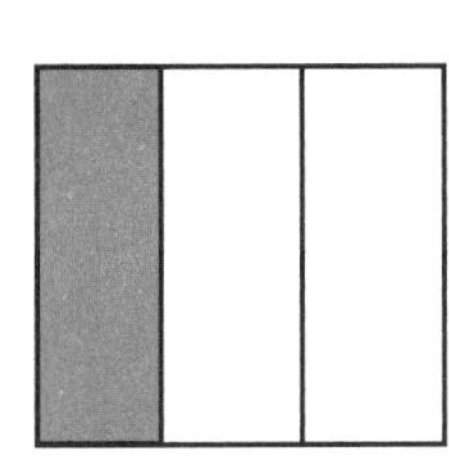

$\frac{1}{2}$ $\frac{1}{3}$

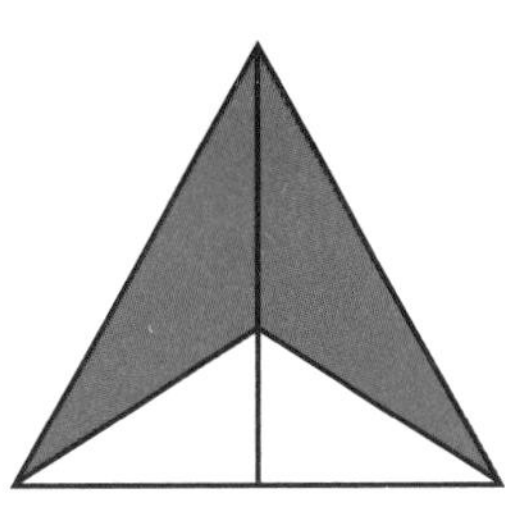

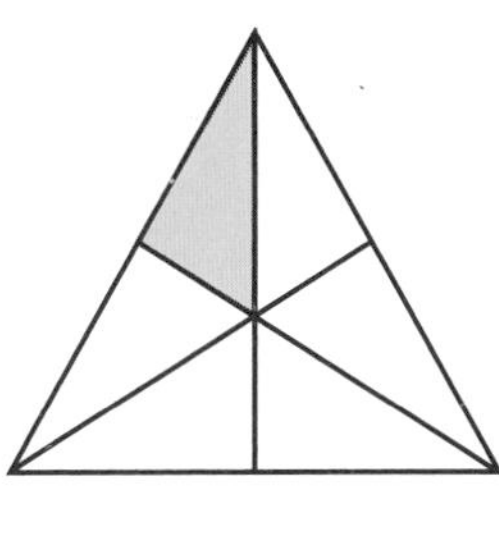

$\frac{2}{3}$ $\frac{1}{6}$

$\frac{1}{4}$ or $\frac{1}{6}$

$\frac{1}{5}$ or $\frac{1}{7}$

$\frac{1}{8}$ or $\frac{1}{4}$

Fortunate Fractions

Directions: Color the correct number of fortune cookies to show each fraction.

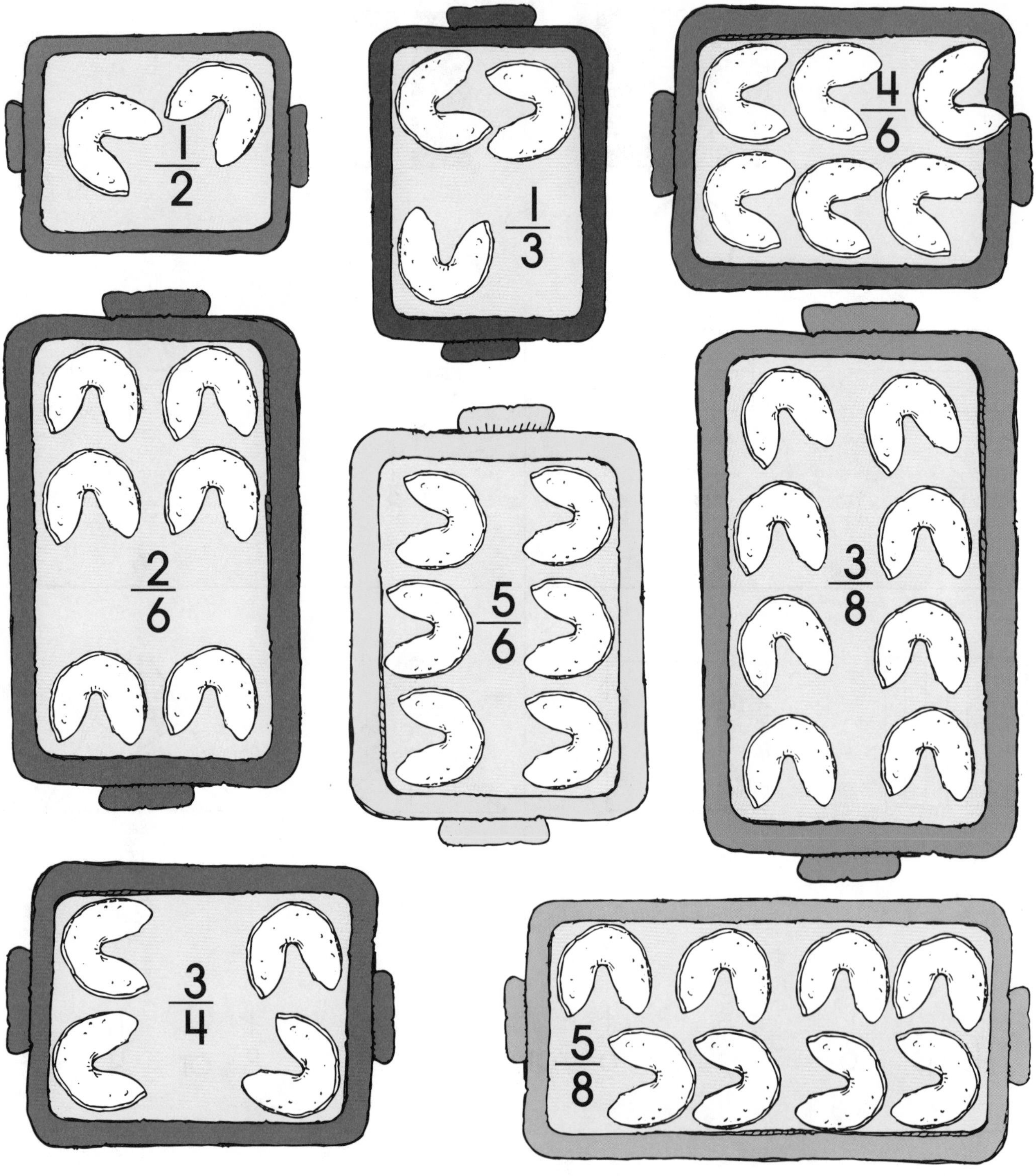

$\frac{1}{2}$

$\frac{1}{3}$

$\frac{4}{6}$

$\frac{2}{6}$

$\frac{5}{6}$

$\frac{3}{8}$

$\frac{3}{4}$

$\frac{5}{8}$

Name ______________________

Fraction Mysteries

Directions: Some mysterious person is sneaking away with pieces of desserts from Sam Sillicook's diner. Help him figure out how much is missing.

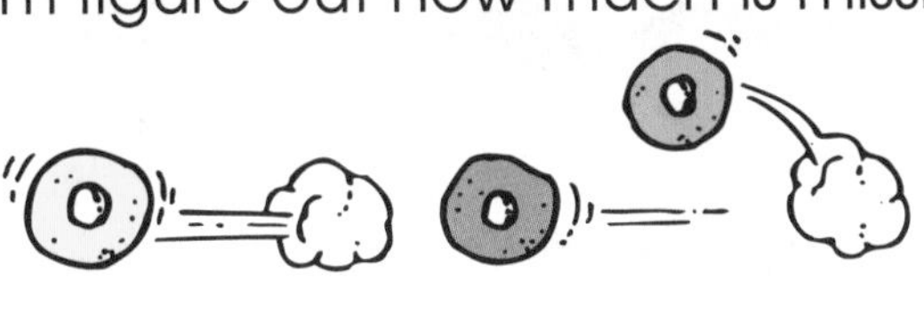

1. What fraction of Sam's Super Sweet Chocolate Cream Cake is missing?

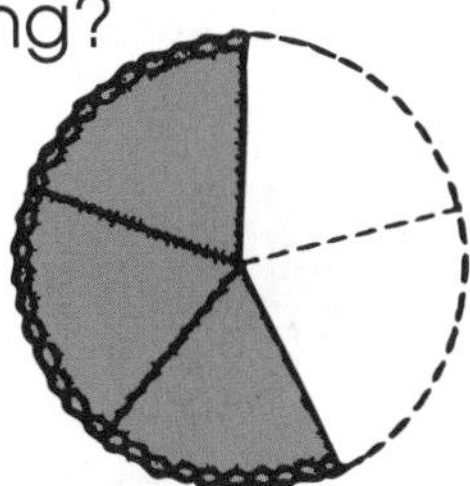

______

2. What fraction of Sam's Heavenly Tasting Cherry Cream Tart is missing?

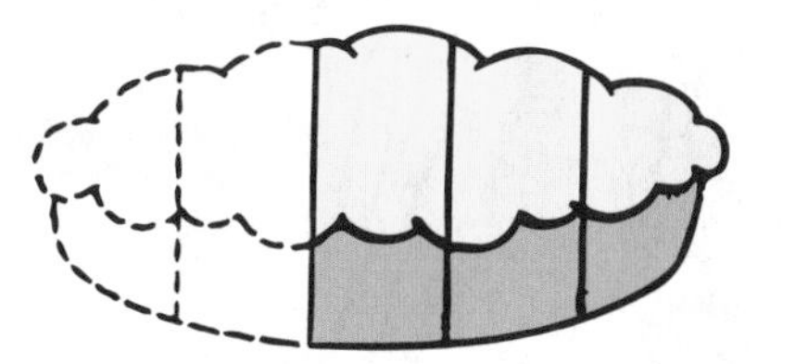

______

3. What fraction of Sam's Tastee Toffee Coffee Cake is missing?

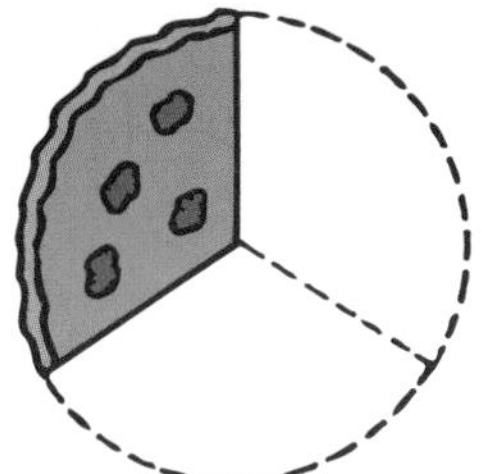

______

4. What fraction of Sam's Luscious Licorice Candy Cake is missing?

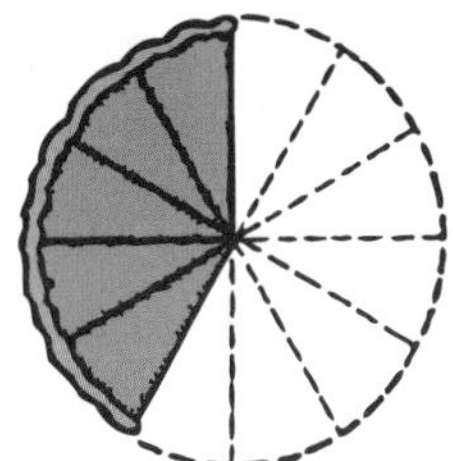

______

5. What fraction of Sam's Tasty Tidbits of Chocolate Ice Cream is missing?

______

6. Sam's Upside-Down Ice-Cream Cake is very famous. What fraction has vanished?

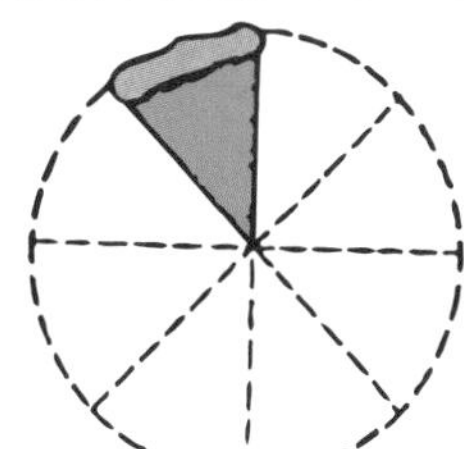

______

Fraction Fun

4 gloves are colored. 9 gloves in all.

$\frac{4}{9}$ of the gloves are colored.

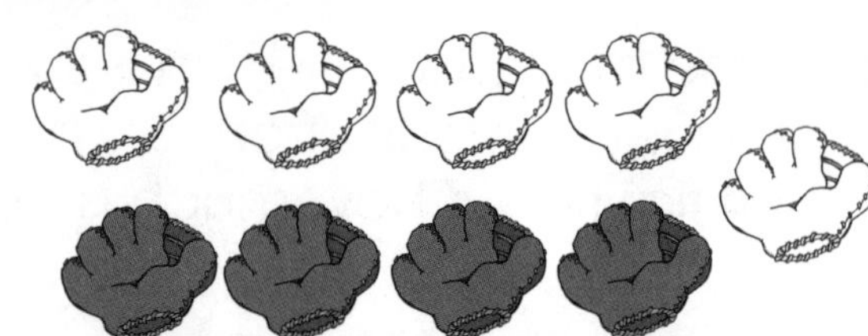

Directions: Write the fractional part for each set.

What fraction of the balls are colored in the window? ________

bottles? ___________ paddles? ___________ whistles? ___________

bags? ___________ pennants? ___________ helmets? ___________

skis? ___________ shoes? ___________ trophies? ___________

Shapes

Directions: Look at the shapes and answer the questions.

How many □s can you find? _____

How many △s can you find? _____

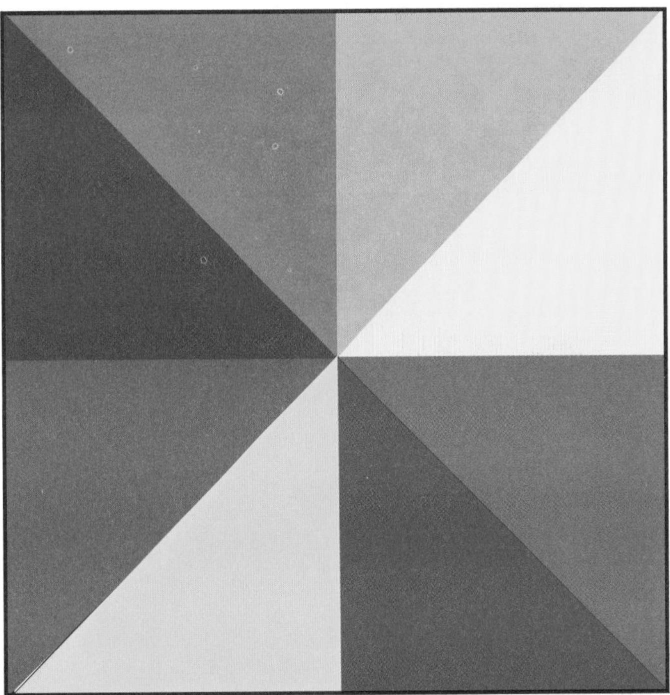

Name ______________________

Shapes: Set! Point! Match!

Directions: Match each polygon to its name.

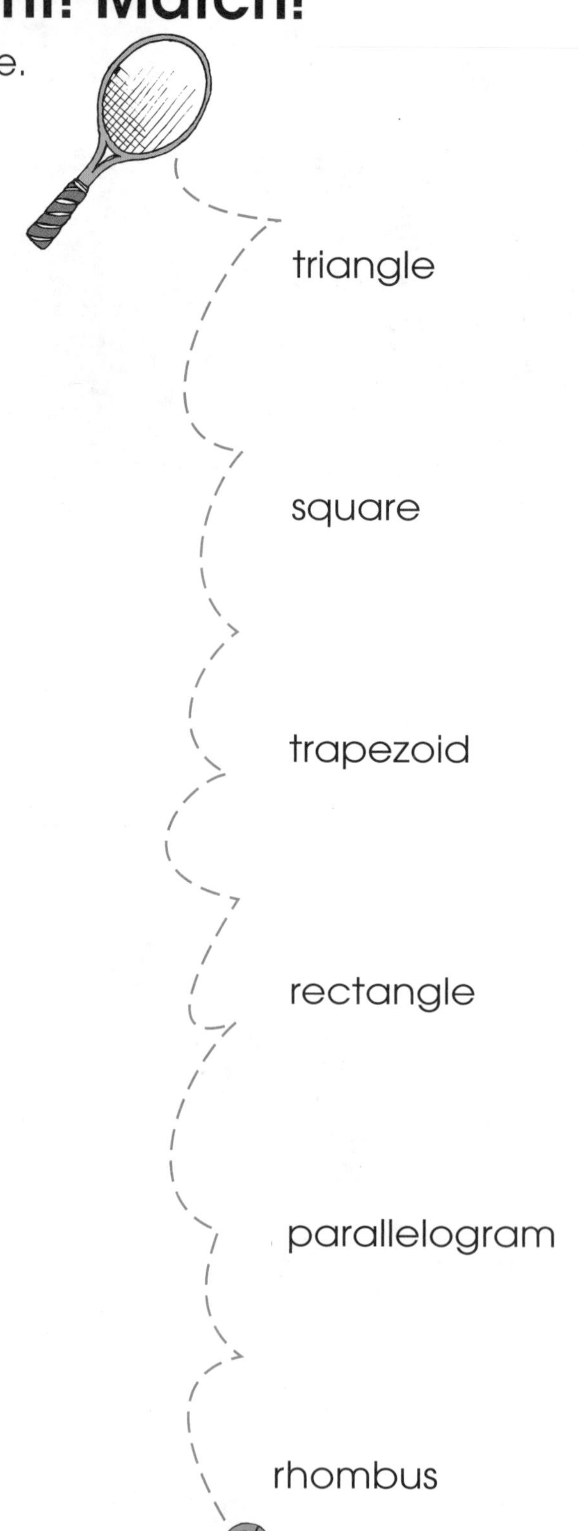

Name ____________________

Shapes: Geometry

Directions: Draw a line from the word to the shape.

Use a red line for circles.

Use a blue line for squares.

Use a yellow line for rectangles.

Use a green line for triangles.

Circle **Square** **Triangle** **Rectangle**

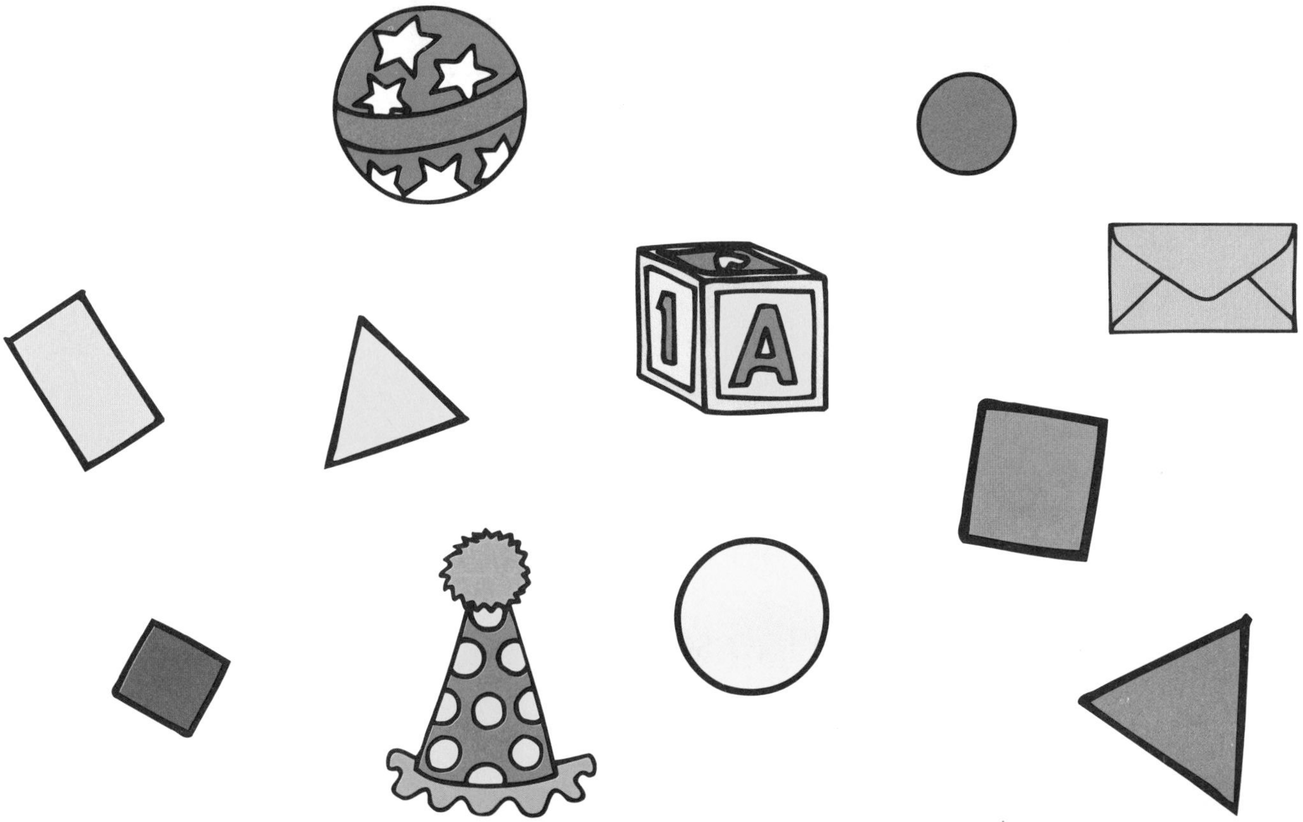

Shapes: Flower Power

Directions: Count the flowers and answer the questions.

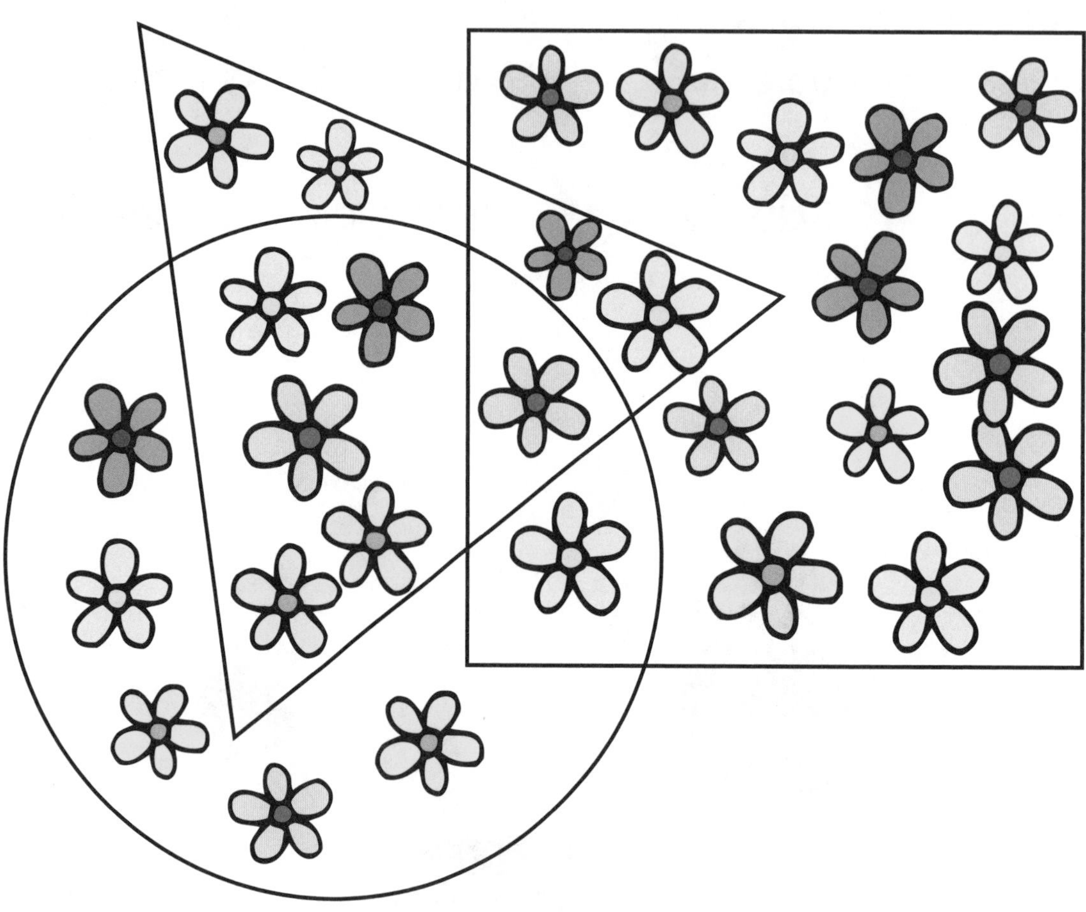

How many  s are in the circle? ________

How many  s are in the triangle? ________

How many  s are in the square? ________

How many  s in all? ________

Name ____________________________

How Many Shapes?

Directions: Find the shapes and color them using the code.

△ red ● blue ◇ yellow ⬭ green ▢ orange ■ black

Name ____________________

Shapes: Geometry

Geometry is the branch of mathematics that has to do with points, lines, and shapes. These shapes are solid, not flat.

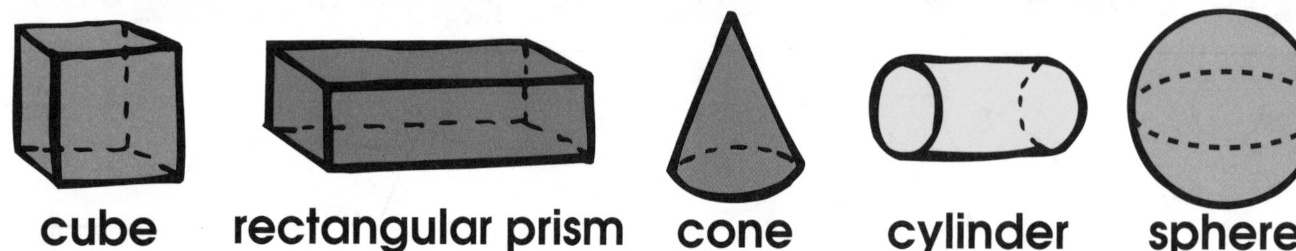

Directions: Use the code to color the picture.

Code:
cubes — blue
rectangular prisms — red
cones — green
cylinders — yellow
spheres — orange

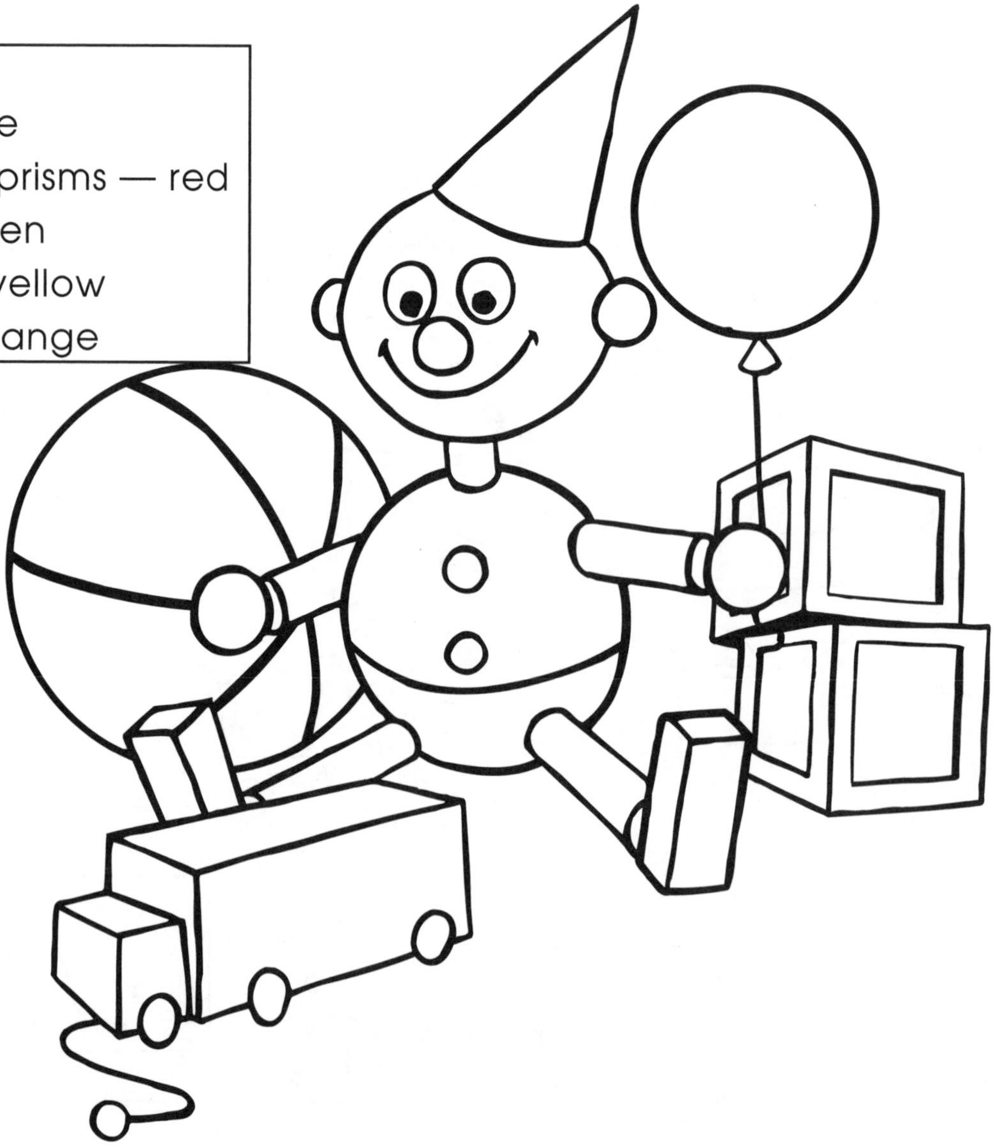

Name ______________________________

Measurement: Inches

Directions: Use a ruler to measure the fish to the nearest inch.

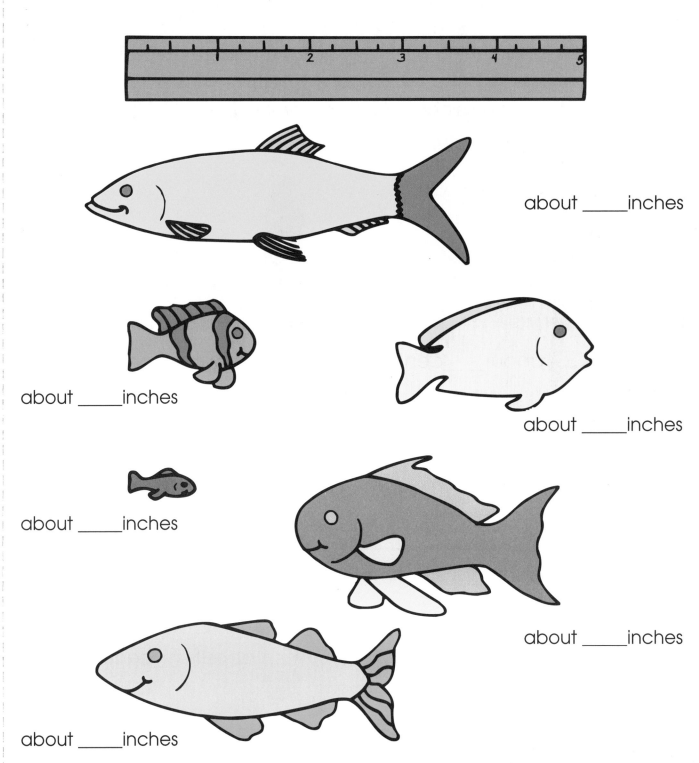

1 2 3 4 5

about _____inches

about _____inches

about _____inches

about _____inches

about _____inches

about _____inches

Name ____________________

Measurement: Centimeters

A centimeter is a unit of length in the metric system. There are 2.54 centimeters in an inch.

Directions: Use a centimeter ruler to measure the crayons to the nearest centimeter.

Example: The first crayon is about 7 centimeters long.

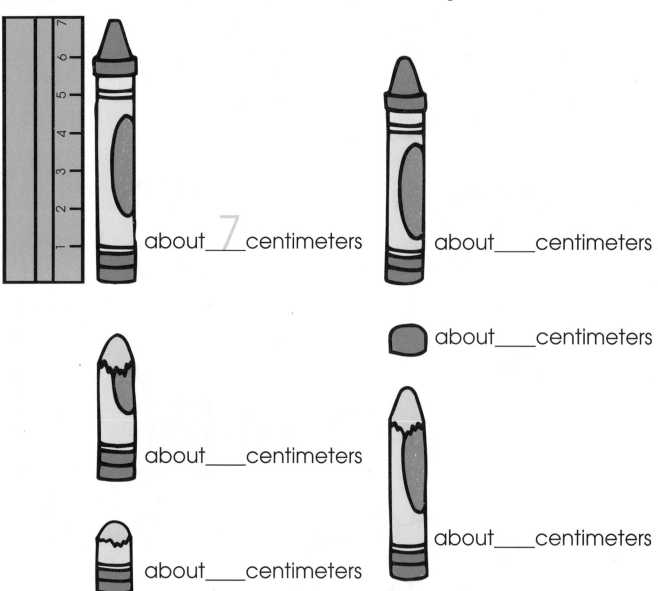

about 7 centimeters

about ____ centimeters

about ____ centimeters

about ____ centimeters

about ____ centimeters

about ____ centimeters

Name ______________________

Measurement: Foot, Yard, Mile

Directions: Decide whether you would use foot, yard, or mile to measure each object.

1 foot = 12 inches
1 yard = 36 inches or 3 feet
1 mile = 1,760 yards

Example:

length of a river ___mile___

height of a tree ____________

width of a room ____________

length of a football field ____________

height of a door ____________

length of a dress ____________

length of a race ____________

height of a basketball hoop ____________

width of a window ____________

distance a plane travels ____________

Directions: Solve the problem.

Tara races Tom in the 100-yard dash. Tara finishes 10 yards in front of Tom. How many feet did Tara finish in front of Tom? ____________

Name ____________________

Measurement: Meter and Kilometer

Meters and kilometers are units of length in the metric system. A meter is equal to 39.37 inches. A kilometer is equal to about $\frac{5}{8}$ of a mile.

Directions: Decide whether you would use meter or kilometer to measure each object.

1 meter = 100 centimeters
1 kilometer = 1,000 meters

Example:

length of a river kilometer

height of a tree ____________

width of a room ____________

length of a football field ____________

height of a door ____________

length of a dress ____________

length of a race ____________

height of a basketball pole ____________

width of a window ____________

distance a plane travels ____________

Directions: Solve the problem.

Anna races Lee in the 100-meter dash. Anna finishes 10 meters in front of Lee. How many centimeters did Anna finish in front of Lee? ____________

Name ______________________

Time to the Half-Hour

This clock face shows the time gone by since 8 o'clock. Thirty minutes or half an hour have gone by.

Directions: There are 3 ways to say time to the half-hour. We say 7:30, thirty past the hour, or half past seven. Write the times below. Draw the hands on the last clock.

half-hour later

9:00 ______ 9:30 ______

30 ______ minutes past 9 ______ o'clock

half-hour later

______ ______

______ minutes past ______ o'clock

Name ____________________

Growing Time

Directions: Each hour has 4 quarter hours. A quarter-hour is 15 minutes. Write the times below.

one quarter-hour later

____________ ____________

____________ minutes past ____________ o'clock

one quarter-hour later

____________ ____________

____________ minutes past ____________ o'clock

Time to the Minute

Each number on the clock face stands for 5 minutes.

Directions: Count by 5's beginning at 12. Write the numbers below.

00 05 10 15 20 25

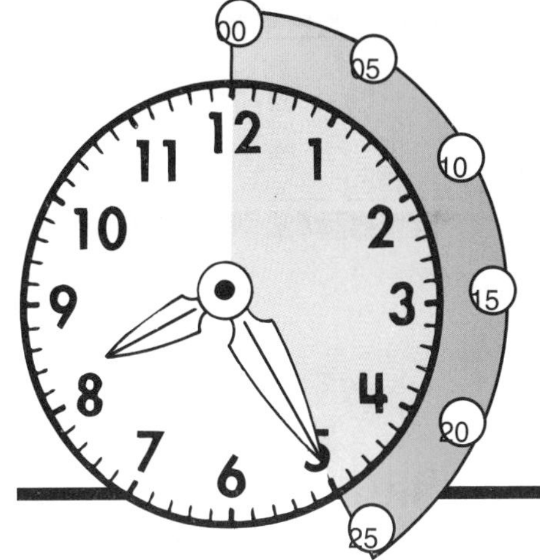

It is 25 minutes after 8 o'clock. It is written 8:25.

Directions: Count by 5's.

00 ______ ______ ______ ______

______ ______ ______

It is ______ minutes after ______ o'clock.
It is written 8:35.

Name ______________________

Digital Magic

Directions: Write the time on the digital clocks.

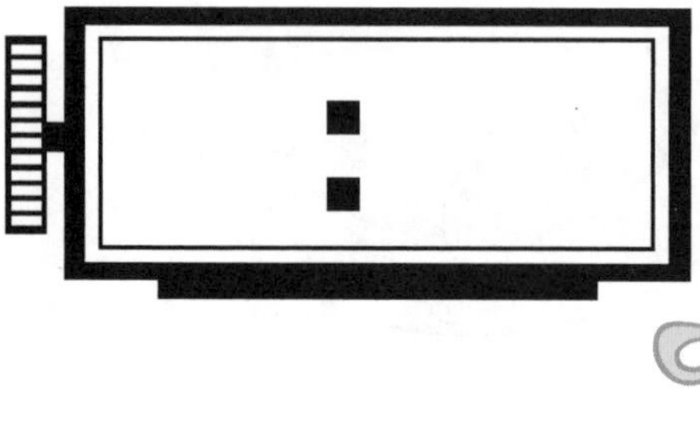

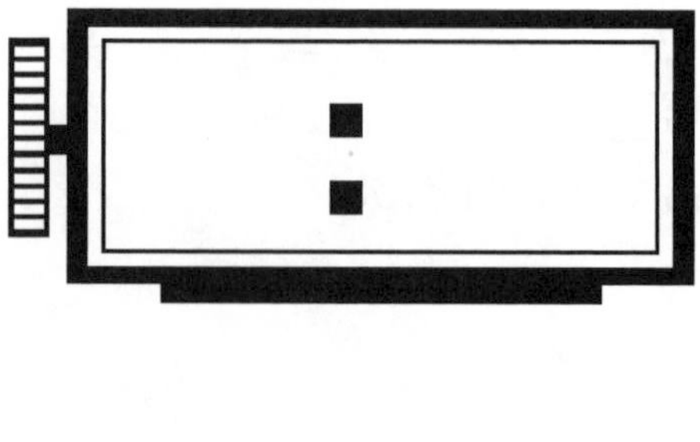

Name ____________________

Matching Digital and Face Clocks

Directions: Trace the time on the digital clocks.

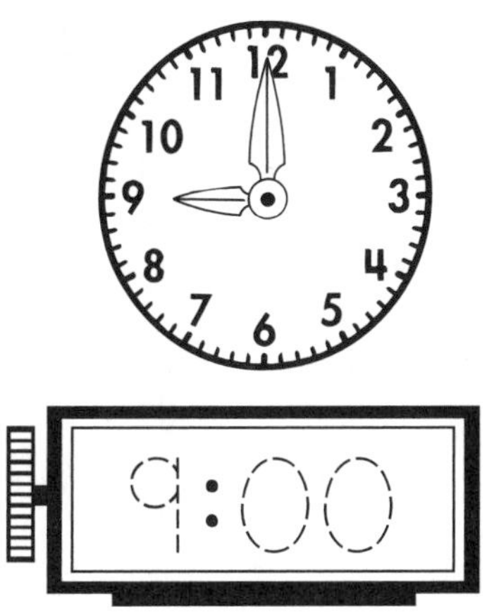

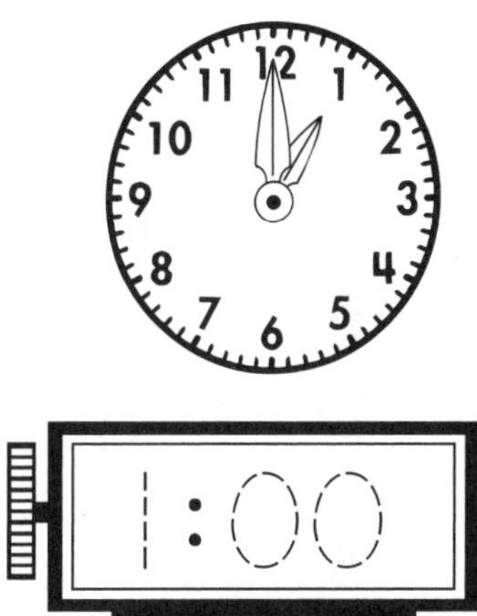

Directions: Draw a line to match the clocks.

Name ______________________

Keeping "Track" of Time

Directions: Write the correct time by each clock.

Monkeying Around

Directions: Nat can't tell time. He needs your help to solve these problems.

1. Nat is supposed to be at school in 10 minutes. What time should he get there?

____

2. Nat started breakfast at 7:10 A.M. It took him 15 minutes to eat. Mark the time he finished.

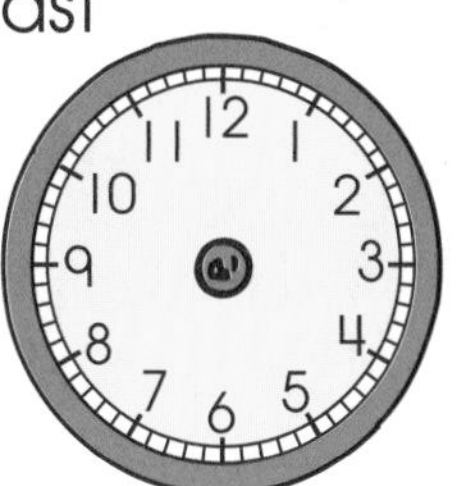

____

3. Nat will leave school in 5 minutes. What time will it be then?

____

4. Nat's family will eat dinner in 15 minutes. When will that be?

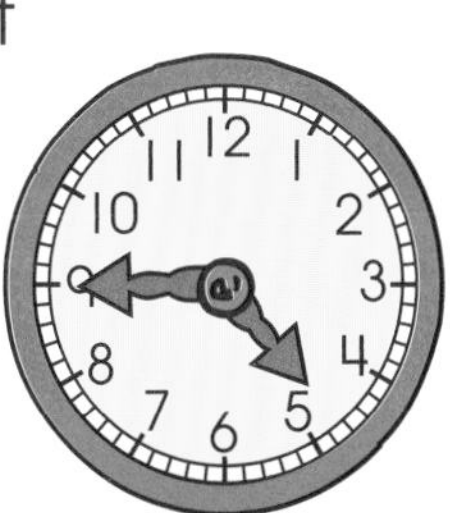

____

5. It is now 6:45 P.M. Nat must start his homework in 5 minutes. Mark the starting time on the clock.

____

6. Nat will go to the park in 15 minutes. It is now 1:25 P.M. Mark the time he will go to the park.

____

Name ______________________________

Time Problems

Directions: Draw the hands on the clocks to show the starting time and the ending time. Then, write the answer to the question.

1. The bike race started at 2:55 P.M. and lasted 2 hours and 10 minutes. What time did the race end?

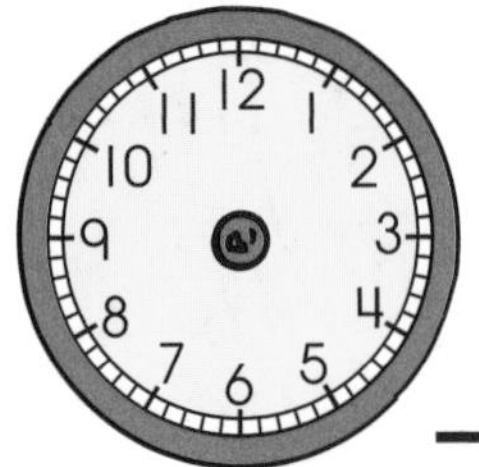

____

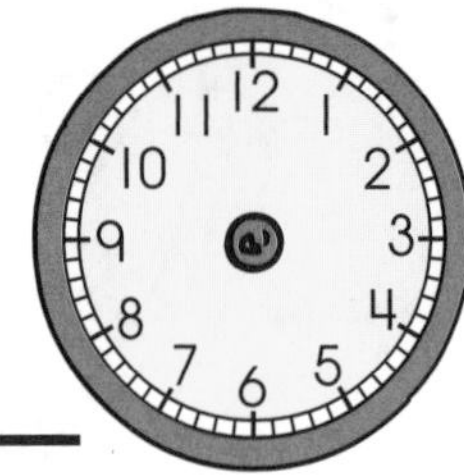

4. Sherry walked in the 12-mile Hunger Walk. She started at 12:30 P.M. and finished at 4:50 P.M. How long did she walk?

____

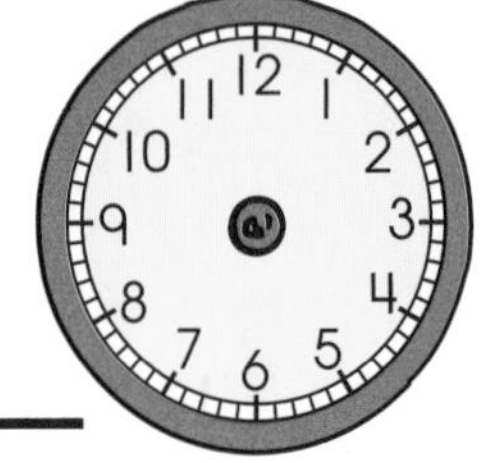

2. The 500-mile auto race started at 11:00 A.M. and lasted 2 hours and 25 minutes. What time did the race end?

____

5. The chili cook-off started at 10:00 A.M., and all the chili was cooked by 4:30 P.M. How long did it take to cook the chili?

____

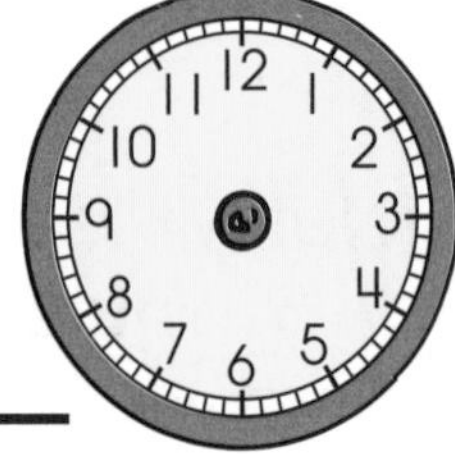

3. The train left Indianapolis at 7:25 A.M. and arrived in Chicago at 10:50 A.M. How long did the trip take?

____

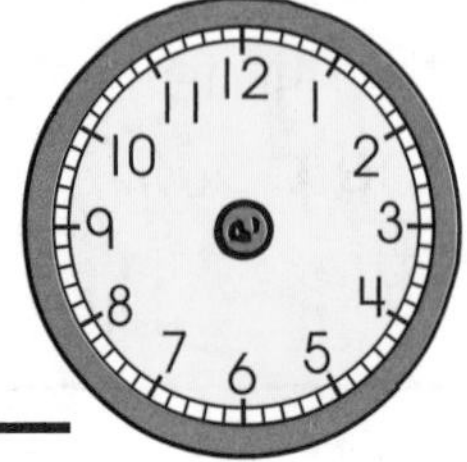

6. The chili judging began at 4:30 P.M. After 3 hours and 45 minutes the chili had all been eaten. At what time was the chili judging finished?

____

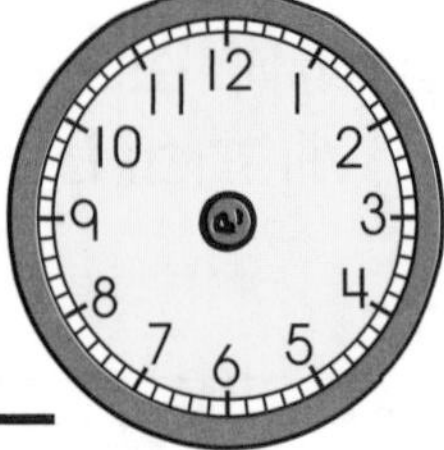

Name ____________________

Feeding Time

The abbreviations **A.M.** and **P.M.** help tell the time of day. At midnight, A.M. begins. At noon, P.M. begins. Ken and Angie enjoy watching the animals being fed at the zoo. However, when they arrived, they were a little confused by the signs. Help them figure out the feeding time for each kind of animal. Be sure to include if it's A.M. or P.M.

Zebras: Feeding time is 2 hours after the monkeys.

____

Tigers: Feeding time is 2 hours after 9:00 A.M.

____

Elephants: Feeding time is 1:00 P.M.

Giraffes: Feeding time is 1 hour before the lions.

____

Monkeys: Feeding time is 3 hours before the giraffes.

____

Lions: Feeding time is 3 hours after the elephants.

____

Directions: Now, trace the path in the zoo that Ken and Angie would take so that they could see all the animals being fed.

Name ______________________

Counting With Nickels and Pennies

Directions: Count the money. Begin by saying 5 for the nickel and add 1 for each penny.

Name ______________________

Counting With Dimes and Nickels

Directions: Count the money. Begin by saying 10 for the dimes, then count the nickels. Write the amount.

10  20  25  30 35 ¢ = 35 ¢
Total

10 20 30 40 59 55

5  10 15 = 15 ¢

I'm counting my money. 10¢, 20¢, 30¢, 35¢, 40¢, 45¢, 50¢...

Solve this puzzle. What coins does the chicken have?

3 dimes and 4 nickels

Name ____________________

Money: Penny, Nickel, Dime

Directions: Draw a line from the toy to the amount of money it costs.

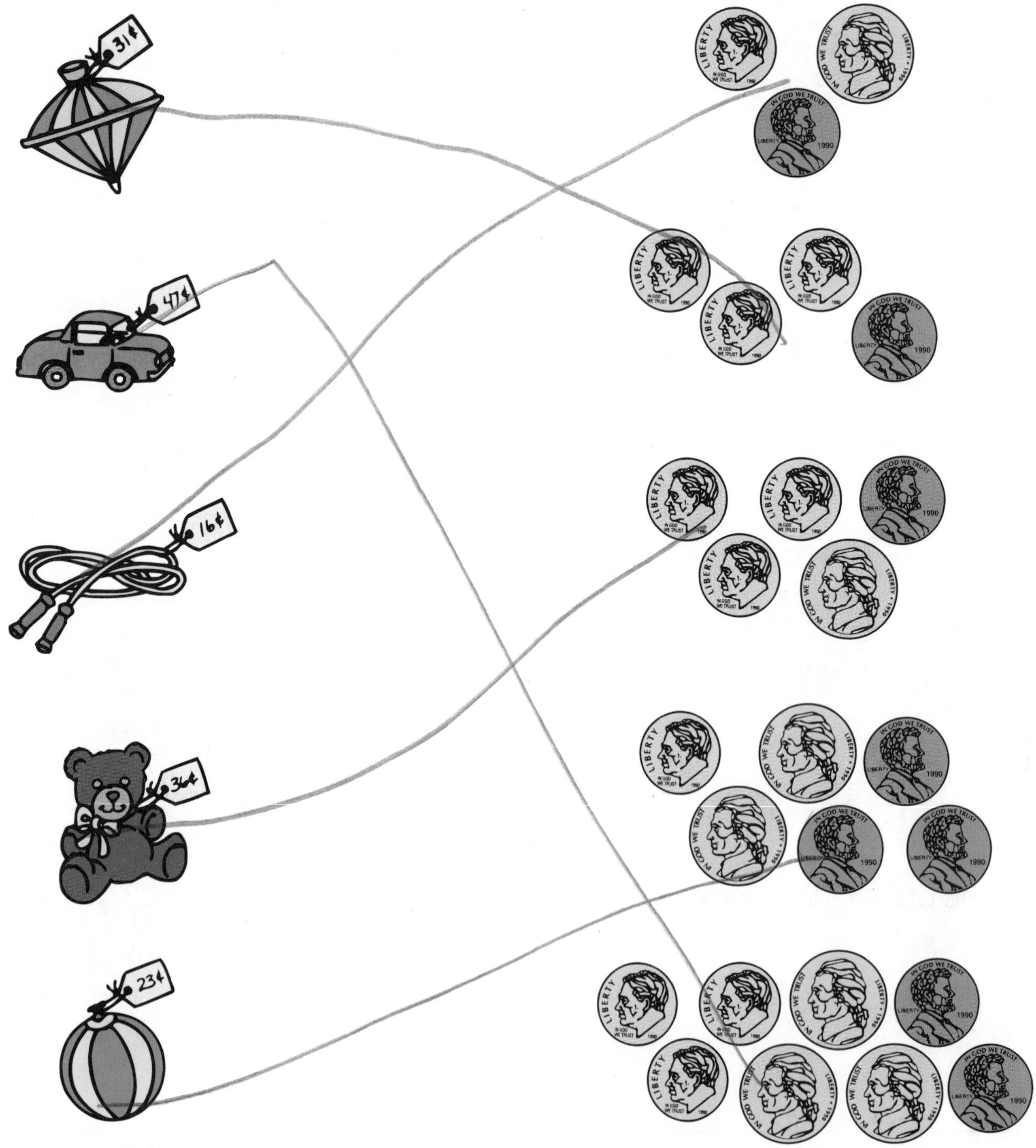

31¢

47¢

16¢

36¢

23¢

Name ____________________

Money: Coins and Dollars

dollar = 100¢ or $1.00

penny = 1¢ or $.01

nickel = 5¢ or $.05

dime = 10¢ or $.10

quarter = 25¢ or $.25

half-dollar = 50¢ or $.50

Directions: Write the amount for each group of money shown. Use a dollar sign and decimal point. The first one is done for you.

$.07

$.11

$.36

32¢

$2.55

116¢

Name ______________________

Adding Money

Directions: Write the amount of money using decimals. Then add to find the total amount.

Example:  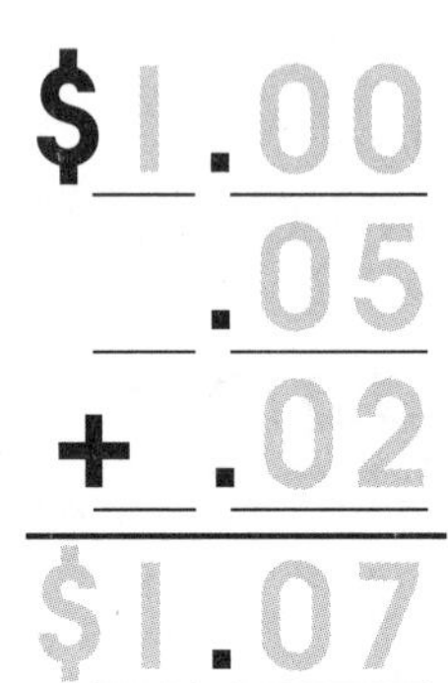

$1.00
.05
+ .02
$1.07

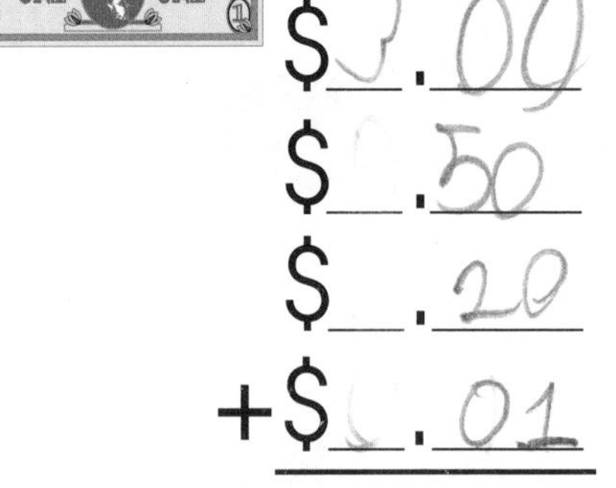
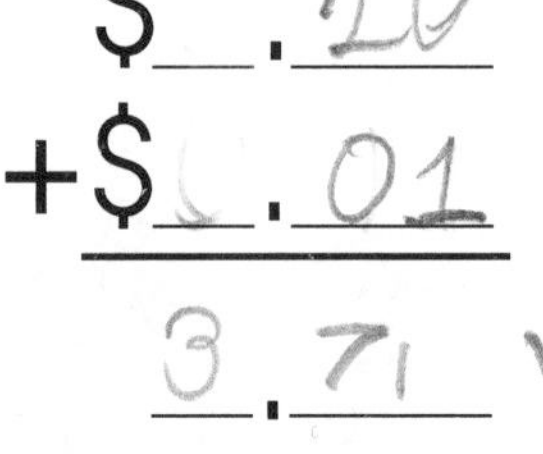

$__.____
$__.____
$__.____
+$__.____
__.____

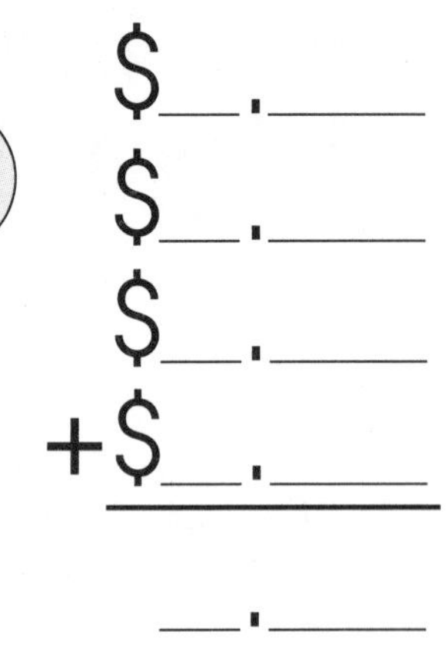

$__.____
$__.____
$__.____
+$__.____
__.____

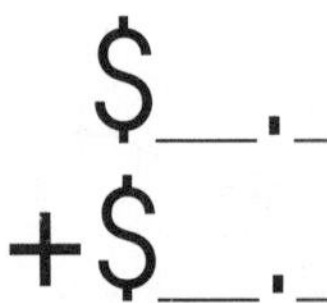

$__.____
$__.____
+$__.____
__.____

$__.____
$__.____
$__.____
+$__.____
__.____

Name ____________________

Money Problems

Directions: Count the money on each tray. Write the name of the food that costs that amount.

Example:

hamburger..$2.45	hot dog......... $1.77	sandwich.... $1.55
milk ....$ .64	soda pop...... $1.26	milkshake.... $1.89
cake........... $2.85	pie.................$2.25	sundae.......... $.95

____

____

____

____

____

____

Name ______________________________

Money Combinations

$3.00 $9.00 $4.00

$6.00 $5.00 $2.00

$1.00 $8.00 $7.00

Directions: You want to buy 3 different items in the hobby store. You have $16.00. Write all the different combinations of items you can buy using the entire $16.00.

1. ________	1. ________	1. ________	1. ________
2. ________	2. ________	2. ________	2. ________
3. ________	3. ________	3. ________	3. ________

1. ________	1. ________	1. ________	1. ________
2. ________	2. ________	2. ________	2. ________
3. ________	3. ________	3. ________	3. ________

Name ____________________

Money: How Many Coins?

Directions: Draw the fewest coins possible to equal the amount shown in each box.

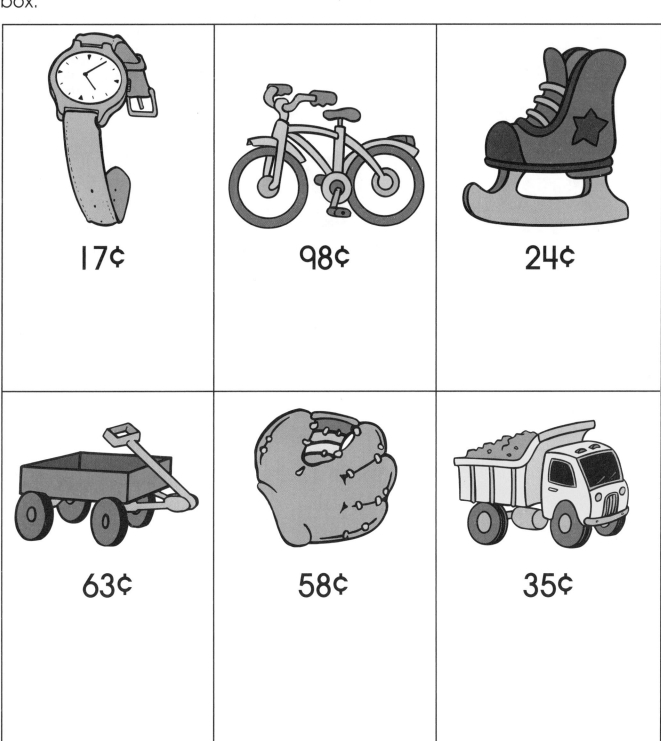

17¢	98¢	24¢
63¢	58¢	35¢

Money: Earnings Add Up!

Wash dishes **$1.50**

Feed cat **$.95**

Mow lawn **$3.50**

Mop floors **$1.25**

Pick tomatoes **$2.75**

Wash windows **$2.85**

Directions: Use the pictures above to help you find out how much you can earn by doing each set of jobs. Write the total amount for each set on each wallet.

1. pick tomatoes ________
2. wash windows ________
3. mow the lawn ________

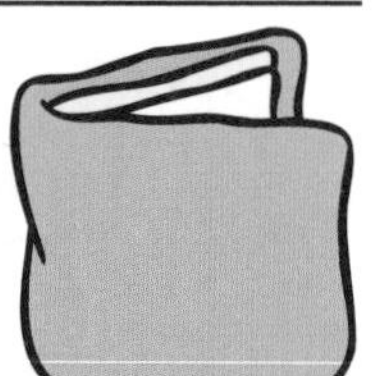
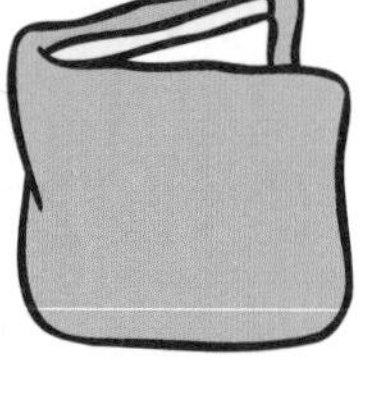

1. wash windows ________
2. mop floors ________
3. mow the lawn ________

1. feed the cat ________
2. pick tomatoes ________
3. wash dishes ________

1. pick tomatoes ________
2. wash windows ________
3. feed the cat ________

Name ____________________

Money: Add 'Em Up!

Directions: Write the prices, then add. Regroup, when needed.

1. skateboard
   + ________ hat

2. dictionary
   + ________ radio

3. wallet
   + ________ goldfish

4. hot dog
   + ________ watch

5. dictionary
   + ________ kite

6. in-line skates
   + ________ trumpet

7. hot dog
   + ________ rocket

8. skateboard
   + ________ goldfish

9. hat
   + ________ kite

10. radio
    + ________ trumpet

11. rocket
    + ________ goldfish

12. skateboard
    + ________ in-line skates

Name ____________________

Money: Making Change

Directions: When you do not have the exact change to buy something at a store, the clerk must give you change. The first amount of money is what you give the clerk. The second amount is what the item costs. In the box, list the fewest number of coins and bills you will receive in change.

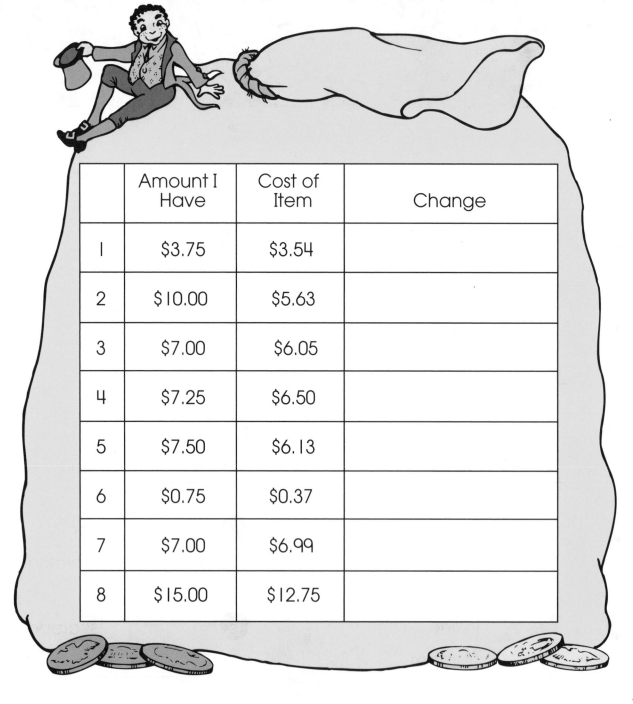

	Amount I Have	Cost of Item	Change
1	$3.75	$3.54	
2	$10.00	$5.63	
3	$7.00	$6.05	
4	$7.25	$6.50	
5	$7.50	$6.13	
6	$0.75	$0.37	
7	$7.00	$6.99	
8	$15.00	$12.75	

Page 8

Counting

Directions: Write the numbers that are:

next in order	one less	one greater
22, 23, 24, 25	15, 16	6, 7
674, 675, 676	246, 247	125, 126
227, 228, 229	549, 550	499, 500
199, 200, 201	332, 333	750, 751
329, 330, 331	861, 862	933, 934

Directions: Write the missing numbers.

13 14 15 16 17 18

163 164 165 166 167 168

821 822 823 824 825 826

Page 9

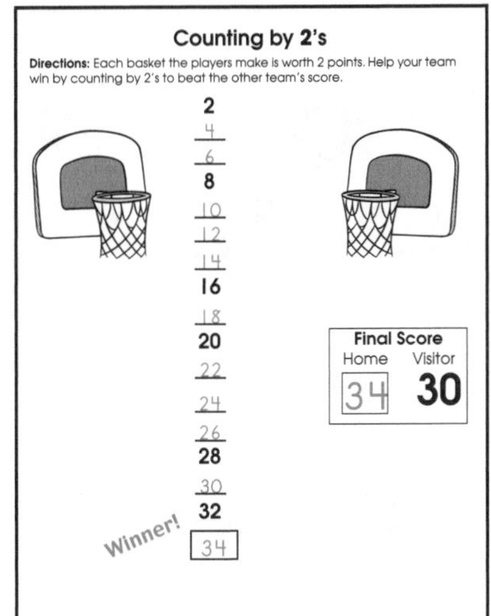

Counting by 2's

Directions: Each basket the players make is worth 2 points. Help your team win by counting by 2's to beat the other team's score.

2, 4, 6, 8, 10, 12, 14, 16, 18, 20, 22, 24, 26, 28, 30, 32, 34

Winner!

Final Score
Home 34 Visitor 30

Page 10

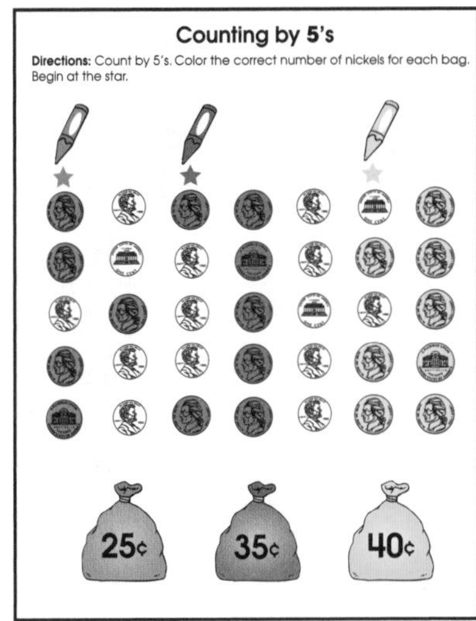

Counting by 5's

Directions: Count by 5's. Color the correct number of nickels for each bag. Begin at the star.

25¢ 35¢ 40¢

Page 11

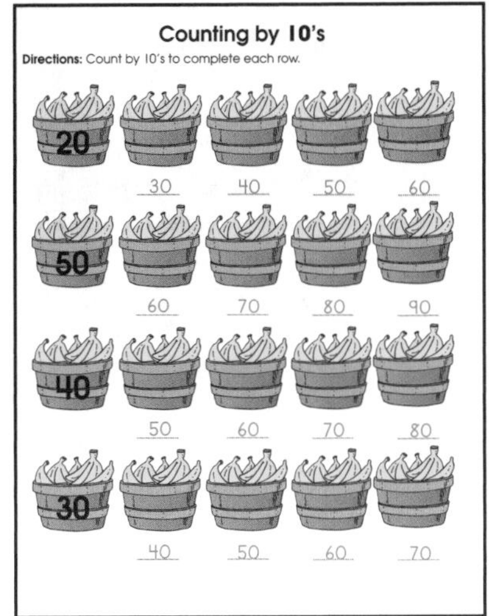

Counting by 10's

Directions: Count by 10's to complete each row.

20, 30, 40, 50, 60

50, 60, 70, 80, 90

40, 50, 60, 70, 80

30, 40, 50, 60, 70

Page 12

Patterns

Directions: Connect the dots in each row to continue the pattern.

Page 13

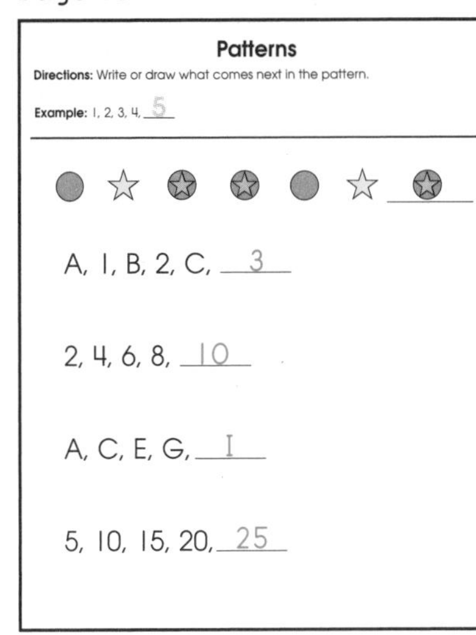

Patterns

Directions: Write or draw what comes next in the pattern.

Example: 1, 2, 3, 4, 5

A, 1, B, 2, C, 3

2, 4, 6, 8, 10

A, C, E, G, I

5, 10, 15, 20, 25

Page 14

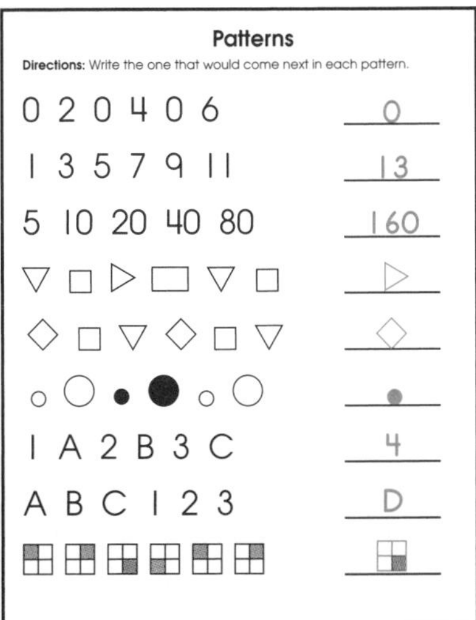

Patterns

Directions: Write the one that would come next in each pattern.

0 2 0 4 0 6 — 0

1 3 5 7 9 11 — 13

5 10 20 40 80 — 160

1 A 2 B 3 C — 4

A B C 1 2 3 — D

Page 15

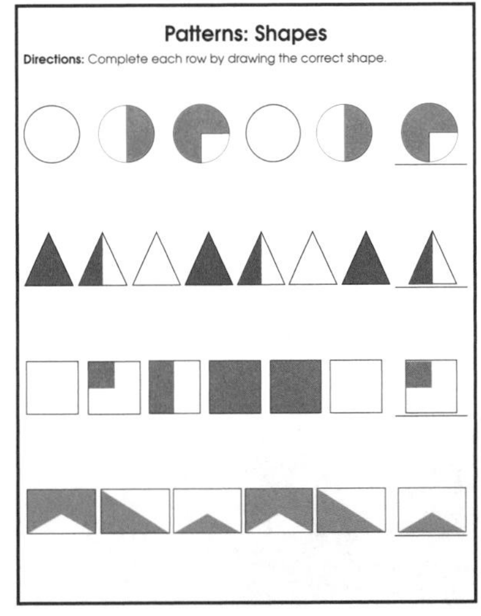

Patterns: Shapes

Directions: Complete each row by drawing the correct shape.

Page 16

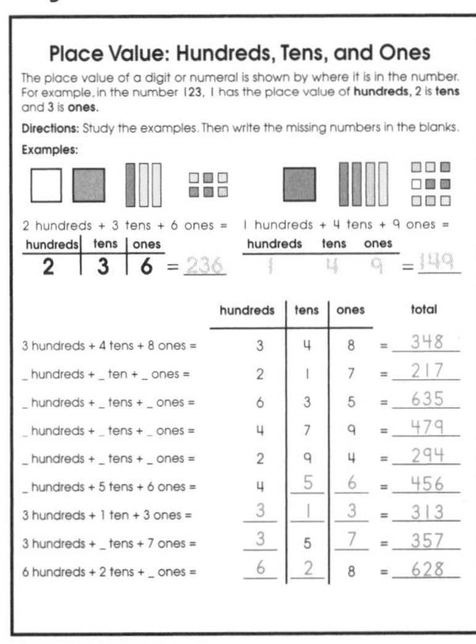

Place Value: Hundreds, Tens, and Ones

The place value of a digit or numeral is shown by where it is in the number. For example, in the number 123, 1 has the place value of **hundreds**, 2 is **tens** and 3 is **ones**.

Directions: Study the examples. Then write the missing numbers in the blanks.

Examples:

2 hundreds + 3 tens + 6 ones = hundreds 2 | tens 3 | ones 6 = 236

1 hundreds + 4 tens + 9 ones = hundreds 1 | tens 4 | ones 9 = 149

	hundreds	tens	ones	total
3 hundreds + 4 tens + 8 ones =	3	4	8	= 348
_ hundreds + _ ten + _ ones =	2	1	7	= 217
_ hundreds + _ tens + _ ones =	6	3	5	= 635
_ hundreds + _ tens + _ ones =	4	7	9	= 479
_ hundreds + _ tens + _ ones =	2	9	4	= 294
_ hundreds + 5 tens + 6 ones =	4	5	6	= 456
3 hundreds + 1 ten + 3 ones =	3	1	3	= 313
3 hundreds + _ tens + 7 ones =	3	5	7	= 357
6 hundreds + 2 tens + _ ones =	6	2	8	= 628

Page 17

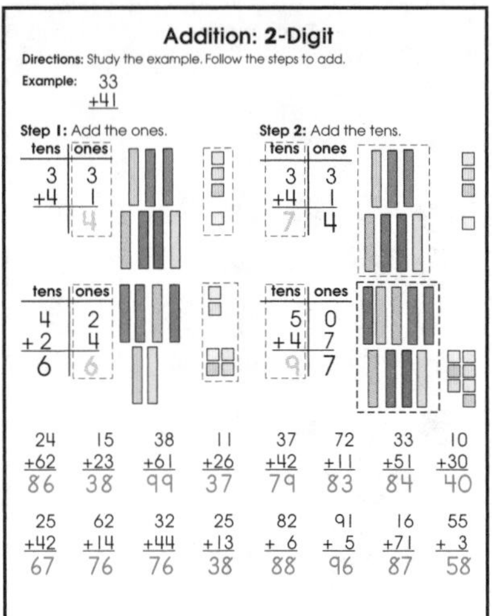

Addition: 2-Digit

Directions: Study the example. Follow the steps to add.

Example: 33 + 41

Step 1: Add the ones. **Step 2:** Add the tens.

tens	ones
3	3
+4	1
7	4

42 + 24 = 66; 50 + 47 = 97

24	15	38	11	37	72	33	10
+62	+23	+61	+26	+42	+11	+51	+30
86	38	99	37	79	83	84	40

25	62	32	25	82	91	16	55
+42	+14	+44	+13	+ 6	+ 5	+71	+ 3
67	76	76	38	88	96	87	58

Page 18

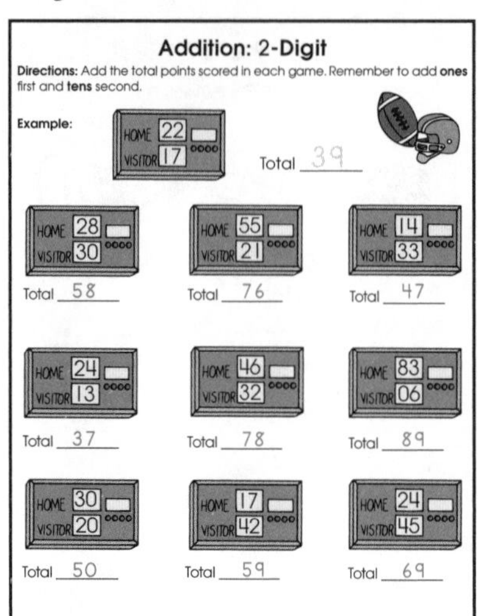

Addition: 2-Digit

Directions: Add the total points scored in each game. Remember to add **ones** first and **tens** second.

Example: HOME 22 VISITOR 17 Total 39

HOME	VISITOR	Total
28	30	58
55	21	76
14	33	47
24	13	37
46	32	78
83	06	89
30	20	50
17	42	59
24	45	69

Page 19

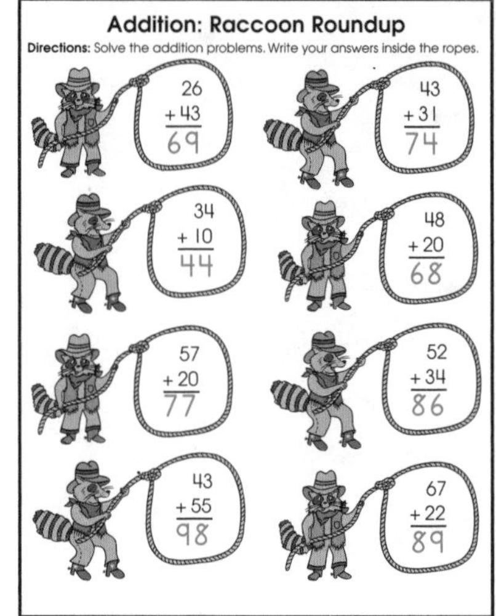

Addition: Raccoon Roundup

Directions: Solve the addition problems. Write your answers inside the ropes.

26	43	34	48	57	52	43	67
+43	+31	+10	+20	+20	+34	+55	+22
69	74	44	68	77	86	98	89

Page 20

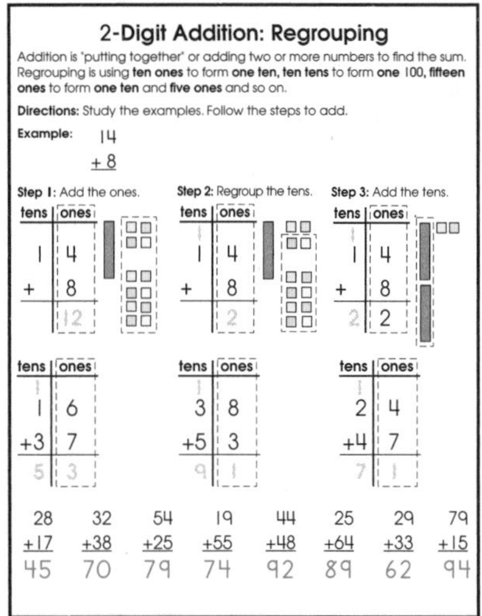

2-Digit Addition: Regrouping

Addition is "putting together" or adding two or more numbers to find the sum. Regrouping is using **ten ones** to form **one ten**, **ten tens** to form **one 100**, **fifteen ones** to form **one ten** and **five ones** and so on.

Directions: Study the examples. Follow the steps to add.

Example: 14 + 8

Step 1: Add the ones. **Step 2:** Regroup the tens. **Step 3:** Add the tens.

16 + 37 = 53; 38 + 53 = 91; 24 + 47 = 71

28	32	54	19	44	25	29	79
+17	+38	+25	+55	+48	+64	+33	+15
45	70	79	74	92	89	62	94

Page 21

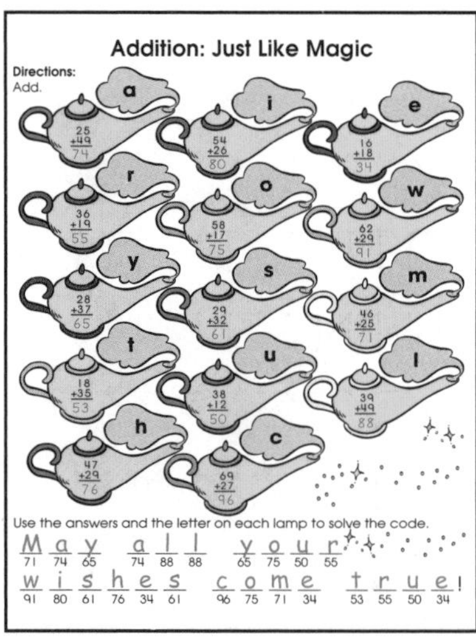

Addition: Just Like Magic

Directions: Add.

a 25 + 49 = 74; i 54 + 26 = 80; e 16 + 18 = 34; r 36 + 19 = 55; o 58 + 17 = 75; w 62 + 29 = 91; y 28 + 37 = 65; s 29 + 32 = 61; m 46 + 25 = 71; t 18 + 35 = 53; u 38 + 12 = 50; l 39 + 49 = 88; h 47 + 29 = 76; c 69 + 27 = 96

Use the answers and the letter on each lamp to solve the code.

May all your wishes come true!

Page 22

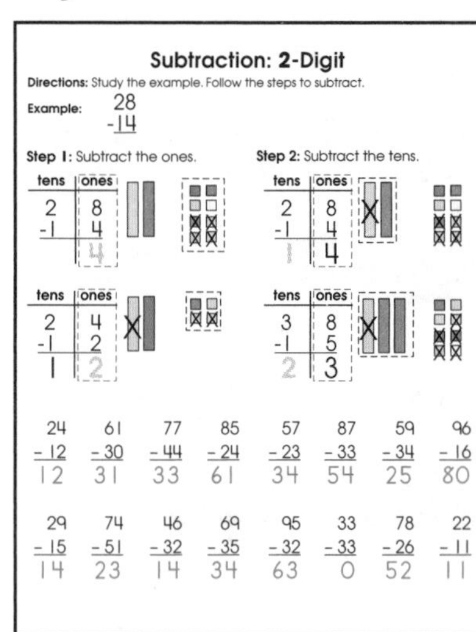

Subtraction: 2-Digit

Directions: Study the example. Follow the steps to subtract.

Example: 28 − 14

Step 1: Subtract the ones. **Step 2:** Subtract the tens.

24 − 12 = 12; 38 − 15 = 23

24	61	77	85	57	87	59	96
−12	−30	−44	−24	−23	−33	−34	−16
12	31	33	61	34	54	25	80

29	74	46	69	95	33	78	22
−15	−51	−32	−35	−32	−33	−26	−11
14	23	14	34	63	0	52	11

Page 23

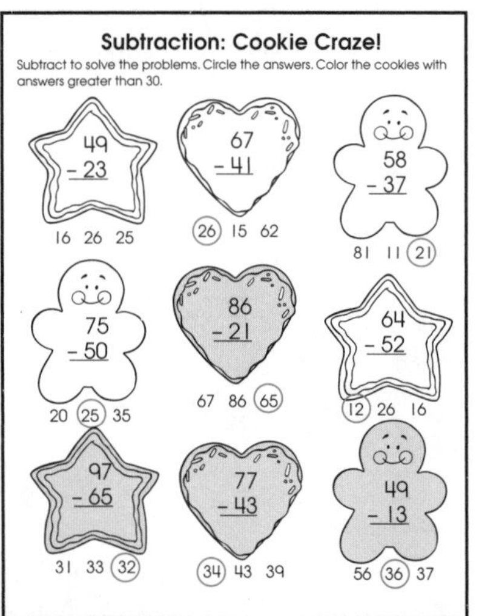

Subtraction: Cookie Craze!

Subtract to solve the problems. Circle the answers. Color the cookies with answers greater than 30.

- 49 − 23: 16 26 25
- 67 − 41: (26) 15 62
- 58 − 37: 81 11 (21)
- 75 − 50: 20 (25) 35
- 86 − 21: 67 86 (65)
- 64 − 52: (12) 26 16
- 97 − 65: 31 33 (32)
- 77 − 43: (34) 43 39
- 49 − 13: 56 (36) 37

Page 24

Subtraction: Prehistoric Problems

Directions: Solve the subtraction problems. Use the code to color the picture.

Code: 25 — blue, 31 — yellow, 21 — brown, 57 — green, 14 — orange, 11 — red

47 − 22 = 25; 52 − 21 = 31; 25 − 11 = 14; 62 − 31 = 31; 77 − 20 = 57; 51 − 40 = 11; 69 − 12 = 57; 98 − 41 = 57; 55 − 34 = 21

Page 25

Subtraction

Subtraction means "taking away" or subtracting one number from another to find the difference. For example, 10 - 3 = 7.

Directions: Subtract.

Example: Subtract the ones. 39 − 24 = 5. Subtract the tens. 39 − 24 = 15

48	95	87	55
-35	-22	-16	-43
13	73	71	12

37	69	44	99
-14	-57	-23	-78
23	12	21	21

66 - 44 = 22 57 - 33 = 24

The yellow car traveled 87 miles per hour. The orange car traveled 66 miles per hour. How much faster was the yellow car traveling? 21 m.p.h.

Page 26

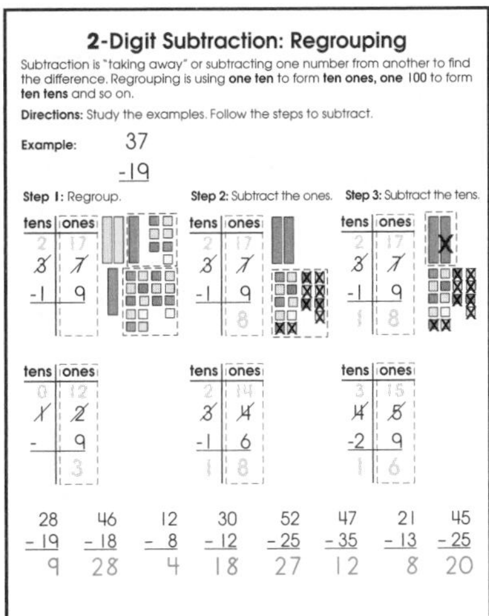

2-Digit Subtraction: Regrouping

Subtraction is "taking away" or subtracting one number from another to find the difference. Regrouping is using **one ten** to form **ten ones**, **one 100** to form **ten tens** and so on.

Directions: Study the examples. Follow the steps to subtract.

Example: 37 − 19

Step 1: Regroup. **Step 2:** Subtract the ones. **Step 3:** Subtract the tens.

28 − 19 = 9; 46 − 18 = 28; 12 − 8 = 4; 30 − 12 = 18; 52 − 25 = 27; 47 − 35 = 12; 21 − 13 = 8; 45 − 25 = 20

Page 27

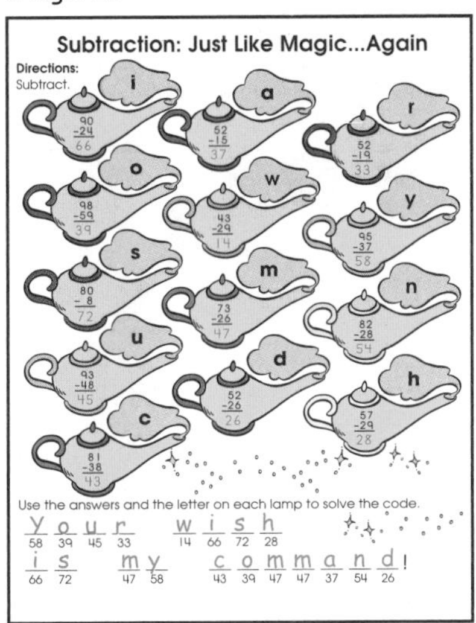

Subtraction: Just Like Magic...Again

Directions: Subtract.

Use the answers and the letter on each lamp to solve the code.

Your wish is my command!

Page 28

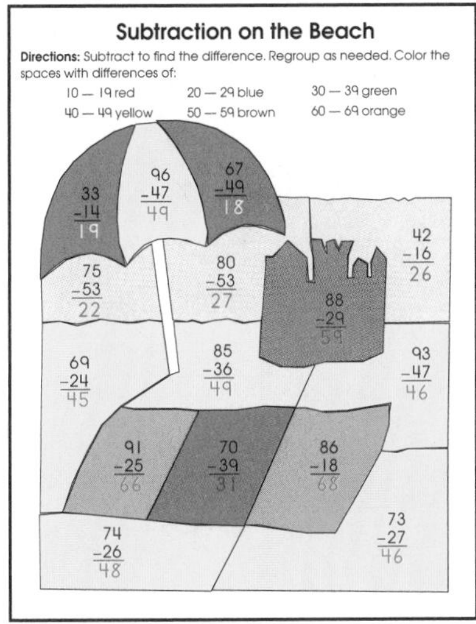

Subtraction on the Beach

Directions: Subtract to find the difference. Regroup as needed. Color the spaces with differences of:

10 — 19 red; 20 — 29 blue; 30 — 39 green; 40 — 49 yellow; 50 — 59 brown; 60 — 69 orange

Page 29

Monster Math

Directions: Add or subtract using regrouping.

84 − 56 = 28; 41 − 17 = 24; 52 − 28 = 24; 84 − 27 = 57; 57 − 39 = 18; 72 − 19 = 53; 33 − 15 = 18; 64 + 17 = 81; 36 − 19 = 17; 65 − 28 = 37; 48 − 30 = 18; 33 + 18 = 51; 25 + 35 = 60

Page 30

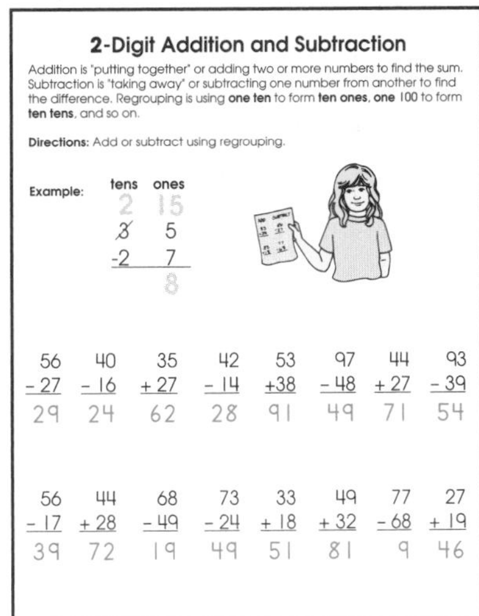

2-Digit Addition and Subtraction

Addition is "putting together" or adding two or more numbers to find the sum. Subtraction is "taking away" or subtracting one number from another to find the difference. Regrouping is using **one ten** to form **ten ones**, **one 100** to form **ten tens**, and so on.

Directions: Add or subtract using regrouping.

Example: 35 − 27 = 8

56 − 27 = 29; 40 − 16 = 24; 35 + 27 = 62; 42 − 14 = 28; 53 + 38 = 91; 97 − 48 = 49; 44 + 27 = 71; 93 − 39 = 54

56 − 17 = 39; 44 + 28 = 72; 68 − 49 = 19; 73 − 24 = 49; 33 + 18 = 51; 49 + 32 = 81; 77 − 68 = 9; 27 + 19 = 46

Page 31

2-Digit Addition and Subtraction

Directions: Add or subtract using regrouping.

23 + 48 = 71; 84 − 56 = 28; 69 + 29 = 98; 41 − 17 = 24

52 − 28 = 24; 73 + 18 = 91; 84 − 27 = 57; 57 − 39 = 18

33 − 15 = 18; 64 + 17 = 81; 37 + 58 = 95; 36 − 19 = 17

65 − 28 = 37; 48 − 30 = 18; 33 + 18 = 51; 25 + 35 = 60

Page 32

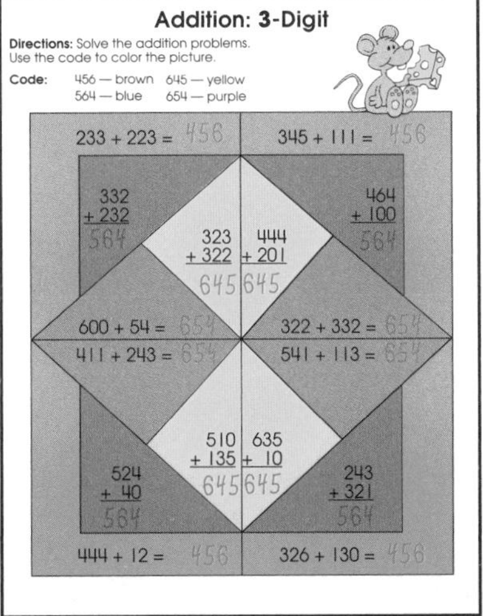

Addition: 3-Digit

Directions: Solve the addition problems. Use the code to color the picture.

Code: 456 — brown; 645 — yellow; 564 — blue; 654 — purple

233 + 223 = 456; 345 + 111 = 456; 332 + 232 = 564; 464 + 100 = 564; 323 + 322 = 645; 444 + 201 = 645; 600 + 54 = 654; 411 + 243 = 654; 322 + 332 = 654; 541 + 113 = 654; 510 + 135 = 645; 635 + 10 = 645; 524 + 40 = 564; 243 + 321 = 564; 444 + 12 = 456; 326 + 130 = 456

Page 33

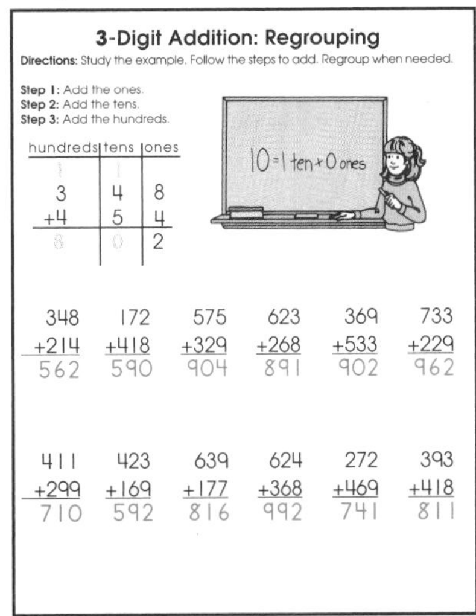

3-Digit Addition: Regrouping

Directions: Study the example. Follow the steps to add. Regroup when needed.

Step 1: Add the ones.
Step 2: Add the tens.
Step 3: Add the hundreds.

348 + 454 = 802

10 = 1 ten + 0 ones

348 + 214 = 562; 172 + 418 = 590; 575 + 329 = 904; 623 + 268 = 891; 369 + 533 = 902; 733 + 229 = 962

411 + 299 = 710; 423 + 169 = 592; 639 + 177 = 816; 624 + 368 = 992; 272 + 469 = 741; 393 + 418 = 811

Page 34

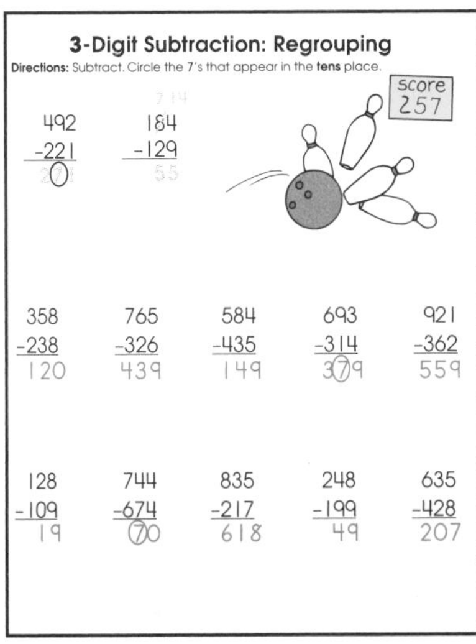

3-Digit Subtraction: Regrouping

Directions: Subtract. Circle the 7's that appear in the **tens** place.

score 257

492 − 221 = 271; 184 − 129 = 55

358 − 238 = 120; 765 − 326 = 439; 584 − 435 = 149; 693 − 314 = 379; 921 − 362 = 559

128 − 109 = 19; 744 − 674 = 70; 835 − 217 = 618; 248 − 199 = 49; 635 − 428 = 207

Page 35

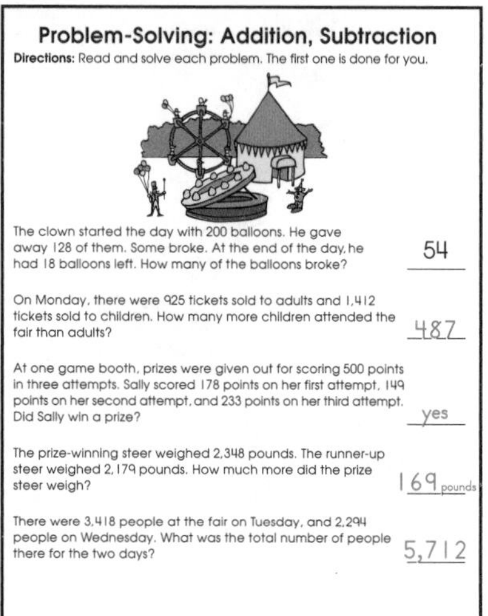

Problem-Solving: Addition, Subtraction

Directions: Read and solve each problem. The first one is done for you.

The clown started the day with 200 balloons. He gave away 128 of them. Some broke. At the end of the day, he had 18 balloons left. How many of the balloons broke? 54

On Monday, there were 925 tickets sold to adults and 1,412 tickets sold to children. How many more children attended the fair than adults? 487

At one game booth, prizes were given out for scoring 500 points in three attempts. Sally scored 178 points on her first attempt, 149 points on her second attempt, and 233 points on her third attempt. Did Sally win a prize? yes

The prize-winning steer weighed 2,348 pounds. The runner-up steer weighed 2,179 pounds. How much more did the prize steer weigh? 169 pounds

There were 3,418 people at the fair on Tuesday, and 2,294 people on Wednesday. What was the total number of people there for the two days? 5,712

Page 36

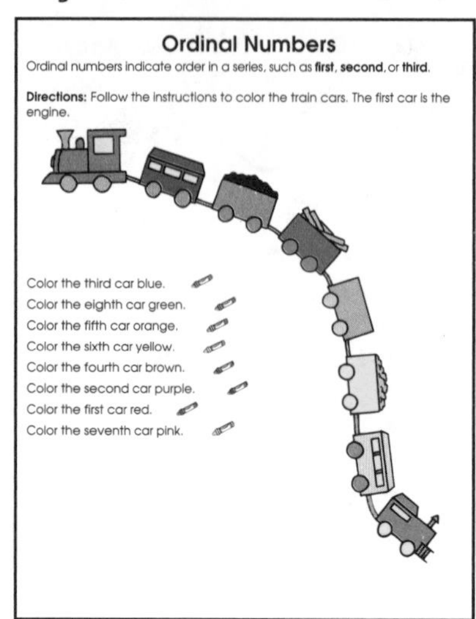

Ordinal Numbers

Ordinal numbers indicate order in a series, such as **first**, **second**, or **third**.

Directions: Follow the instructions to color the train cars. The first car is the engine.

Color the third car blue.
Color the eighth car green.
Color the fifth car orange.
Color the sixth car yellow.
Color the fourth car brown.
Color the second car purple.
Color the first car red.
Color the seventh car pink.

Page 37

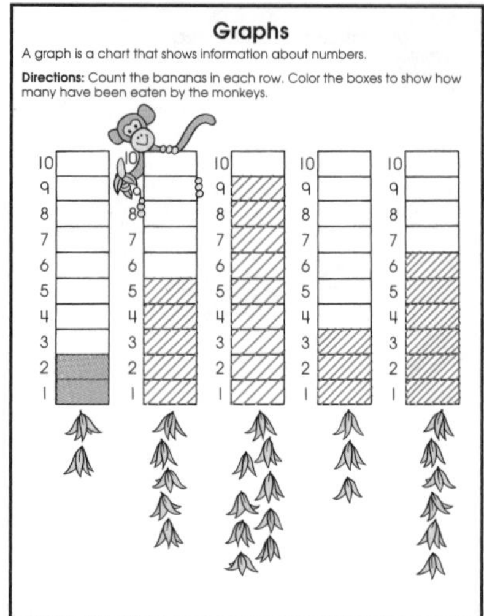

Graphs

A graph is a chart that shows information about numbers.

Directions: Count the bananas in each row. Color the boxes to show how many have been eaten by the monkeys.

Page 38

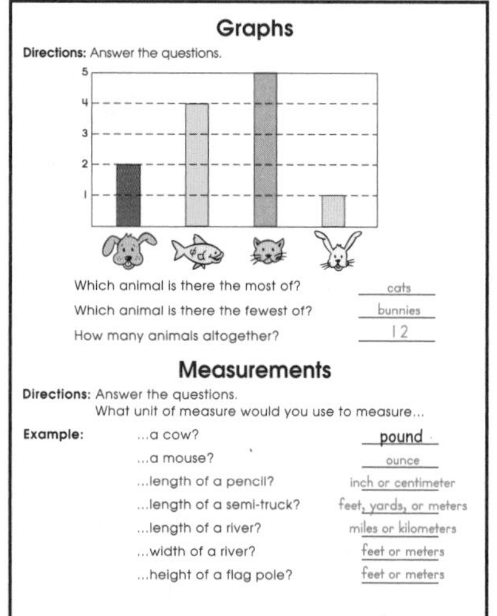

Graphs

Directions: Answer the questions.

Which animal is there the most of? cats
Which animal is there the fewest of? bunnies
How many animals altogether? 12

Measurements

Directions: Answer the questions.
What unit of measure would you use to measure...

Example:	...a cow?	pound
	...a mouse?	ounce
	...length of a pencil?	inch or centimeter
	...length of a semi-truck?	feet, yards, or meters
	...length of a river?	miles or kilometers
	...width of a river?	feet or meters
	...height of a flag pole?	feet or meters

Page 39

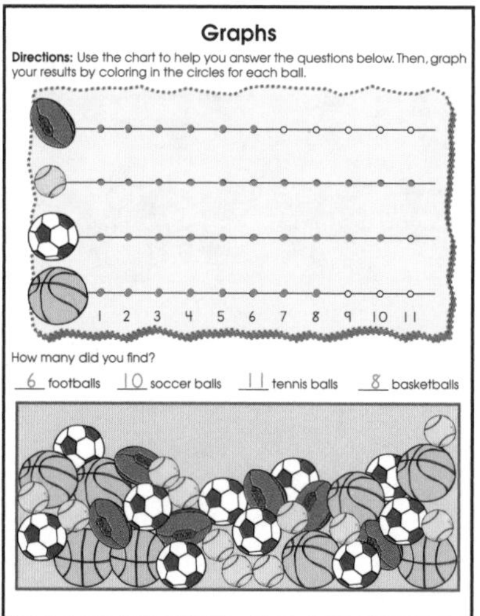

Graphs

Directions: Use the chart to help you answer the questions below. Then, graph your results by coloring in the circles for each ball.

How many did you find?
6 footballs 10 soccer balls 11 tennis balls 8 basketballs

Page 40

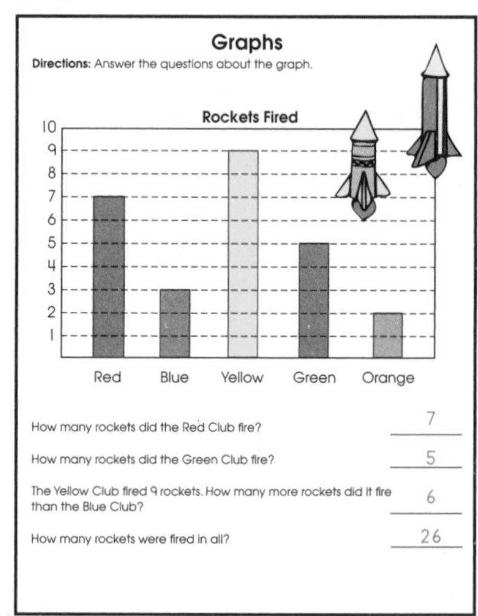

Graphs

Directions: Answer the questions about the graph.

How many rockets did the Red Club fire? 7

How many rockets did the Green Club fire? 5

The Yellow Club fired 9 rockets. How many more rockets did it fire than the Blue Club? 6

How many rockets were fired in all? 26

Page 41

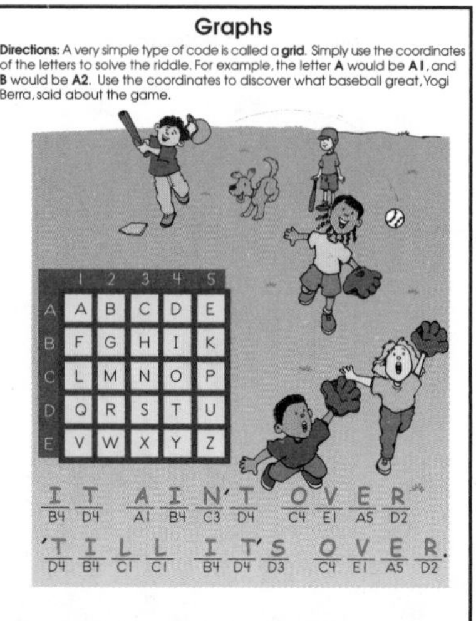

Graphs

Directions: A very simple type of code is called a **grid**. Simply use the coordinates of the letters to solve the riddle. For example, the letter **A** would be **A1**, and **B** would be **A2**. Use the coordinates to discover what baseball great, Yogi Berra, said about the game.

	1	2	3	4	5
A	A	B	C	D	E
B	F	G	H	I	K
C	L	M	N	O	P
D	Q	R	S	T	U
E	V	W	X	Y	Z

IT AIN'T OVER 'TILL IT'S OVER.

Page 42

Graphs

Directions: Use the pictograph of the World Cup champions to answer the questions below.

1. Which country won the most World Cups? Brazil
2. Which countries won the fewest? England and France
3. How many more World Cups did Brazil win than England? 3
4. Which two teams are tied for second place in number of championships? Italy and Germany
5. What is the total number of World Cup championships played? 16
6. Brazil won the 1994 World Cup Championship. Before 1994, which three teams were tied for the most championships? Brazil, Italy, and Germany
7. Which teams are from South America? Argentina, Brazil, and Uruguay
8. How many championships were won by South American teams? 8

Page 43

Greater Than, Less Than

Directions: Write < or > in each circle. Make sure the "mouth" is open toward the greater number!

36 < 49	35 < 53
20 > 18	74 > 21
53 < 76	68 < 80
29 > 26	45 > 19
90 > 89	70 > 67

Page 44

Greater Than, Less Than

Directions: Circle the numbers in each line that make the sentence correct.

3 < 0 1 2 3 (4)(5)(6)(7)(8)(9)(10)
7 > (0)(1)(2)(3)(4)(5)(6) 7 8 9 10
4 = 0 1 2 3 (4) 5 6 7 8 9 10
8 < 0 1 2 3 4 5 6 7 8 (9)(10)
2 > (0)(1) 2 3 4 5 6 7 8 9 10
5 < 0 1 2 3 4 5 (6)(7)(8)(9)(10)
10 > (9)(5)(4)
1 > 9 4 (0)
0 < (2)(7)(10)
9 = 4 8 (9)

Page 45

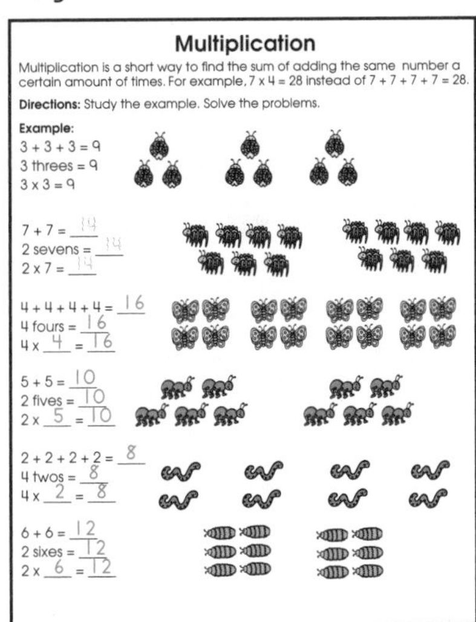

Multiplication

Multiplication is a short way to find the sum of adding the same number a certain amount of times. For example, 7 x 4 = 28 instead of 7 + 7 + 7 + 7 = 28.

Directions: Study the example. Solve the problems.

Example:
3 + 3 + 3 = 9
3 threes = 9
3 x 3 = 9

7 + 7 = 14
2 sevens = 14
2 x 7 = 14

4 + 4 + 4 + 4 = 16
4 fours = 16
4 x 4 = 16

5 + 5 = 10
2 fives = 10
2 x 5 = 10

2 + 2 + 2 + 2 = 8
4 twos = 8
4 x 2 = 8

6 + 6 = 12
2 sixes = 12
2 x 6 = 12

Page 46

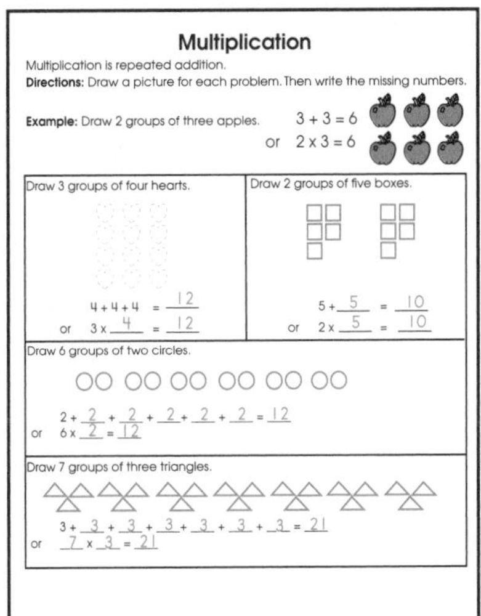

Multiplication

Multiplication is repeated addition.
Directions: Draw a picture for each problem. Then write the missing numbers.

Example: Draw 2 groups of three apples. 3 + 3 = 6 or 2 x 3 = 6

Draw 3 groups of four hearts. 4 + 4 + 4 = 12 or 3 x 4 = 12

Draw 2 groups of five boxes. 5 + 5 = 10 or 2 x 5 = 10

Draw 6 groups of two circles. 2 + 2 + 2 + 2 + 2 + 2 = 12 or 6 x 2 = 12

Draw 7 groups of three triangles. 3 + 3 + 3 + 3 + 3 + 3 + 3 = 21 or 7 x 3 = 21

Page 47

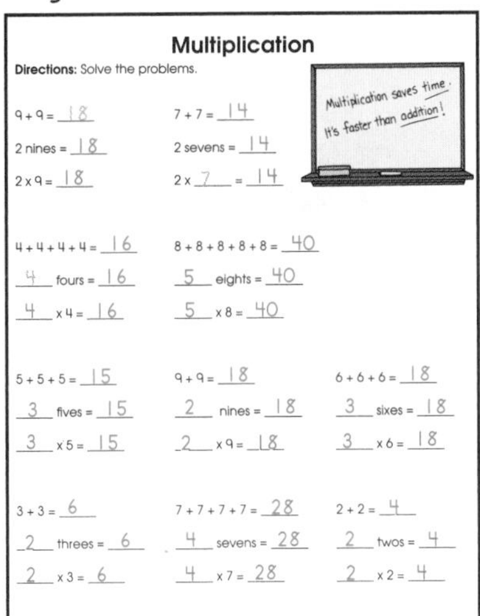

Multiplication

Directions: Solve the problems.

9 + 9 = 18
2 nines = 18
2 x 9 = 18

7 + 7 = 14
2 sevens = 14
2 x 7 = 14

4 + 4 + 4 + 4 = 16
4 fours = 16
4 x 4 = 16

8 + 8 + 8 + 8 + 8 = 40
5 eights = 40
5 x 8 = 40

5 + 5 + 5 = 15
3 fives = 15
3 x 5 = 15

9 + 9 = 18
2 nines = 18
2 x 9 = 18

6 + 6 + 6 = 18
3 sixes = 18
3 x 6 = 18

3 + 3 = 6
2 threes = 6
2 x 3 = 6

7 + 7 + 7 + 7 = 28
4 sevens = 28
4 x 7 = 28

2 + 2 = 4
2 twos = 4
2 x 2 = 4

Page 48

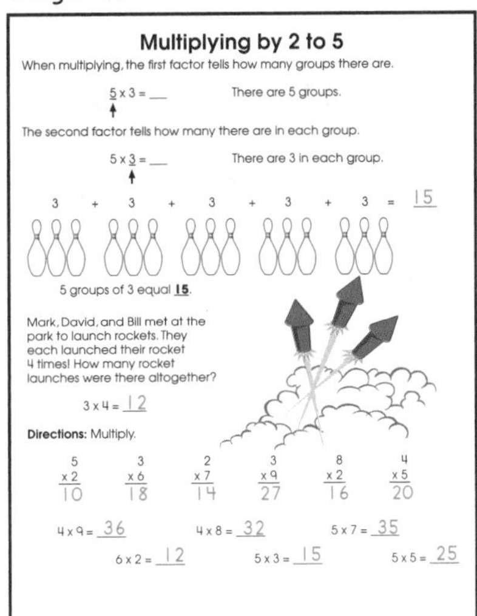

Multiplying by 2 to 5

When multiplying, the first factor tells how many groups there are.

5 x 3 = ___ There are 5 groups.

The second factor tells how many there are in each group.

5 x 3 = ___ There are 3 in each group.

3 + 3 + 3 + 3 + 3 = 15

5 groups of 3 equal **15**.

Mark, David, and Bill met at the park to launch rockets. They each launched their rocket 4 times! How many rocket launches were there altogether?

3 x 4 = 12

Directions: Multiply.

5 x 2 = 10; 3 x 6 = 18; 2 x 7 = 14; 3 x 9 = 27; 8 x 2 = 16; 4 x 5 = 20

4 x 9 = 36; 4 x 8 = 32; 5 x 7 = 35
6 x 2 = 12; 5 x 3 = 15; 5 x 5 = 25

Page 49

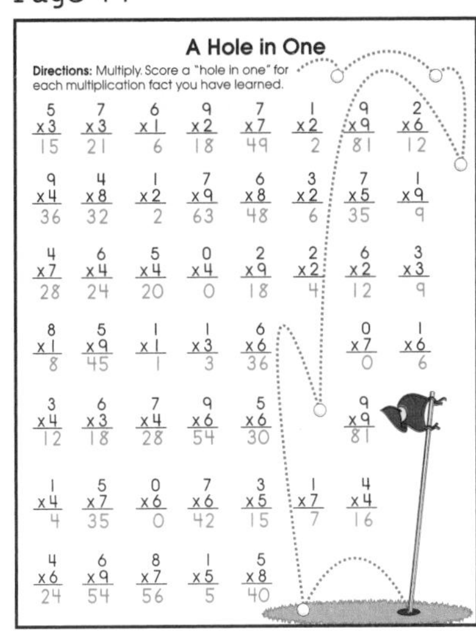

A Hole in One

Directions: Multiply. Score a "hole in one" for each multiplication fact you have learned.

5 x 3 = 15; 7 x 3 = 21; 6 x 1 = 6; 9 x 2 = 18; 7 x 7 = 49; 1 x 2 = 2; 9 x 9 = 81; 2 x 6 = 12
9 x 4 = 36; 4 x 8 = 32; 1 x 2 = 2; 7 x 9 = 63; 6 x 8 = 48; 3 x 2 = 6; 7 x 5 = 35; 1 x 9 = 9
4 x 7 = 28; 6 x 4 = 24; 5 x 4 = 20; 0 x 4 = 0; 2 x 9 = 18; 2 x 2 = 4; 6 x 2 = 12; 3 x 3 = 9
8 x 1 = 8; 5 x 9 = 45; 1 x 1 = 1; 1 x 3 = 3; 6 x 6 = 36; 0 x 7 = 0; 1 x 6 = 6
3 x 4 = 12; 6 x 3 = 18; 7 x 4 = 28; 9 x 6 = 54; 5 x 6 = 30; 9 x 9 = 81
1 x 4 = 4; 5 x 7 = 35; 0 x 6 = 0; 7 x 6 = 42; 3 x 5 = 15; 1 x 7 = 7; 4 x 4 = 16
4 x 6 = 24; 6 x 9 = 54; 8 x 7 = 56; 1 x 5 = 5; 5 x 8 = 40

Page 50

Slam Dunk Multiplication

Directions: Solve each multiplication problem. If the product ends in an odd number, color the net yellow. If the product ends in an even number, color the net orange.

Page 51

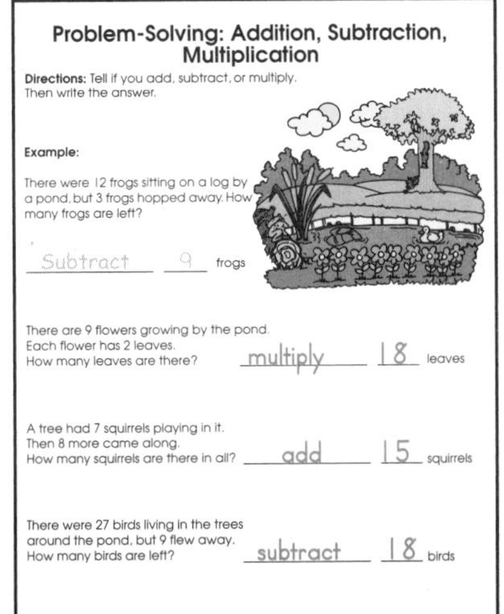

Problem-Solving: Addition, Subtraction, Multiplication

Directions: Tell if you add, subtract, or multiply. Then write the answer.

Example:

There were 12 frogs sitting on a log by a pond, but 3 frogs hopped away. How many frogs are left? Subtract 9 frogs

There are 9 flowers growing by the pond. Each flower has 2 leaves. How many leaves are there? multiply 18 leaves

A tree had 7 squirrels playing in it. Then 8 more came along. How many squirrels are there in all? add 15 squirrels

There were 27 birds living in the trees around the pond, but 9 flew away. How many birds are left? subtract 18 birds

Page 52

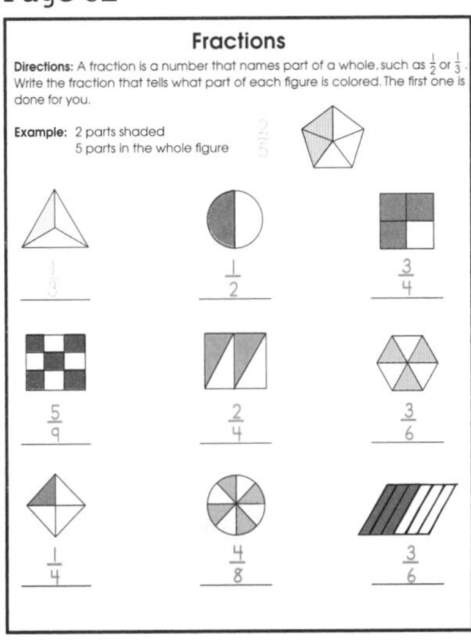

Fractions

Directions: A fraction is a number that names part of a whole, such as $\frac{1}{2}$ or $\frac{1}{3}$. Write the fraction that tells what part of each figure is colored. The first one is done for you.

Example: 2 parts shaded, 5 parts in the whole figure $\frac{2}{5}$

$\frac{1}{3}$ $\frac{1}{2}$ $\frac{3}{4}$

$\frac{5}{9}$ $\frac{2}{4}$ $\frac{3}{6}$

$\frac{1}{4}$ $\frac{4}{8}$ $\frac{3}{6}$

Page 53

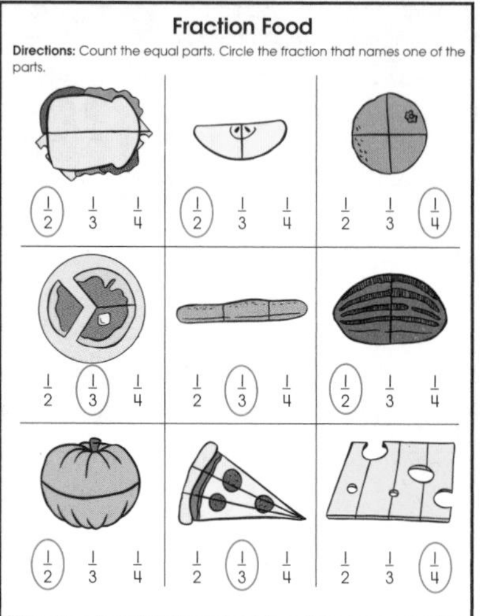

Page 54

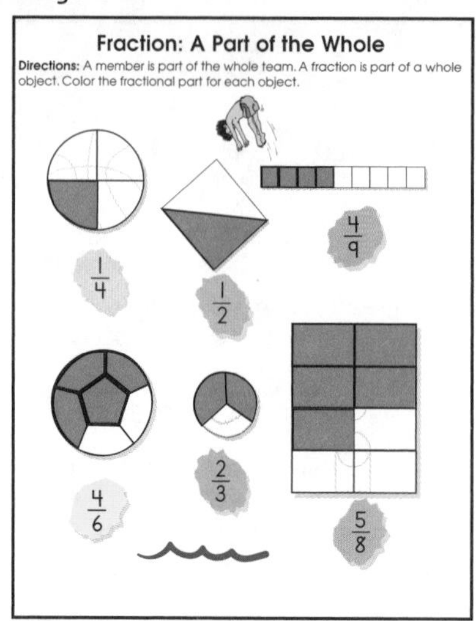

Page 55

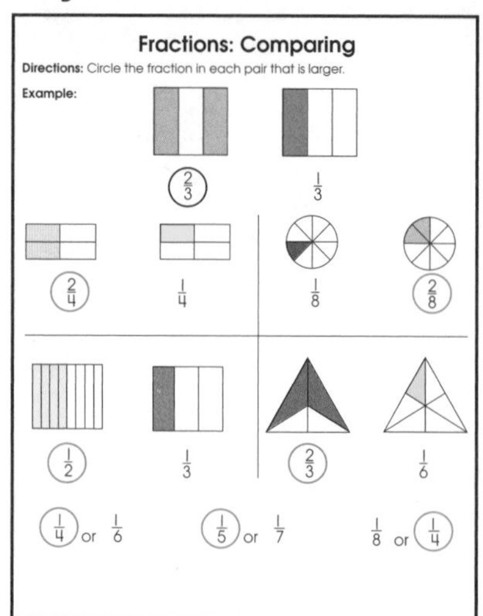

Page 56

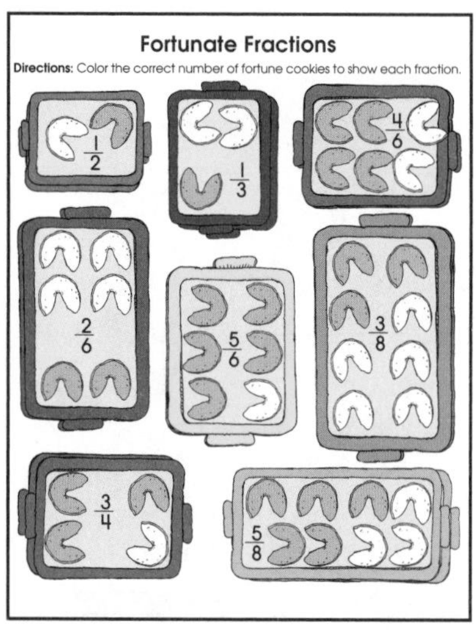

Page 57

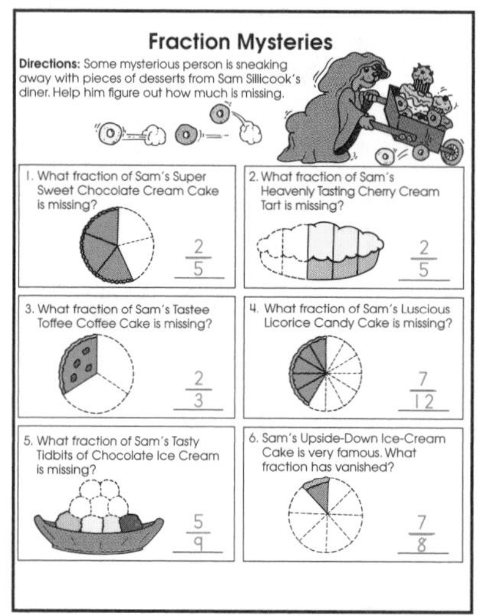

Page 58

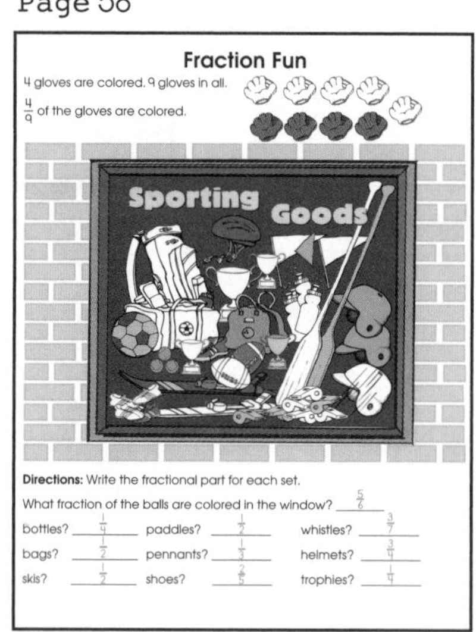

Page 59

Page 60

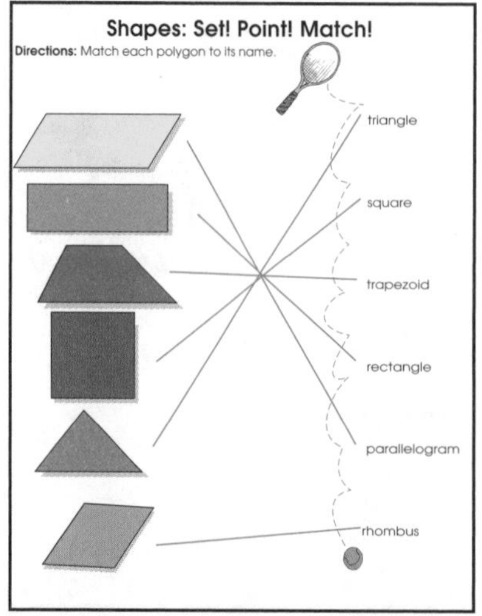

Page 61

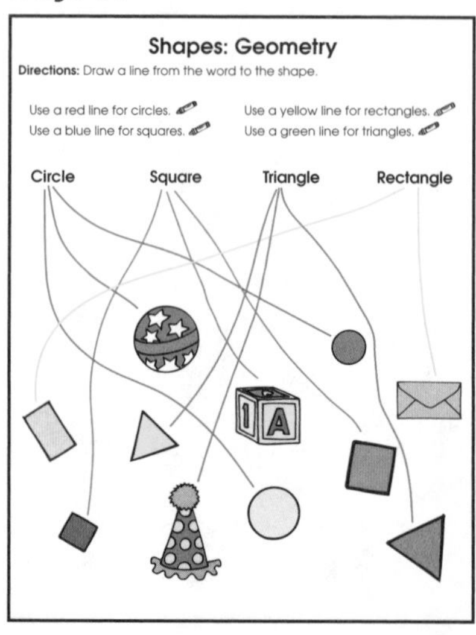

Page 62

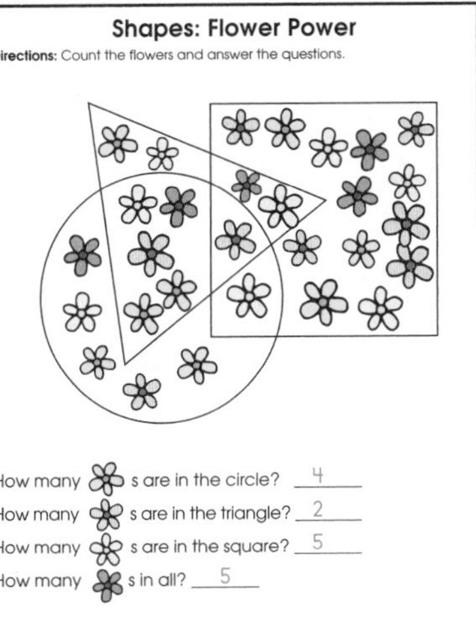

Shapes: Flower Power

Directions: Count the flowers and answer the questions.

How many ✿s are in the circle? 4

How many ✿s are in the triangle? 2

How many ✿s are in the square? 5

How many ✿s in all? 5

Page 63

How Many Shapes?

Directions: Find the shapes and color them using the code.

red blue yellow green orange black

Page 64

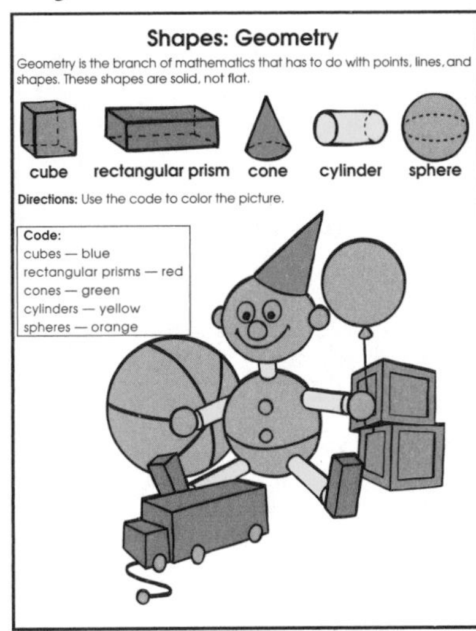

Shapes: Geometry

Geometry is the branch of mathematics that has to do with points, lines, and shapes. These shapes are solid, not flat.

cube rectangular prism cone cylinder sphere

Directions: Use the code to color the picture.

Code:
cubes — blue
rectangular prisms — red
cones — green
cylinders — yellow
spheres — orange

Page 65

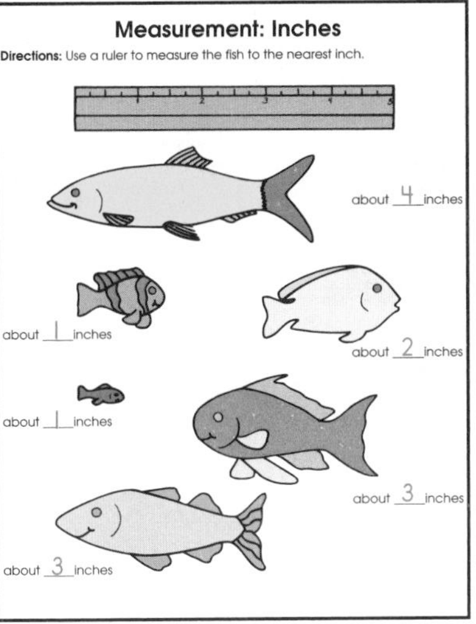

Measurement: Inches

Directions: Use a ruler to measure the fish to the nearest inch.

about 4 inches

about 1 inches

about 2 inches

about 1 inches

about 3 inches

about 3 inches

Page 66

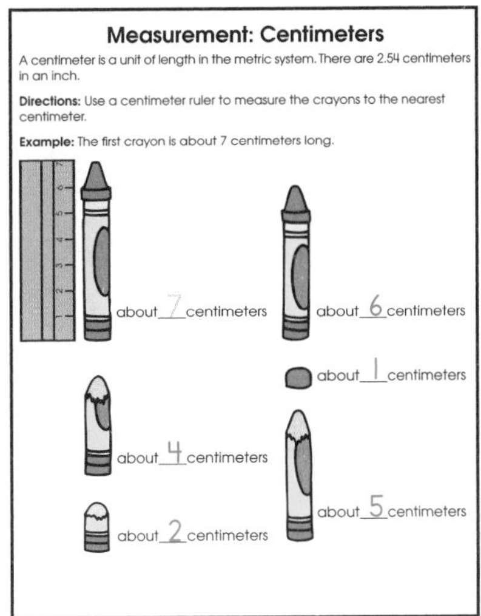

Measurement: Centimeters

A centimeter is a unit of length in the metric system. There are 2.54 centimeters in an inch.

Directions: Use a centimeter ruler to measure the crayons to the nearest centimeter.

Example: The first crayon is about 7 centimeters long.

about 7 centimeters

about 6 centimeters

about 1 centimeters

about 4 centimeters

about 5 centimeters

about 2 centimeters

Page 67

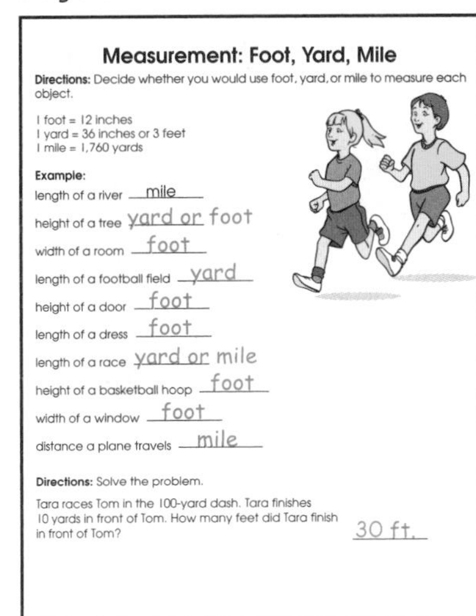

Measurement: Foot, Yard, Mile

Directions: Decide whether you would use foot, yard, or mile to measure each object.

1 foot = 12 inches
1 yard = 36 inches or 3 feet
1 mile = 1,760 yards

Example:

length of a river mile

height of a tree yard or foot

width of a room foot

length of a football field yard

height of a door foot

length of a dress foot

length of a race yard or mile

height of a basketball hoop foot

width of a window foot

distance a plane travels mile

Directions: Solve the problem.

Tara races Tom in the 100-yard dash. Tara finishes 10 yards in front of Tom. How many feet did Tara finish in front of Tom? 30 ft.

Page 68

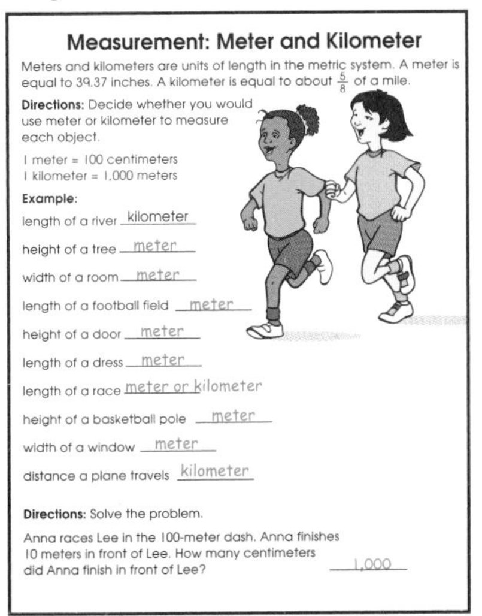

Measurement: Meter and Kilometer

Meters and kilometers are units of length in the metric system. A meter is equal to 39.37 inches. A kilometer is equal to about $\frac{5}{8}$ of a mile.

Directions: Decide whether you would use meter or kilometer to measure each object.

1 meter = 100 centimeters
1 kilometer = 1,000 meters

Example:

length of a river kilometer

height of a tree meter

width of a room meter

length of a football field meter

height of a door meter

length of a dress meter

length of a race meter or kilometer

height of a basketball pole meter

width of a window meter

distance a plane travels kilometer

Directions: Solve the problem.

Anna races Lee in the 100-meter dash. Anna finishes 10 meters in front of Lee. How many centimeters did Anna finish in front of Lee? 1,000

Page 69

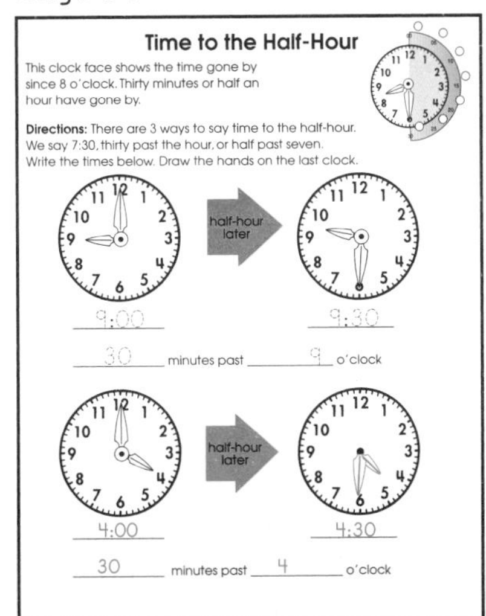

Time to the Half-Hour

This clock face shows the time gone by since 8 o'clock. Thirty minutes or half an hour have gone by.

Directions: There are 3 ways to say time to the half-hour. We say 7:30, thirty past the hour, or half past seven. Write the times below. Draw the hands on the last clock.

half-hour later

9:00 9:30

30 minutes past 9 o'clock

half-hour later

4:00 4:30

30 minutes past 4 o'clock

Page 70

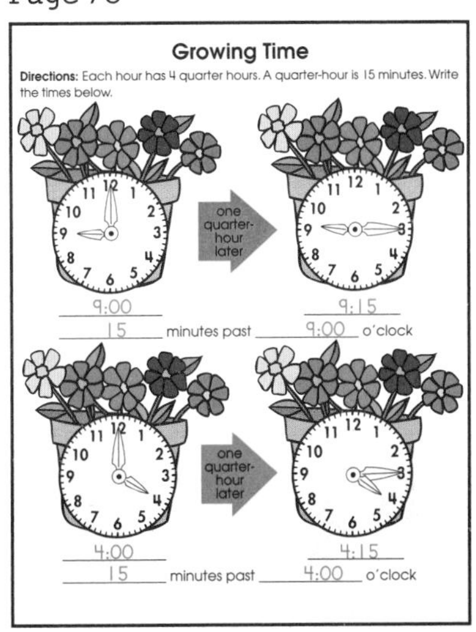

Growing Time

Directions: Each hour has 4 quarter hours. A quarter-hour is 15 minutes. Write the times below.

one quarter-hour later

9:00 9:15

15 minutes past 9:00 o'clock

one quarter-hour later

4:00 4:15

15 minutes past 4:00 o'clock

Time to the Minute

Each number on the clock face stands for 5 minutes.

Directions: Count by 5's beginning at 12. Write the numbers below.

00 05 10 15 20 25

It is 25 minutes after 8 o'clock. It is written 8:25.

Directions: Count by 5's.

00 05 10 15 20

25 30 35

It is 35 minutes after 8 o'clock. It is written 8:35.

Page 72

Digital Magic

Directions: Write the time on the digital clocks.

5:00 12:00

8:00 3:00

Page 73

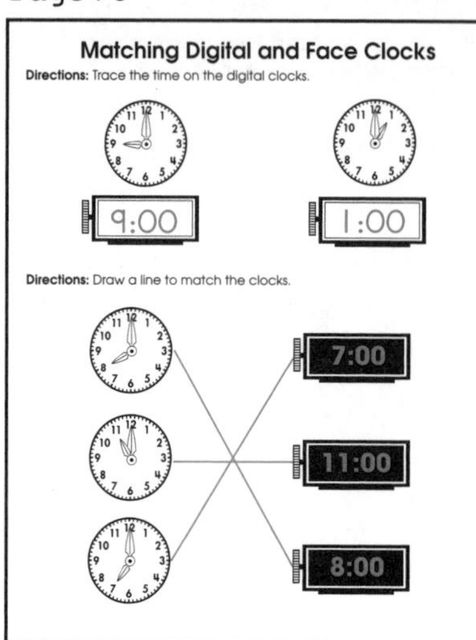

Matching Digital and Face Clocks

Directions: Trace the time on the digital clocks.

9:00 1:00

Directions: Draw a line to match the clocks.

7:00

11:00

8:00

Page 74

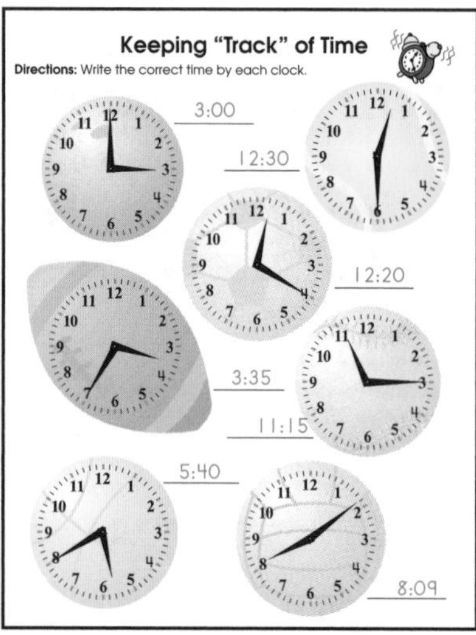

Keeping "Track" of Time

Directions: Write the correct time by each clock.

3:00

12:30

12:20

3:35

11:15

5:40

8:09

Page 75

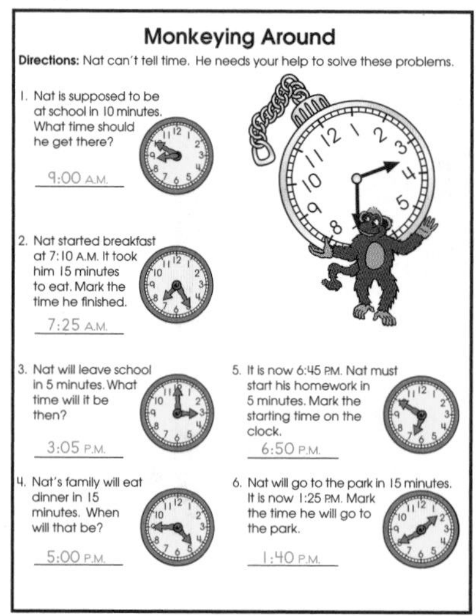

Monkeying Around

Directions: Nat can't tell time. He needs your help to solve these problems.

1. Nat is supposed to be at school in 10 minutes. What time should he get there? 9:00 A.M.
2. Nat started breakfast at 7:10 A.M. It took him 15 minutes to eat. Mark the time he finished. 7:25 A.M.
3. Nat will leave school in 5 minutes. What time will it be then? 3:05 P.M.
4. Nat's family will eat dinner in 15 minutes. When will that be? 5:00 P.M.
5. It is now 6:45 P.M. Nat must start his homework in 5 minutes. Mark the starting time on the clock. 6:50 P.M.
6. Nat will go to the park in 15 minutes. It is now 1:25 P.M. Mark the time he will go to the park. 1:40 P.M.

Page 76

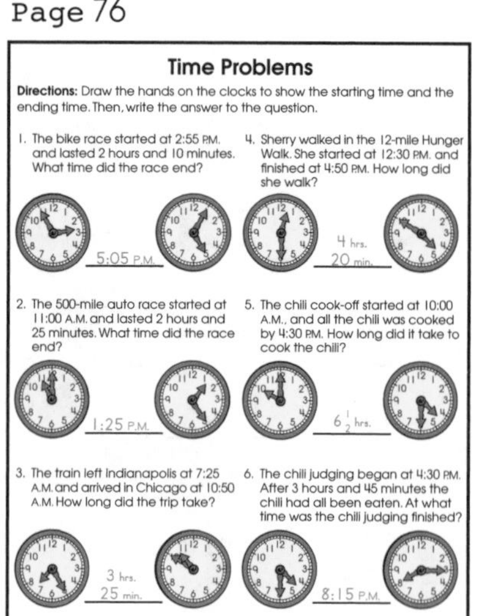

Time Problems

Directions: Draw the hands on the clocks to show the starting time and the ending time. Then, write the answer to the question.

1. The bike race started at 2:55 P.M. and lasted 2 hours and 10 minutes. What time did the race end? 5:05 P.M.
2. The 500-mile auto race started at 11:00 A.M. and lasted 2 hours and 25 minutes. What time did the race end? 1:25 P.M.
3. The train left Indianapolis at 7:25 A.M. and arrived in Chicago at 10:50 A.M. How long did the trip take? 3 hrs. 25 min.
4. Sherry walked in the 12-mile Hunger Walk. She started at 12:30 P.M. and finished at 4:50 P.M. How long did she walk? 4 hrs. 20 min.
5. The chili cook-off started at 10:00 A.M., and all the chili was cooked by 4:30 P.M. How long did it take to cook the chili? $6\frac{1}{2}$ hrs.
6. The chili judging began at 4:30 P.M. After 3 hours and 45 minutes the chili had all been eaten. At what time was the chili judging finished? 8:15 P.M.

Page 77

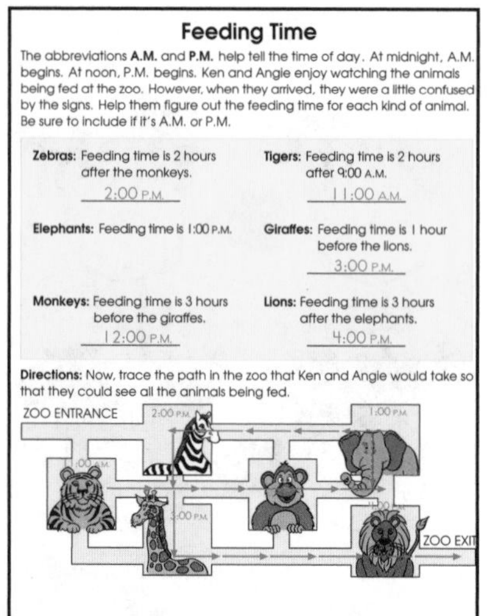

Feeding Time

The abbreviations **A.M.** and **P.M.** help tell the time of day. At midnight, A.M. begins. At noon, P.M. begins. Ken and Angie enjoy watching the animals being fed at the zoo. However, when they arrived, they were a little confused by the signs. Help them figure out the feeding time for each kind of animal. Be sure to include if it's A.M. or P.M.

Zebras: Feeding time is 2 hours after the monkeys. 2:00 P.M.

Tigers: Feeding time is 2 hours after 9:00 A.M. 11:00 A.M.

Elephants: Feeding time is 1:00 P.M.

Giraffes: Feeding time is 1 hour before the lions. 3:00 P.M.

Monkeys: Feeding time is 3 hours before the giraffes. 12:00 P.M.

Lions: Feeding time is 3 hours after the elephants. 4:00 P.M.

Directions: Now, trace the path in the zoo that Ken and Angie would take so that they could see all the animals being fed.

Page 78

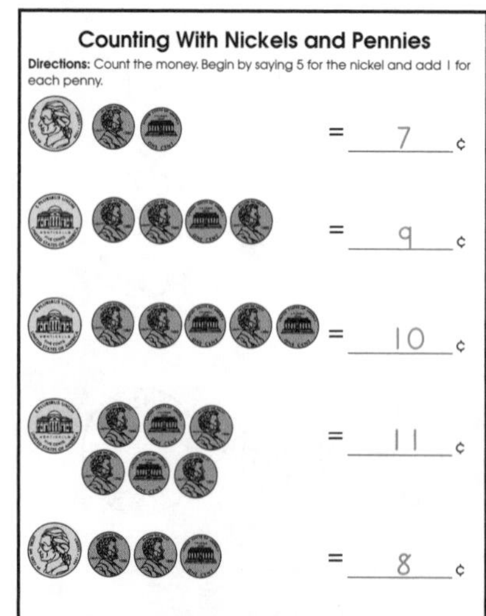

Counting With Nickels and Pennies

Directions: Count the money. Begin by saying 5 for the nickel and add 1 for each penny.

= 7 ¢

= 9 ¢

= 10 ¢

= 11 ¢

= 8 ¢

Page 79

Counting With Dimes and Nickels

Directions: Count the money. Begin by saying 10 for the dimes, then count the nickels. Write the amount.

10 20 25 30 35 ¢ = 35 ¢ Total

10 20 30 40 50 55

60 65 70 = 70 ¢

I'm counting my money. 10¢, 20¢, 30¢, 35¢, 40¢, 45¢, 50¢...

Solve this puzzle. What coins does the chicken have?

dimes and nickels

Page 80

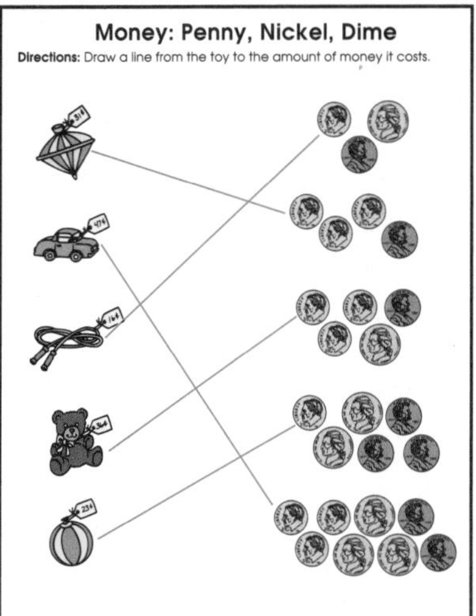

Money: Penny, Nickel, Dime

Directions: Draw a line from the toy to the amount of money it costs.

Page 81

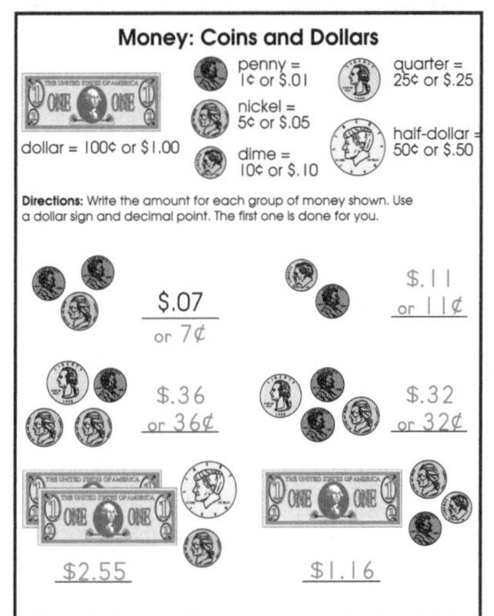

Money: Coins and Dollars

dollar = 100¢ or $1.00

penny = 1¢ or $.01

nickel = 5¢ or $.05

dime = 10¢ or $.10

quarter = 25¢ or $.25

half-dollar = 50¢ or $.50

Directions: Write the amount for each group of money shown. Use a dollar sign and decimal point. The first one is done for you.

$.07 or 7¢

$.11 or 11¢

$.36 or 36¢

$.32 or 32¢

$2.55

$1.16

Page 82

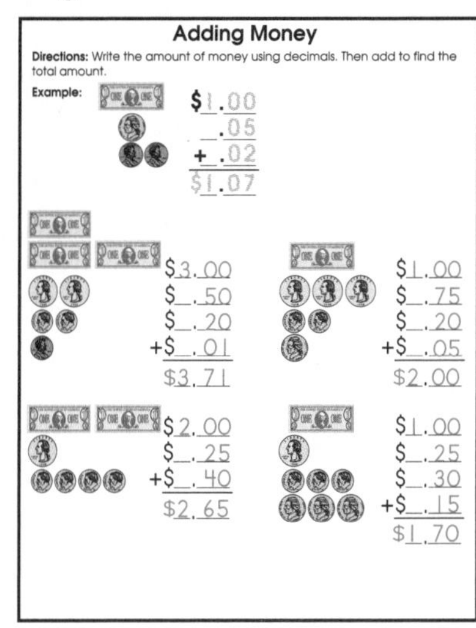

Adding Money

Directions: Write the amount of money using decimals. Then add to find the total amount.

Example:

$1.00
.05
+ .02
$1.07

$3.00 $.50 $.20 +$.01 $3.71	$1.00 $.75 $.20 +$.05 $2.00
$2.00 $.25 +$.40 $2.65	$1.00 $.25 $.30 +$.15 $1.70

Page 83

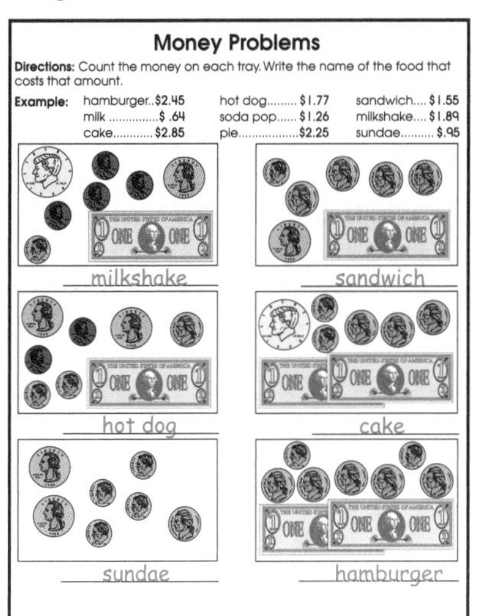

Money Problems

Directions: Count the money on each tray. Write the name of the food that costs that amount.

Example:

hamburger..$2.45	hot dog.........$1.77	sandwich.... $1.55
milk ....$ .64	soda pop...... $1.26	milkshake.... $1.89
cake............ $2.85	pie.................$2.25	sundae.......... $.95

milkshake

sandwich

hot dog

cake

sundae

hamburger

Page 84

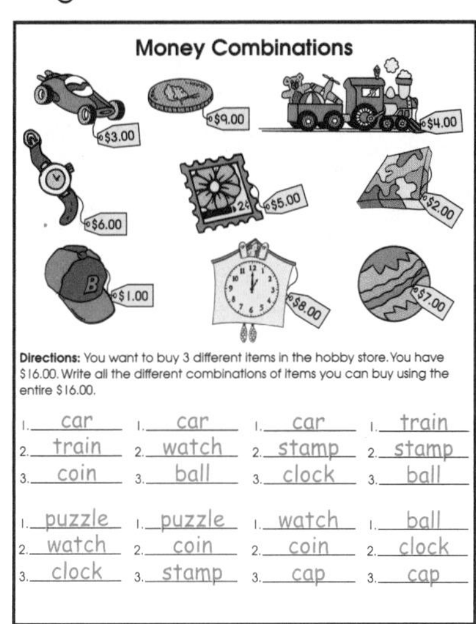

Money Combinations

$3.00

$9.00

$4.00

$6.00

$5.00

$2.00

$1.00

$8.00

$7.00

Directions: You want to buy 3 different items in the hobby store. You have $16.00. Write all the different combinations of items you can buy using the entire $16.00.

1. car 2. train 3. coin	1. car 2. watch 3. ball	1. car 2. stamp 3. clock	1. train 2. stamp 3. ball
1. puzzle 2. watch 3. clock	1. puzzle 2. coin 3. stamp	1. watch 2. coin 3. cap	1. ball 2. clock 3. cap

Page 85

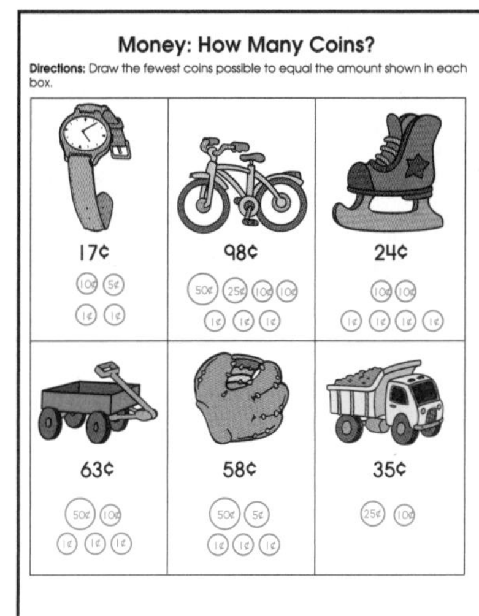

Money: How Many Coins?

Directions: Draw the fewest coins possible to equal the amount shown in each box.

17¢ 10¢ 5¢ 1¢ 1¢	98¢ 50¢ 25¢ 10¢ 10¢ 1¢ 1¢ 1¢	24¢ 10¢ 10¢ 1¢ 1¢ 1¢ 1¢
63¢ 50¢ 10¢ 1¢ 1¢ 1¢	58¢ 50¢ 5¢ 1¢ 1¢ 1¢	35¢ 25¢ 10¢

Page 86

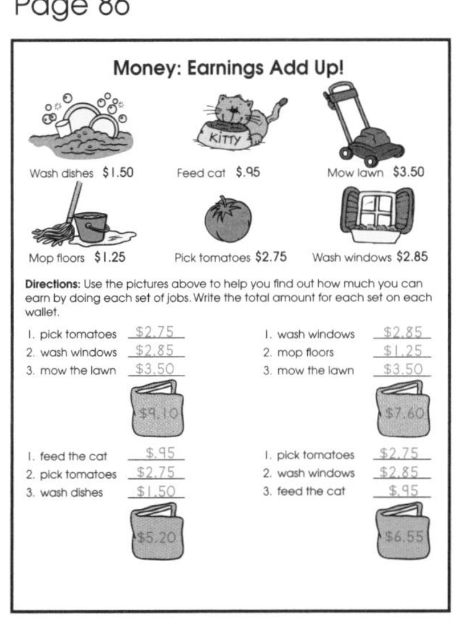

Money: Earnings Add Up!

Wash dishes $1.50

Feed cat $.95

Mow lawn $3.50

Mop floors $1.25

Pick tomatoes $2.75

Wash windows $2.85

Directions: Use the pictures above to help you find out how much you can earn by doing each set of jobs. Write the total amount for each set on each wallet.

1. pick tomatoes $2.75 2. wash windows $2.85 3. mow the lawn $3.50 $9.10	1. wash windows $2.85 2. mop floors $1.25 3. mow the lawn $3.50 $7.60
1. feed the cat $.95 2. pick tomatoes $2.75 3. wash dishes $1.50 $5.20	1. pick tomatoes $2.75 2. wash windows $2.85 3. feed the cat $.95 $6.55

Page 87

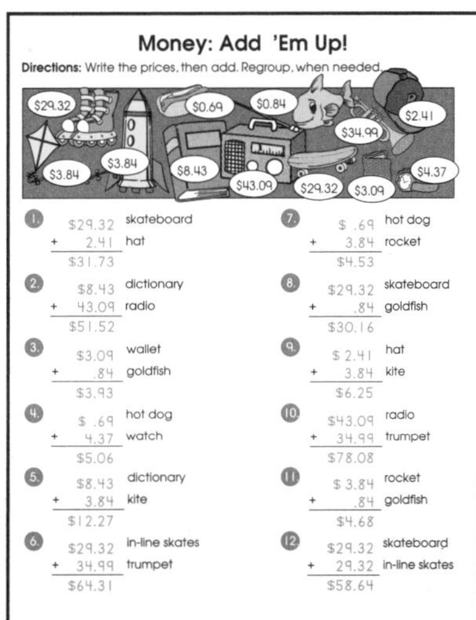

Money: Add 'Em Up!

Directions: Write the prices, then add. Regroup, when needed.

1. $29.32 skateboard + 2.41 hat $31.73	7. $ .69 hot dog + 3.84 rocket $4.53
2. $8.43 dictionary + 43.09 radio $51.52	8. $29.32 skateboard + .84 goldfish $30.16
3. $3.09 wallet + .84 goldfish $3.93	9. $2.41 hat + 3.84 kite $6.25
4. $ .69 hot dog + 4.37 watch $5.06	10. $43.09 radio + 34.99 trumpet $78.08
5. $8.43 dictionary + 3.84 kite $12.27	11. $3.84 rocket + .84 goldfish $4.68
6. $29.32 in-line skates + 34.99 trumpet $64.31	12. $29.32 skateboard + 29.32 in-line skates $58.64

Page 88

Money: Making Change

Directions: When you do not have the exact change to buy something at a store, the clerk must give you change. The first amount of money is what you give the clerk. The second amount is what the item costs. In the box, list the fewest number of coins and bills you will receive in change.

	Amount I Have	Cost of Item	Change
1	$3.75	$3.54	2 dimes, 1 penny
2	$10.00	$5.63	four 1 dollar bills, 1 quarter, 1 dime, 2 pennies
3	$7.00	$6.05	3 quarters, 2 dimes
4	$7.25	$6.50	3 quarters
5	$7.50	$6.13	1 dollar bill, 1 quarter, 1 dime, 2 pennies
6	$0.75	$0.37	1 quarter, 1 dime, 2 pennies
7	$7.00	$6.99	1 penny
8	$15.00	$12.75	two 1 dollar bills, 1 quarter

Developmental Skills for Third Grade Math Success

Parents and educators alike know that the School Specialty name ensures outstanding educational experience and content. Summer Link Math was designed to help your child retain those skills learned during the past school year. With Summer Link Math, your child will be ready to review and take on new material with confidence when he or she returns to school in the fall. The skills reviewed here will help your child be prepared for proficiency testing.

You can use this checklist to evaluate your child's progress. Place a check mark in the box if the appropriate skill has been mastered. If your child needs more work with a particular skill, place an "R" in the box and come back to it for review.

Math Skills

- [ ] Counts by 2's to 100
- [ ] Counts by 5's to 100
- [ ] Counts by 10's to 100
- [ ] Recognizes number symbols 0—1,000
- [ ] Completes simple patterns
- [ ] Names basic geometric shapes
- [ ] Sort objects using at least one attribute
- [ ] Can add up to 100
- [ ] Can subtract from 100
- [ ] Interprets and creates graphs
- [ ] Indicates order using ordinal numbers
- [ ] Can identify > and < signs
- [ ] Can write fractions from numeric pictures
- [ ] Understands numbers having place values to 3 digits
- [ ] Completes two-digit addition; no regrouping
- [ ] Completes two-digit addition with regrouping
- [ ] Completes two-digit subtraction; no regrouping
- [ ] Completes two-digit subtraction with regrouping
- [ ] Completes three-digit addition; no regrouping
- [ ] Completes three-digit subtraction; no regrouping
- [ ] Performs (3 single digits) column addition
- [ ] Knows values of coins in combination
- [ ] Can solve money addition problems
- [ ] Can measure items using simple standard units
- [ ] Understands basic concept of multiplication
- [ ] Can tell time at various intervals
- [ ] Makes estimations based on past experiences
- [ ] Can name fractions of objects using $\frac{1}{4}$, $\frac{1}{3}$, and $\frac{1}{2}$
- [ ] Uses problem-solving strategies

SUMMER LINK

READING

Recommended Reading
Summer Before Grade 3

• **Animal Close-Ups Series**	Barbara Taylor
• **Araminta's Paint Box; Song and Dance Man**	Karen Ackerman
• **The Arctic; The Desert; The Ocean; The Rain Forest**	Alan Baker
• **Barn Dance!**	Bill Martin, Jr.
• **Bird Watch: A Book of Poetry**	Jane Yolen
• **Chester's Way; Julius, the Baby of the World**	Kevin Henkes
• **Chickens Aren't the Only Ones**	Ruth Heller
• **Dandelions; Fly Away Home**	Eve Bunting
• **Eleanor, Ellatony, Ellencake, and Me!**	C.M. Rubin
• **Emmett's Dream; Molly and Emmett's Camping Adventure; Molly and Emmett's Surprise Garden**	Marylin Hafner
• **Fox In Love** (first readers)	Edward Marshall
• **Good Driving, Amelia Bedelia**	Herman Parish
• **The Great Kapok Tree**	Lynne Cherry
• **Henry and Mudge Series** (first readers)	Cynthia Rylant
• **Ira Says Goodbye**	Bernard Waber
• **Little Critter Series** (first readers)	Mercer Mayer
• **Miss Rumphius**	Barbara Cooney
• **The Napping House**	Audrey and Don Wood
• **Noisy Nora**	Rosemary Wells
• **The Ox-Cart Man**	Donald Hall
• **Why Mosquitos Buzz in People's Ears**	Verna Aardema
• **Wolves**	R.D. Lawrence

Name ______________________________

Consonant Teams

Consonant teams are two or three consonant letters that have a single sound.
Examples: sh and **tch**

Directions: Write each word from the word box next to its picture. Underline the consonant team in each word. Circle the consonant team in each word in the box.

bench	match	shoe	thimble
shell	brush	peach	watch
whale	teeth	chair	wheel

shoe — thimble

wheel — watch

chair — peach

whale — match

bench — shell

brush — teeth

Name ______________________________

Consonant Teams

Directions: Circle the consonant teams in each word in the word box. Write a word from the word box to finish each sentence. Circle the consonant teams in your words.

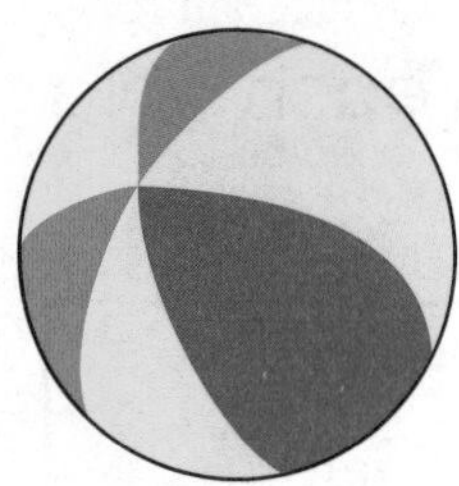

trash	splash	chain
shut	chicken	catch
ship	when	patch
	which	

1. My ____chicken____ won't lay eggs.
2. I put a ____chain____ on my bicycle so nobody can take it.
3. We watched the big ____ship____ dock and let off its passengers.
4. It is my job to take out the ____trash____ .
5. I have to wear a ____patch____ over my eye until it is better.
6. The baby likes to ____splash____ in the bathtub.
7. Can you ____catch____ the ball with one hand?
8. Please ____shut____ the windows before it rains.
9. ____when____ are we going to leave for school?
10. I don't know ____which____ of these books is mine.

Name ____________________

Double Vowel Words

Usually when two vowels appear together, the first one says its name and the second one is silent.

Example: be̲an

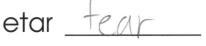

Directions: Unscramble the double vowel words below. Write the correct word on the line.

 ocat  coat

etar tear

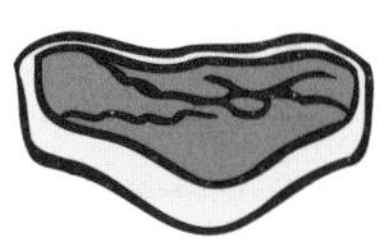 mtea 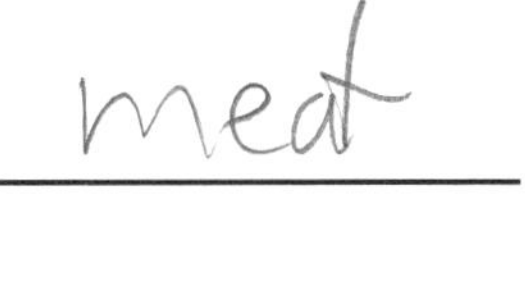 meat

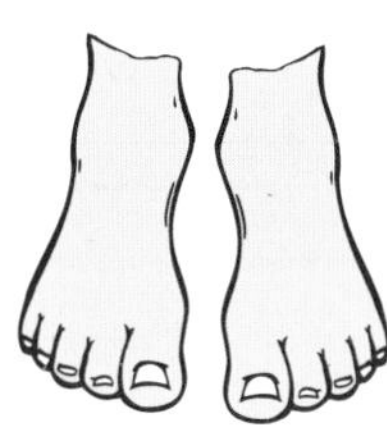 eetf feet

 teas  seat

 otab boat

 ogat goat

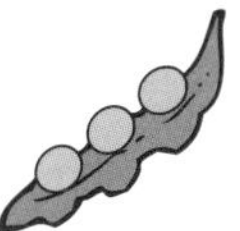 spea peas

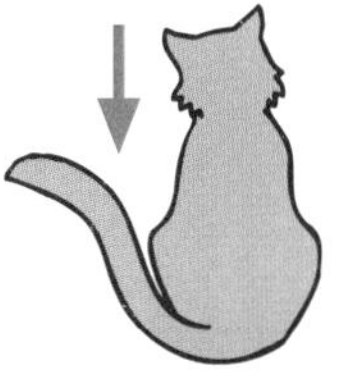 atli tail

 apil pail

Silent Letters

Some words have letters you can not hear at all, such as the **gh** in **night**, the **w** in **wrong**, the **l** in **walk**, the **k** in **knee**, the **b** in **climb**, and the **t** in **listen**.

Directions: Look at the words in the word box. Write the word under its picture. Underline the silent letters.

knife	light	calf	wrench	lamb	eight
wrist	whistle	comb	thumb	knob	knee

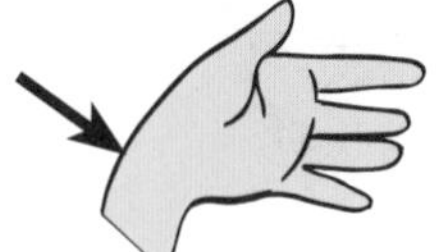

_______________ _______________ _______________ _______________

_______________ _______________ _______________ _______________

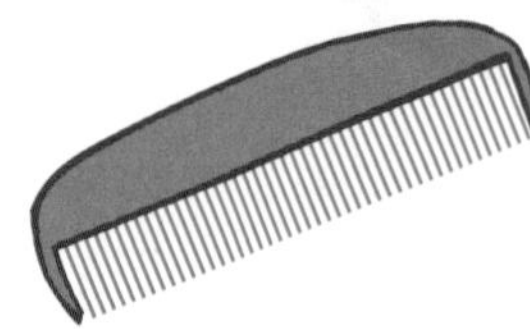

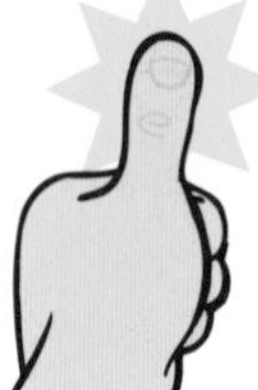

_______________ _______________ _______________ _______________

Name ____________________

Review

Directions: Read the story. Circle the consonant teams (two or three letters) and silent letters in the underlined words. Be sure to check for more than one team in a word! One has been done for you.

One day last spring, my family went on a picnic. My father picked out a pretty spot next to a stream. While my brother and I climbed a tree, my mother spread out a sheet and placed the food on it. But before we could eat, a skunk walked out of the woods! Mother screamed and scared the skunk. It sprayed us with a terrible smell! Now, we think it is a funny story. But that day, we ran!

Directions: Write the words with three-letter blends on the lines.

____________________ ____________________ ____________________

____________________ ____________________

Name ____________________

Review

Directions: Look through a magazine. Cut out pictures of nouns and glue them below. Write the name of the noun next to the picture.

PLACE THING PERSON PLACE THING PERSON PLACE THING PERSON PLACE THING

NOUNS

PERSON PLACE THING PERSON PLACE THING PERSON PLACE THING PERSON PLACE THING

PERSON PLACE THING PERSON PLACE THING PERSON PLACE THING PERSON PLACE THING

PERSON PLACE THING PERSON PLACE THING PERSON PLACE THING PERSON PLACE

Name ______________________________

Plurals

Plurals are words that mean more than one. You usually add an **s** or **es** to the word. In some words ending in **y**, the **y** changes to an **i** before adding **es**. For example, **baby** changes to **babies**.

Directions: Look at the following lists of plural words. Write the word that means one next to it. The first one has been done for you.

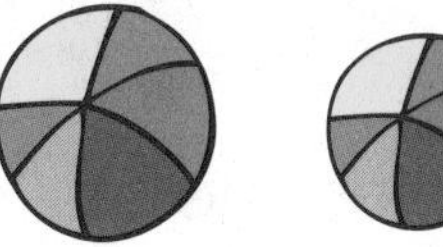
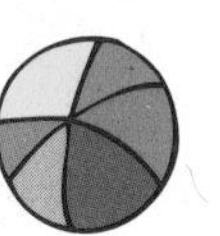
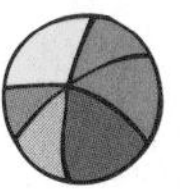

foxes	**fox**	balls	______________
bushes	______________	candies	______________
dresses	______________	wishes	______________
chairs	______________	boxes	______________
shoes	______________	ladies	______________
stories	______________	bunnies	______________
puppies	______________	desks	______________
matches	______________	dishes	______________
cars	______________	pencils	______________
glasses	______________	trucks	______________

Name ______________________

Compound Subjects

Two similar sentences can be joined into one sentence if the predicate is the same. A **compound subject** is made up of two subjects joined together by the word **and**.

Example: Jamie can sing.
Sandy can sing.

Jamie **and** Sandy can sing.

Directions: Combine the sentences. Write the new sentence on the line.

1. The cats are my pets.
   The dogs are my pets.

____

2. Chairs are in the store.
   Tables are in the store.

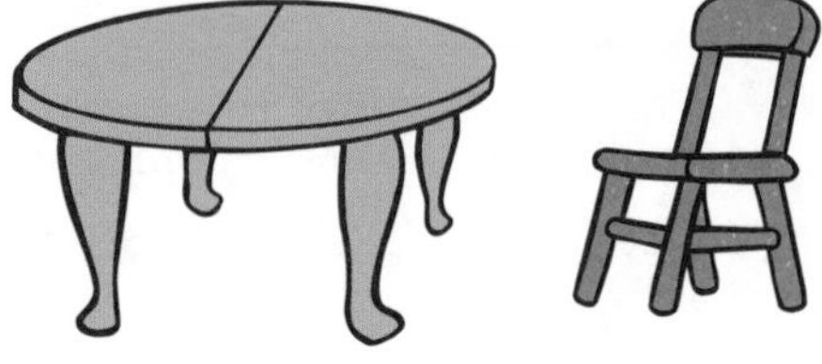

____

3. Tom can ride a bike.
   Jack can ride a bike.

____

Name ____________________

Verbs

Directions: Write each verb in the correct column.

rake	talked	look	hopped	skip
cooked	fished	call	clean	sewed

Yesterday	Today
____________	____________
____________	____________
____________	____________
____________	____________
____________	____________

Name ______________________________

Compound Subjects and Predicates

The following sentences have either a **compound subject** or a **compound predicate.**

Directions: If the sentence has a compound subject (more than one thing doing the action), **underline** the subject. If it has a compound predicate (more than one action), **circle** the predicate.

Example: Bats and owls like the night.

The fox (slinks and spies.)

1. Raccoons and mice steal food.

2. Monkeys and birds sleep in trees.

3. Elephants wash and play in the river.

4. Bears eat honey and scratch trees.

5. Owls hoot and hunt.

Name ______________________

Ownership

Directions: Read the sentences. Choose the correct word and write it in the sentences below.

1. The ______________ lunchbox is broken.	boys	boy's
2. The ______________ played in the cage.	gerbil's	gerbils
3. ______________ hair is brown.	Anns	Ann's
4. The ______________ ran in the field.	horse's	horses
5. My ______________ coat is torn.	sister's	sisters
6. The ______________ fur is brown.	cats	cat's
7. Three ______________ flew past our window.	birds	bird's
8. The ______________ paws are muddy.	dogs	dog's
9. The ______________ neck is long.	giraffes	giraffe's
10. The ______________ are big and powerful.	lion's	lions

Name ____________________

Synonyms

Directions: Read each sentence. Fill in the blanks with the synonyms.

friend	tired	story
presents	little	

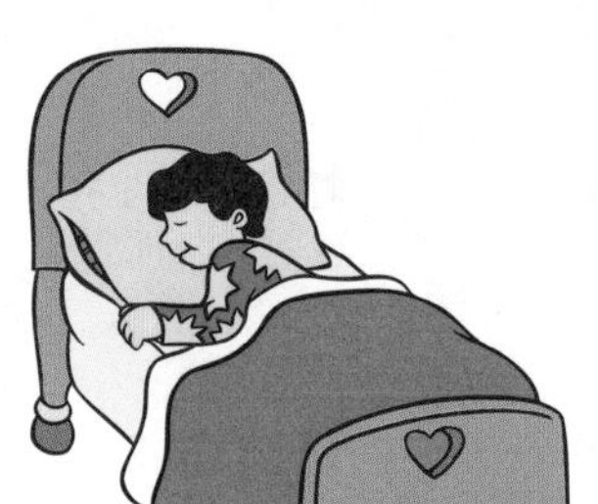

I want to go to bed because I am very <u>sleepy</u>. ____________________

On my birthday I like to open my <u>gifts</u>. ____________________

My <u>pal</u> and I like to play together. ____________________

My favorite <u>tale</u> is Cinderella. ____________________

The mouse was so <u>tiny</u> that it was hard to catch him. ____________________

Antonyms

Antonyms are words that are opposites.

Directions: Read the words next to the pictures. Draw a line to the antonyms.

	dark	empty
	hairy	dry
	closed	happy
	dirty	bald
	sad	clean
	full	light
	wet	open

Name ____________________

Antonyms: Completing a Story

Directions: Write opposite words in the blanks to complete the story.

hot	hard	top	cold	bottom
soft	quickly	happy	slowly	sad

One day, Grandma came for a visit. She gave my sister Jenny and me a box of chocolate candy. We said, "Thank you!" Then Jenny ____________ took the __________ off the box. The pieces all looked the same! I couldn't tell which pieces were _________ inside and which were __________ ! I only liked the _________ ones. Jenny didn't care. She was ______________ to get any kind of candy!

I _____________ looked at all the pieces. I didn't know which one to pick. Just then Dad called us. Grandma was going home. He wanted us to say good-bye to her. I hurried to the front door where they were standing. Jenny came a minute later.

I told Grandma I hoped I would see her soon. I always feel ________ when she leaves. Jenny stood behind me and didn't say anything. After Grandma went home, I found out why. Jenny had most of our candy in her mouth! Only a few pieces were left in the ____________ of the box! Then I was ________ ! That Jenny!

Name ______________________

Homophones

Directions: Read each word. Circle the picture that goes with the word.

1. sun

4. hi

2. ate

5. four

3. buy

6. hear

Name ______________________________

Is, Are, and Am

Is, **are**, and **am** are special action words that tell us something is happening now.

Use **am** with **I**. **Example: I am**.
Use **is** to tell about one person or thing. **Example: He is**.
Use **are** to tell about more than one. **Example: We are**.
Use **are** with **you**. **Example: You are.**

Directions: Write **is**, **are**, or **am** in the sentences below.

1. My friends __________________ helping me build a tree house.

2. It __________________ in my backyard.

3. We __________________ using hammers, wood, and nails.

4. It __________________ a very hard job.

5. I __________________ lucky to have good friends.

Name ______________________

Was and Were

Was and **were** tell us about something that already happened.

Use **was** to tell about one person or thing. **Example:** I **was**, he **was**. Use **were** to tell about more than one person or thing or when using the word you. **Example:** We **were**, you **were**.

Directions: Write **was** or **were** in each sentence.

1. Lily ____________ eight years old on her birthday.

2. Tim and Steve ____________ happy to be at the party.

3. Megan ____________ too shy to sing "Happy Birthday."

4. Ben ____________ sorry he dropped his cake.

5. All of the children ____________ happy to be invited.

Name ______________________________

Go, Going, and Went

We use **go** or **going** to tell about now or later. Sometimes we use **going** with the words **am** or **are**. We use **went** to tell about something that already happened.

Directions: Write **go**, **going**, or **went** in the sentences below.

1. Today, I will ____________ to the store.

2. Yesterday, we ____________ shopping.

3. I am ____________ to take Muffy to the vet.

4. Jan and Steve ____________ to the party.

5. They are ____________ to have a good day.

Name ______________________________

Have, Has, and Had

We use **have** and **has** to tell about now. We use **had** to tell about something that already happened.

Directions: Write **has, have**, or **had** in the sentences below.

1. We ________________ three cats at home.

2. Ginger ________________ brown fur.

3. Bucky and Charlie ________________ gray fur.

4. My friend Tom ________________ one cat, but he died.

5. Tom ________________ a new cat now.

See, Saw, and Sees

We use **see** or **sees** to tell about now. We use **saw** to tell about something that already happened.

Directions: Write **see**, **sees**, or **saw** in the sentences below.

1. Last night, we ____________ the stars.

2. John can ____________ the stars from his window.

3. He ____________ them every night.

4. Last week, he ____________ the Big Dipper.

5. Can you ____________ it in the night sky, too?

6. If you ____________ it, you would remember it!

7. John ____________ it often now.

8. How often do you ____________ it?

Name ______________________________

Eat, Eats, and Ate

We use **eat** or **eats** to tell about now. We use **ate** to tell about what already happened.

Directions: Write **eat**, **eats**, or **ate** in the sentences below.

1. We like to ____________ in the lunchroom.

2. Today, my teacher will ____________ in a different room.

3. She ____________ with the other teachers.

4. Yesterday, we ____________ pizza, pears, and peas.

5. Today, we will ____________ turkey and potatoes.

Name ____________________

Leave, Leaves, and Left

We use **leave** and **leaves** to tell about now. We use **left** to tell about what already happened.

Directions: Write **leave**, **leaves**, or **left** in the sentences below.

1. Last winter, we ________________ seeds in the bird feeder everyday.

2. My mother likes to ________________ food out for the squirrels.

3. When it rains, she ________________ bread for the birds.

4. Yesterday, she ________________ popcorn for the birds.

Name ______________________

Sentences

Directions: Write capital letters where they should appear in the sentences below.

Example: joe can play in january.

1. we celebrate thanksgiving on the third thursday in november.

____

____

2. in june, michelle and mark will go camping every friday.

____

____

3. on mondays in october, i will take piano lessons.

____

____

Parts of a Sentence

Directions: Look at the pictures. Draw a line from the naming part of the sentence to the action part to complete the sentence.

The boy	delivered the mail.

A small dog	threw a football.

The mailman	fell down.

The goalie	chased the ball.

Name ______________________

Complete the Sentences

Directions: Write your own endings to make the sentences tell a complete idea.

Example:

The Wizard of Oz is a story about Dorothy and her dog, Toto.

1. Dorothy and Toto live on ______________________.
2. A big storm ______________________.
3. Dorothy and Toto are carried off to ______________________.
4. Dorothy meets ______________________.
5. Dorothy, Toto, and their friends follow the ______________________.
6. Dorothy tries to find ______________________.
7. The Wizard turns out to be ______________________.
8. A scary person in the story is ______________________.
9. The wicked witch is killed by ______________________.
10. The hot air balloon leaves without ______________________.
11. Dorothy uses her magic shoes to ______________________.

Statements and Questions

Statements are sentences that tell about something. Statements begin with a capital letter and end with a period. **Questions** are sentences that ask about something. Questions begin with a capital letter and end with a question mark.

Directions: Rewrite the sentences using capital letters and either a period or a question mark.

Example: walruses live in the Arctic

Walruses live in the Arctic.

1. are walruses large sea mammals or fish

____

2. they spend most of their time in the water and on ice

____

3. are floating sheets of ice called ice floes

____

4. are walruses related to seals

____

5. their skin is thick, wrinkled, and almost hairless

____

Name ____________________

Commands

Commands tell someone to do something. **Example: "Be careful."** It can also be written as "Be careful!" if it tells a strong feeling.

Directions: Put a period at the end of the command sentences. Use an exclamation point if the sentence tells a strong feeling. Write your own commands on the lines below.

1. Clean your room

2. Now

3. Be careful with your goldfish

4. Watch out

5. Be a little more careful

____

____

Name ______________________

Questions

Questions are sentences that ask something. They begin with a capital letter and end with a question mark.

Directions: Write the questions on the lines below. Begin each sentence with a capital letter and end it with a question mark.

1. will you be my friend

____

2. what is your name

____

3. are you eight years old

____

4. do you like rainbows

____

Name ______________________________

Main Idea

Directions: Circle the sentence in each paragraph that does not support the main idea.

The school picnic was so much fun! When we arrived, we each made a name tag. Then we signed up for the contests we wanted to enter. My best friend was my partner for every contest. The hen laid so many eggs that I needed a basket to carry them. All that exercise made us very hungry. We were glad to see those tables full of food.

The storm howled outside, so we stayed in for an evening of fun. The colorful rainbow stretched across the sky. The dining room table was stacked with games and puzzles. The delightful smell of popcorn led us into the kitchen where Dad led a parade around the kitchen table. Then we carried our bowls of popcorn into the dining room. We laughed so hard and ate so much, we didn't care who won the games. It was a great evening!

The city championship game would be played on Saturday at Brookside Park. Coach Metzger called an extra practice Friday evening. He said he knew we were good, because we had made it this far. He didn't want us to get nervous and forget everything we knew. School starts on Monday, but I'm not ready to go back yet. After working on some drills, Coach told us to relax, get lots of rest, and come back ready to play.

Name ______________________

Main Idea: Chewing Gum

Directions: Read about chewing gum, then answer the questions.

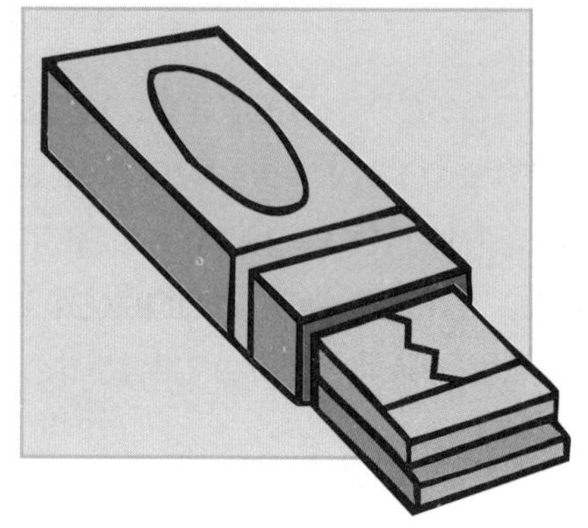

Thomas Adams was an American inventor. In 1870, he was looking for a substitute for rubber. He was working with **chicle** (chick-ul), a substance that comes from a certain kind of tree in Mexico. Years ago, Mexicans chewed chicle. Thomas Adams decided to try it for himself. He liked it so much he started selling it. Twenty years later, he owned a large factory that produced chewing gum.

1. Who was the American inventor who started selling chewing gum? ______________________

2. What was he hoping to invent? ______________________

3. When did he invent chewing gum? ______________________

4. Where does the chicle come from? ______________________

5. Why did Thomas Adams start selling chewing gum? ______________________

6. How long was it until Adams owned a large factory that produced chewing gum? ______________________

Name ______________________________

Main Idea: Clay Homes

Directions: Read about adobe houses, then answer the questions.

Pueblo Native Americans live in houses made of clay. They are called **adobe** (ah-doe-bee) **houses.** Adobe is a yellow-colored clay that comes from the ground. The hot sun in New Mexico and Arizona helps dry the clay to make strong bricks. The Pueblos have used adobe to build their homes for many years.

Pueblos use adobe for other purposes, too. The women in the tribes make beautiful pottery out of adobe. While the clay is still damp, they form it into shapes. After they have made the bowls and other containers, they paint them with lovely designs.

1. What is the subject of this story? ______________________________

2. Who uses clay to make their houses? ______________________________

3. How long have they been building adobe houses? ______________________________

4. Why do adobe bricks need to be dried? ______________________________

5. How do the Pueblos make pottery from adobe? ______________________________

Name ______________________________

Noting Details

Directions: Read the story. Then answer the questions.

The giant panda is much smaller than a brown bear or a polar bear. In fact, a horse weighs about four times as much as a giant panda. So why is it called "giant"? It is giant next to another kind of panda called the red panda.

The red panda also lives in China. The red panda is about the size of a fox. It has a long, fluffy, striped tail and beautiful reddish fur. It looks very much like a raccoon.

Many people think the giant pandas are bears. They look like bears. Even the word panda is Chinese for "white bear." But because of its relationship to the red panda, many scientists now believe that the panda is really more like a raccoon!

1. Why is the giant panda called "giant"?

____

2. Where does the red panda live?

____

3. How big is the red panda?

____

4. What animal does the red panda look like?

____

5. What does the word panda mean?

____

Name ________________________

Recalling Details: Nikki's Pets

Directions: Read about Nikki's pets, then answer the questions.

Nikki has two cats, Tiger and Sniffer, and two dogs, Spot and Wiggles. Tiger is an orange striped cat who likes to sleep under a big tree and pretend she is a real tiger. Sniffer is a gray cat who likes to sniff the flowers in Nikki's garden. Spot is a Dalmatian with many black spots. Wiggles is a big furry brown dog who wiggles all over when he is happy.

1. Which dog is brown and furry? ________________________
2. What color is Tiger? ________________________
3. What kind of dog is Spot? ________________________
4. Which cat likes to sniff flowers? ________________________
5. Where does Tiger like to sleep? ________________________
6. Who wiggles all over when he is happy? ________________________

Name ____________________

Reading for Details

Directions: Read the story about bike safety. Answer the questions below the story.

Mike has a red bike. He likes his bike. Mike wears a helmet. Mike wears knee pads and elbow pads. They keep him safe. Mike stops at signs. Mike looks both ways. Mike is safe on his bike.

1. What color is Mike's bike? ____________________

2. Which sentence in the story tells why Mike wears pads and a helmet? Write it here.

   ____

3. What else does Mike do to keep safe?

   He ____________ at signs and ____________ both ways.

Following Directions

Directions: Read the story. Answer the questions. Try the recipe.

Cows Give Us Milk

Cows live on a farm. The farmer milks the cow to get milk. Many things are made from milk. We make ice cream, sour cream, cottage cheese, and butter from milk. Butter is fun to make! You can learn to make your own butter. First, you need cream. Put the cream in a jar and shake it. Then you need to pour off the liquid. Next, you put the butter in a bowl. Add a little salt and stir! Finally, spread it on crackers and eat!

1. What animal gives us milk? ____________________

2. What 4 things are made from milk?

____________ ____________ ____________ ____________

3. What did the story teach you to make? ____________________

4. Put the steps in order. Place 1, 2, 3, or 4 by the sentence.

_____ Spread the butter on crackers and eat!

_____ Shake cream in a jar.

_____ Start with cream.

_____ Add salt to the butter.

Sequencing: 1, 2, 3, 4!

Directions: Write numbers by each sentence to show the order of the story.

The pool is empty. ____________

Ben plays in the pool. ____________

Ben gets out. ____________

Ben fills the pool. ____________

Sequencing: Yo-Yo Trick

Directions: Read about the yo-yo trick.

Wind up the yo-yo string. Hold the yo-yo in your hand. Now, hold your palm up. Throw the yo-yo downward on the string. Hold your palm down. Now, swing the yo-yo forward. Make it "walk." This yo-yo trick is called "walk the dog."

Directions: Number the directions in order.

________ Swing the yo-yo forward and make it "walk."

________ Hold your palm up and drop the yo-yo.

________ Turn your palm down as the yo-yo reaches the ground.

Name ______________________________

Sequencing/Predicting: A Game for Cats

Directions: Read about what cats like. Then follow the instructions.

Cats like to play with paper bags. Pull a paper bag open. Take everything out. Now, lay it on its side.

1. Write 1, 2, and 3 to put the pictures in order.

2. In box 4, draw what you think the cat will do.

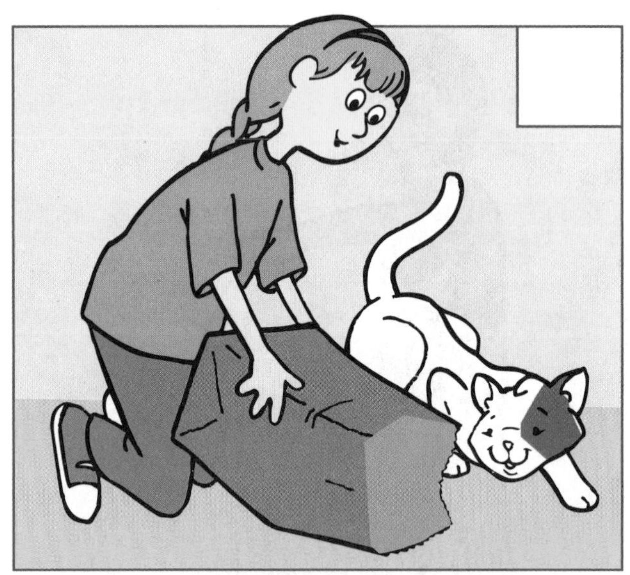

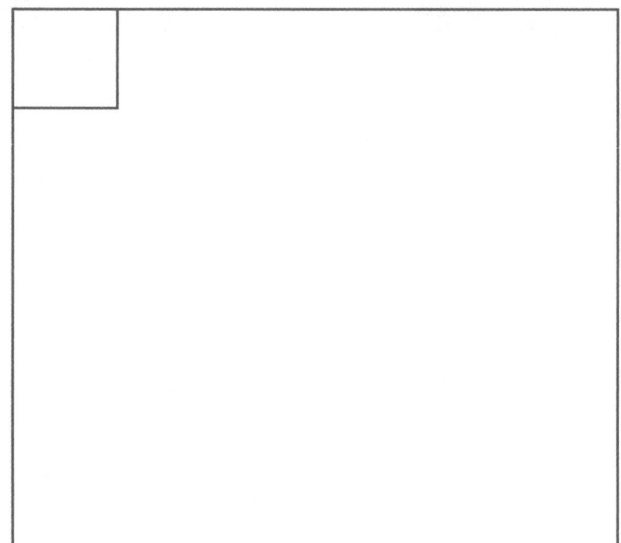

Name ____________________

Sequencing: Story Events

Mari was sick yesterday.

Directions: Number the events in 1, 2, 3 order to tell the story about Mari.

____ She went to the doctor's office.

____ Mari felt much better.

____ Mari felt very hot and tired.

____ Mari's mother went to the drugstore.

____ The doctor wrote down something.

____ The doctor looked in Mari's ears.

____ Mari took a pill.

____ The doctor gave Mari's mother the piece of paper.

____ Mari drank some water with her pill.

Name ______________________

Sequencing: Why Does It Rain?

Directions: Read about rain, then follow the instructions.

Clouds are made up of little drops of ice and water. They push and bang into each other. Then they join together to make bigger drops and begin to fall. More raindrops cling to them. They become heavy and fall quickly to the ground.

Write **first, second, third, fourth,** and **fifth** to put the events in order.

______________ More raindrops cling to them.

______________ Clouds are made up of little drops of ice and water.

______________ They join together and make bigger drops that begin to fall.

______________ The drops of ice and water bang into each other.

______________ The drops become heavy and fall quickly to the ground.

Name ______________________________

Sequencing: A Story

This is a story from *The McGuffey Second Reader*. This is a very old book your great-great-grandparents may have used to learn to read.

Directions: Read the story on pages 141 and 142, then answer the questions on page 143.

The Crow and the Robin

One morning in the early spring, a crow was sitting on the branch of an old oak tree. He felt very ugly and cross and could only say, "Croak! Croak!" Soon, a little robin, who was looking for a place to build her nest, came with a merry song into the same tree. "Good morning to you," she said to the crow.

But the crow made no answer; he only looked at the clouds and croaked something about the cold wind. "I said, 'Good morning to you,'" said the robin, jumping from branch to branch.

"I wonder how you can be so merry this morning," croaked the crow.

"Why shouldn't I be merry?" asked the robin. "Spring has come and everyone ought to be happy."

"I am not happy," said the crow. "Don't you see those black clouds above us? It is going to snow."

"Very well," said the robin, "I shall keep on singing until the snow comes. A merry song will not make it any colder."

"Caw, caw, caw," croaked the crow. "I think you are very foolish."

Sequencing: A Story

The Crow and the Robin

The robin flew to another tree and kept on singing, but the crow sat still and made himself very unhappy. "The wind is so cold," he said. "It always blows the wrong way for me."

Very soon the sun came out, warm and bright, and the clouds went away, but the crow was as cross as ever.

The grass began to spring up in the meadows. Green leaves and flowers were seen in the woods. Birds and bees flew here and there in the glad sunshine. The crow sat and croaked on the branch of the old oak tree.

"It is always too warm or too cold," said he. "To be sure, it is a little pleasant just now, but I know that the sun will soon shine warm enough to burn me up. Then before night, it will be colder than ever. I do not see how anyone can sing at such a time as this."

Just then the robin came back to the tree with a straw in her mouth for her nest. "Well, my friend," asked she, "where is your snow?"

"Don't talk about that," croaked the crow. "It will snow all the harder for this sunshine."

"And snow or shine," said the robin, "you will keep on croaking. For my part, I shall always look on the bright side of things and have a song for every day in the year."

Which will you be like—the crow or the robin? ___________________________

Name ______________________

Sequencing: The Story

These sentences retell the story of "The Crow and the Robin" but are out of order.

Directions: Write the numbers 1 through 10 on he lines to show the correct sequence. The first one has been done for you.

___ Although the sun came out and the clouds went away, the crow was still as cross as ever.

___ "I shall always . . . have a song for every day in the year," said the robin.

_1_ The crow sat on the branch of an old oak tree and could only say, "Croak! Croak!"

___ "This wind is so cold. It always blows the wrong way," the crow said.

___ The crow said, "It is going to snow."

___ The robin said good morning to the crow.

___ The crow told the robin that he thought she was very foolish.

___ The grass began to spring up in the meadows.

___ The robin was jumping from branch to branch as she talked to the crow.

___ The robin came back with straw in her mouth for her nest.

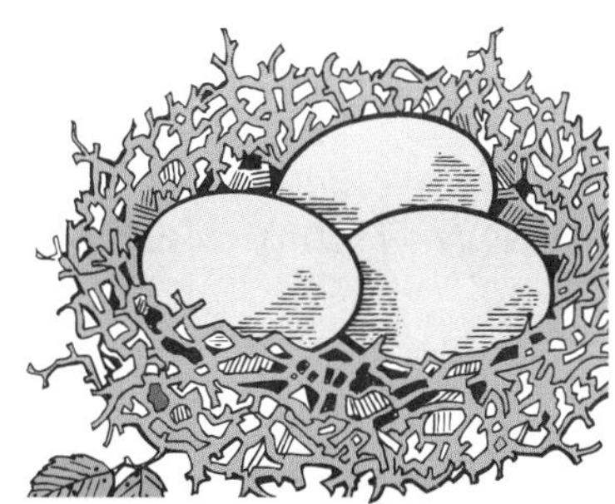

Name ______________________

Tracking: Alternate Paths

Look at Spotty Dog's home. Look at the paths he takes to the oven and the back door. The numbers by each path show how many steps Spotty must take to get there.

Directions: Follow the instructions.

1. Spotty Dog's cookies are done. Trace Spotty's path from his chair to the oven.
2. How many steps does Spotty take? ____________
3. While Spotty is looking in his oven, he hears a noise in the backyard. Trace Spotty's path to the door.
4. How many steps has Spotty taken in all? ____________
5. Spotty goes back to his chair. How many steps must he take? __________
6. How many steps has he taken in all? ____________
7. Spotty's path has made a shape. What shape is it? ______________

Name ______________________

Same/Different: Venn Diagram

A **Venn diagram** is a diagram that shows how two things are the same and different.

Directions: Choose two outdoor sports. Then follow the instructions to complete the Venn diagram.

1. Write the first sport name under the first circle. Write some words that describe the sport. Write them in the first circle.
2. Write the second sport name under the second circle. Write some words that describe the sport. Write them in the circle.
3. Where the 2 circles overlap, write some words that describe both sports.

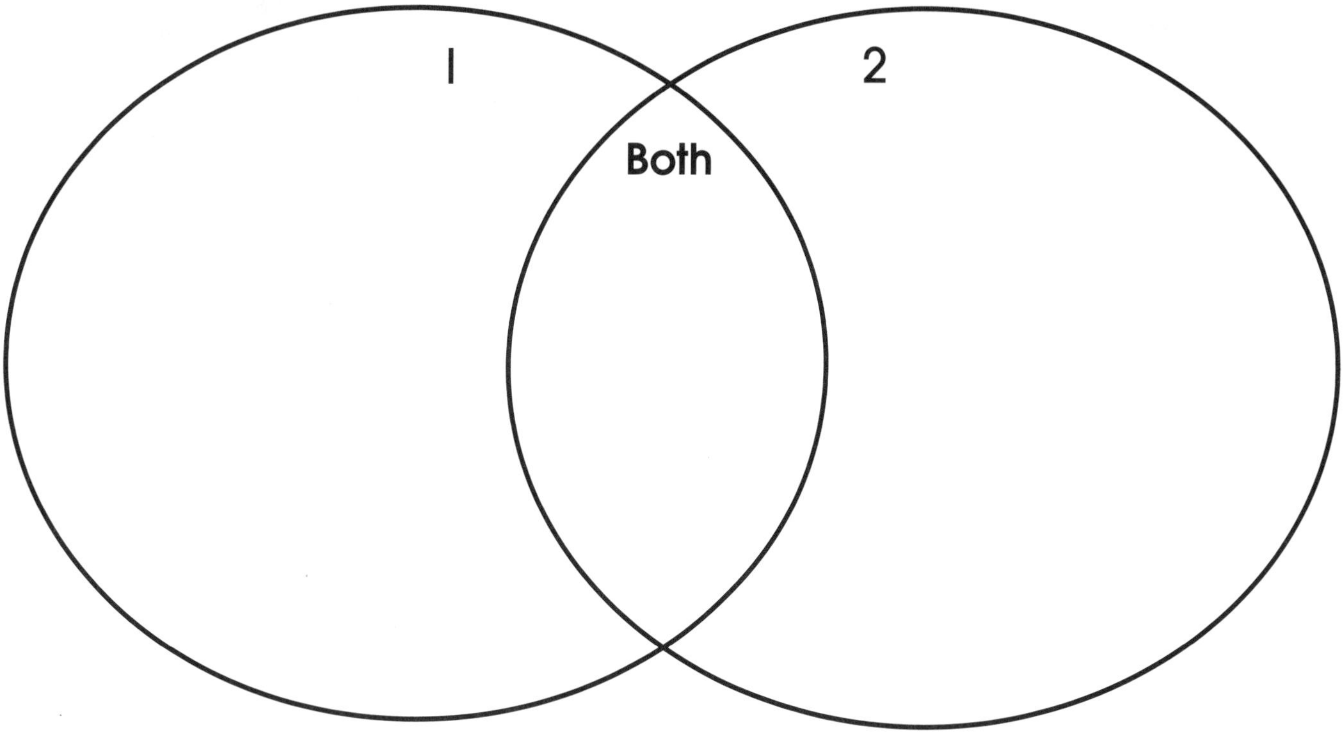

1

2

Both

____
(Sport #1)

____
(Sport #2)

Name ______________________________

Same/Different: Marvin and Mugsy

Directions: Read about Marvin and Mugsy. Then complete the Venn diagram, telling how they are the same and different.

Marcy has two dogs, Marvin and Mugsy. Marvin is a black-and-white spotted Dalmatian. Marvin likes to run after balls in the backyard. His favorite food is Canine Crunchy Crunch. Marcy likes to take Marvin for walks, because dogs need exercise. Marvin loves to sleep in his doghouse. Mugsy is a big furry brown dog, who wiggles when she is happy. Since she is big, she needs lots of exercise. So Marcy takes her for walks in the park. Her favorite food is Canine Crunchy Crunch. Mugsy likes to sleep on Marcy's bed.

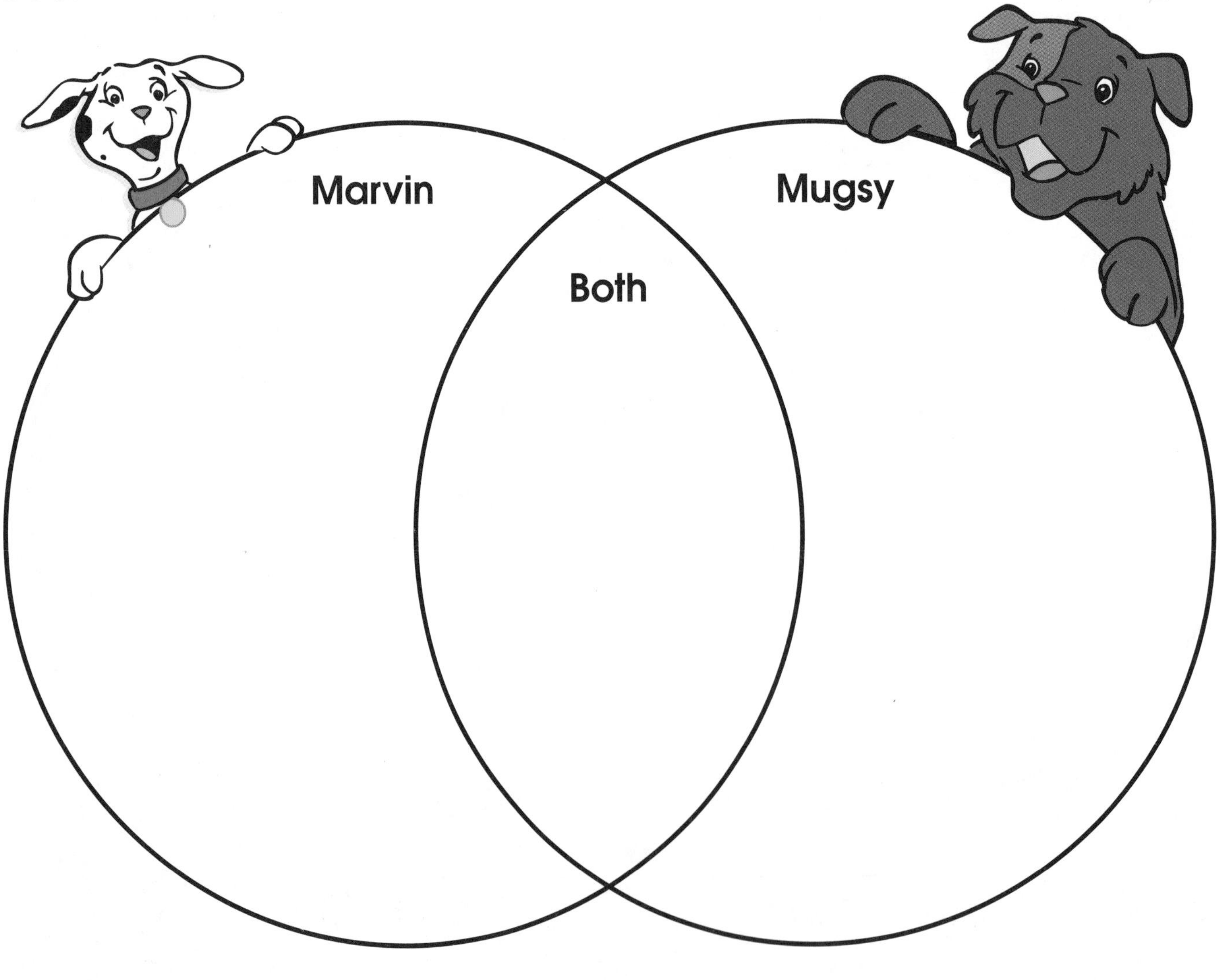

Marvin

Both

Mugsy

Name ____________________

Same/Different: Ann and Lee Have Fun

Directions: Read about Ann and Lee. Then write how they are the same and different in the Venn diagram.

Ann and Lee like to play ball. They like to jump rope. Lee likes to play a card game called "Old Maid." Ann likes to play a card game called "Go Fish." What do you do to have fun?

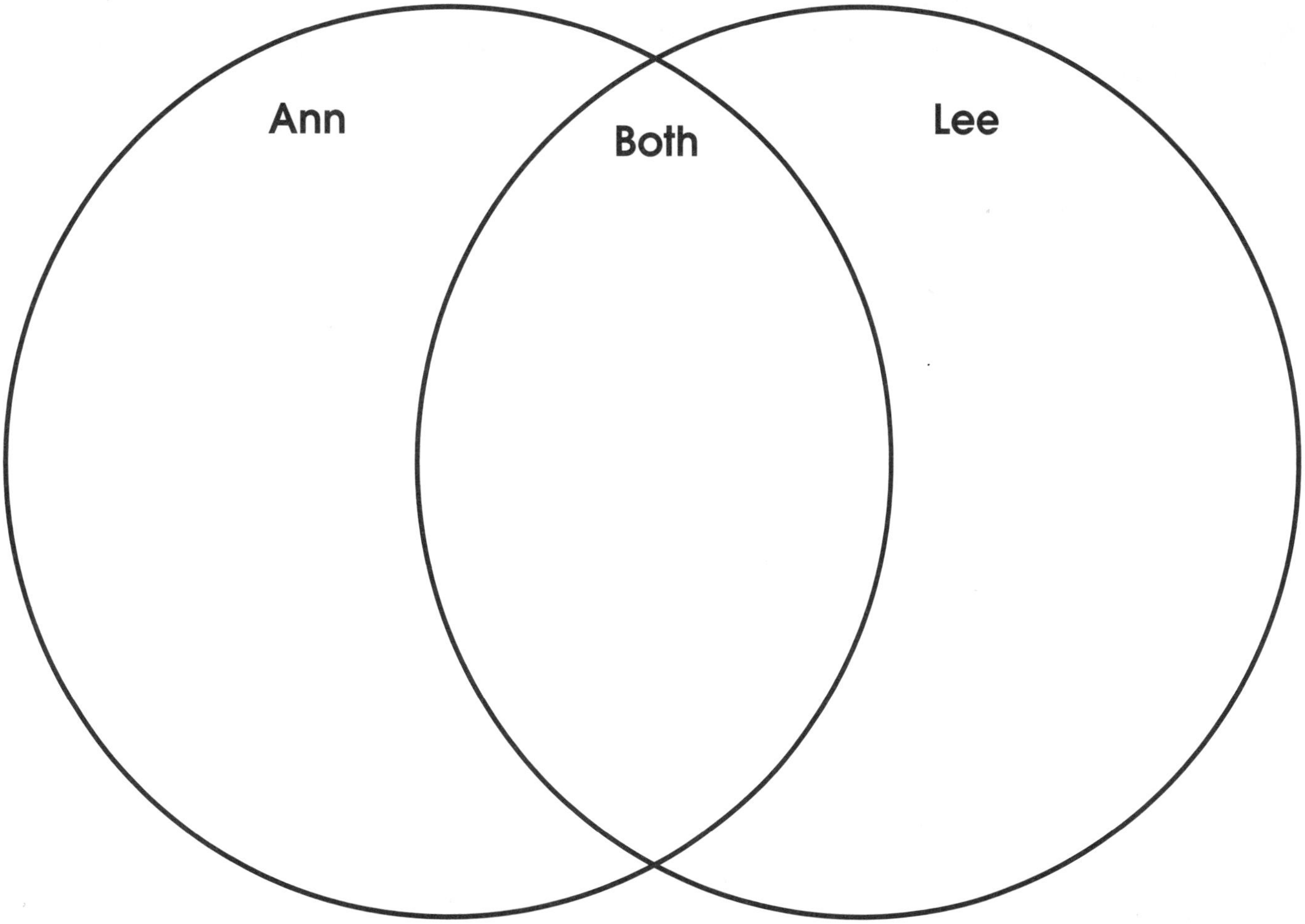

Ann

Both

Lee

Name ______________________________

Classifying

Directions: Read each animal story. Then look at the fun facts. Write an **H** for horse, **P** for panda, or **D** for dog next to each fact.

Horses

Horses are fun to ride. You can ride them in the woods or in fields. Horses usually have pretty names. Sometimes, if they are golden, they are called Amber. Horses swish their tails when it is hot. That keeps the flies away from them.

Pandas

Pandas are from China. They like to climb trees. They scratch bark to write messages to their friends in the trees. When pandas get hungry, they gnaw on bamboo shoots.

Dogs

Dogs are good pets. People often call them by names like Spot or Fido. Sometimes they are named after their looks. For example, a brown dog is sometimes named Brownie. Some people have special, small doors for their dogs to use.

Fun Facts

_______ 1. My name is often Spot or Fido.

_______ 2. I am from China.

_______ 3. I make a good house pet.

_______ 4. I like to carry people into the fields.

_______ 5. My favorite food is bamboo.

_______ 6. Flies bother me when I am hot.

_______ 7. Amber is often my name when I am golden.

_______ 8. I leave messages for my friends by scratching bark.

_______ 9. Sometimes I have my own special door on a house.

Name ______________________________

Classifying

Classifying is putting similar things into groups.

Directions: Write each word from the word box on the correct line.

baby	donkey	whale	family	fox
uncle	goose	grandfather	kangaroo	policeman

people

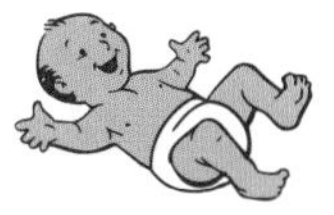 ______________________

 ______________________

 ______________________

 ______________________

 ______________________

animal

 ______________________

 ______________________

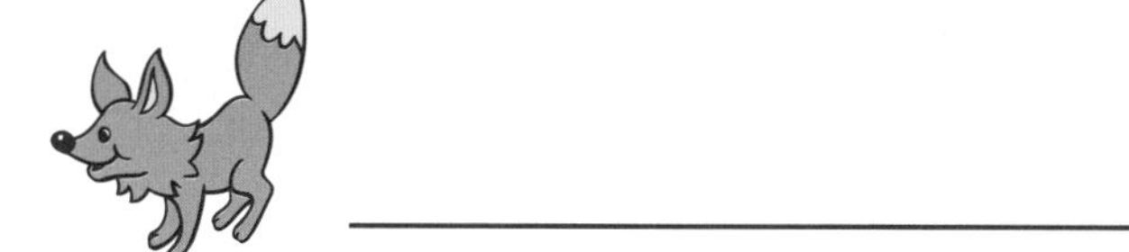 ______________________

 ______________________

 ______________________

Name ____________________

Classifying: Watch Out for Poison Ivy!

Poison ivy is not safe. If you touch it, it can make your skin red and itchy. It can hurt. It grows on the ground. It has three leaves. It can be green or red. Watch out, Jay! There is poison ivy in these woods.

Directions: Color the poison ivy leaves red. Then color the "safe" leaves other colors.

Name ________________________________

Comprehension: Sea Horses Look Strange!

Directions: Read about sea horses. Then answer the questions.

Sea horses are fish, not horses. A sea horse's head looks like a horse's head. It has a tail like a monkey's tail. A sea horse looks very strange!

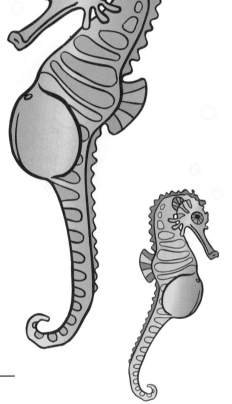

1. (Circle the correct answer.)
A sea horse is a kind of

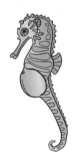

horse.

monkey.

fish.

2. What does a sea horse's head look like?

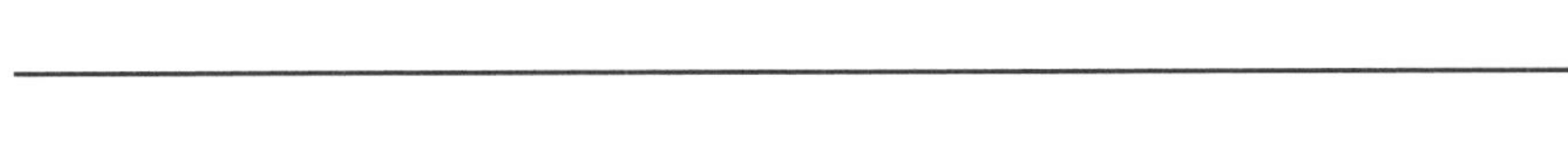

____

____

3. What makes a sea horse look strange?

a. ____

b. ____

Name ____________________

Comprehension: How to Stop a Dog Fight

Directions: Read about how to stop a dog fight. Then answer the questions.

Sometimes dogs fight. They bark loudly. They may bite. Do not try to pull apart fighting dogs. Turn on a hose and spray them with water. This will stop the fight.

1. Name some things dogs may do if they are mad.

____

____

2. Why is it unwise to pull on dogs that are fighting?

____

____

3. Do you think dogs like to get wet?

____

Comprehension: A Winter Story

Directions: Read about winter. Then follow the instructions.

It is cold in winter. Snow falls. Water freezes. Most kids like to play outdoors. Some kids make a snowman. Some kids skate. What do you do in winter?

1. Circle the main idea:

   Snow falls in winter.

   In winter, there are many things to do outside.

2. Write two things about winter weather.

   1) ______________________

   2) ______________________

3. Write what you like to do in winter.

Name ______________________

Comprehension: More About Snakes!

Directions: Read more about snakes. Then follow the instructions.

Unlike people, snakes have cold blood. They like to be warm. They hunt for food when it is warm. They lie in the sun. When it is cold, snakes curl up into a ball.

1. What do snakes do when it is warm?

   a. ______________________

   b. ______________________

2. Why do you think snakes curl up when it is cold? ______________________

   ____

3. (Circle the correct answer.)

People have: (cold blood / warm blood).

Name ______________________

Comprehension: Ant Farms

Directions: Read about ant farms. Then answer the questions.

Ant farms are sold at toy stores and pet stores. Ant farms come in a flat frame. The frame has glass on each side. Inside the glass is sand. The ants live in the sand.

1. Where are ant farms sold? ______________________

2. The frame has ______________________ on each side.

Circle the correct answer.

3. The ants live in (water / sand).

4. The ant farm frame is (flat / round).

Comprehension: Sharks Are Fish, Too!

Directions: Read the story. Then follow the instructions.

Angela learned a lot about sharks when her class visited the city aquarium. She learned that sharks are fish. Some sharks are as big as an elephant, and some can fit into a small paper bag. Sharks have no bones. They have hundreds of teeth, and when they lose them, they grow new ones. They eat animals of any kind. Whale sharks are the largest of all fish.

1. Circle the main idea:

   Angela learned a lot about sharks at the aquarium.

   Some sharks are as big as elephants.

2. When sharks lose teeth, they ________________________________

   ____

3. ________________________________ are the largest of all fish.

4. Sharks have bones. (Circle the answer.)

   Yes   No

Name ____________________

Comprehension: Outdoor/Indoor Games

Directions: Read the story. Then answer the questions.

Derrick likes to play outdoor and indoor games. His favorite outdoor game is baseball because he likes to hit the ball with the bat and run around the bases. He plays this game in the park with the neighborhood kids.

When it rains, he plays checkers with Lorenzo on the dining-room table in his apartment. He likes the game, because he has to use his brain to think about his next move, and the rules are easy to follow.

1. What is your favorite outdoor game? ____________________

2. Why do you like this game? ____________________

____

3. Where is this game played? ____________________

4. What is your favorite indoor game? ____________________

5. Why do you like this game? ____________________

____

6. Where is this game played? ____________________

Comprehension: Early Trucks

What would we do without trucks? Your family may not own a truck, but everyone depends on trucks. Trucks bring our food to stores. Trucks deliver our furniture. Trucks carry new clothes to shopping centers. The goods of the world move on trucks.

Trucks are harder to make than cars. They must be sturdy. They carry heavy loads. They cannot break down.

The first trucks were on the road in 1900. Like trains, they were powered by steam engines. They did not use gasoline. The first trucks did not have heavy wheels. Their engines often broke down.

Trucks changed when the U.S. entered World War I in 1917. Big, heavy tires were put on trucks. Gasoline engines were used. Trucks used in war had to be sturdy. Lives were at stake!

Directions: Answer these questions about the first trucks.

1. What powered the first trucks?

____

2. When did early trucks begin using gasoline engines?

____

3. How do trucks serve us?

____

____

4. Why did trucks used in war have to be sturdy?

____

Name ______________________________

Predicting: A Rainy Game

Predicting is telling what is likely to happen based on the facts.

Directions: Read the story. Then check each sentence below that tells how the story could end.

One cloudy day, Juan and his baseball team, the Bears, played the Crocodiles. It was the last half of the fifth inning, and it started to rain. The coaches and umpires had to decide what to do.

__________ They kept playing until nine innings were finished.

__________ They ran for cover and waited until the rain stopped.

__________ Each player grabbed an umbrella and returned to the field to finish the game.

__________ They canceled the game and played it another day.

__________ They acted like crocodiles and slid around the wet bases.

__________ The coaches played the game while the players sat in the dugout.

Name ______________________________

Predicting Outcome

Directions: Read the story. Complete the story in the last box.

1. "Look at that elephant! He sure is big!"

2. "I'm hungry." "I bet that elephant is, too."

3. "Stop, Amy! Look at that sign!"

4. ______________________________

____

____

Name ______________________________

Fact and Opinion

A **fact** is something that can be proven. An **opinion** is a feeling or belief about something and cannot be proven.

Directions: Read these sentences about different games. Then write **F** next to each fact and **O** next to each opinion.

_____ 1. Tennis is cool!

_____ 2. There are red and black markers in a Checkers game.

_____ 3. In football, a touchdown is worth six points.

_____ 4. Being a goalie in soccer is easy.

_____ 5. A yo-yo moves on a string.

_____ 6. June's sister looks like the queen on the card.

_____ 7. The six kids need three more players for a baseball team.

_____ 8. Table tennis is more fun than court tennis.

_____ 9. Hide-and-Seek is a game that can be played outdoors or indoors.

_____ 10. Play money is used in many board games.

Name ______________________

Fact and Opinion

Directions: Read the story. Then follow the instructions.

Tashi's family likes to go to the zoo. Her favorite animals are all the different kinds of birds. Tashi likes birds because they can fly, they have colorful feathers, and they make funny noises.

Write **F** next to each fact and **O** next to each opinion.

_____ 1. Birds have two feet.

_____ 2. All birds lay eggs.

_____ 3. Parrots are too noisy.

_____ 4. All birds have feathers and wings.

_____ 5. It would be great to be a bird and fly south for the winter.

_____ 6. Birds have hard beaks or bills instead of teeth.

_____ 7. Pigeons are fun to watch.

_____ 8. Some birds cannot fly.

_____ 9. Parakeets make good pets.

_____ 10. A penguin is a bird.

Name ______________________________

Making Inferences

Directions: Read the story. Then answer the questions.

Mrs. Sweet looked forward to a visit from her niece, Candy. In the morning, she cleaned her house. She also baked a cherry pie. An hour before Candy was to arrive, the phone rang. Mrs. Sweet said, "I understand." When she hung up the phone, she looked very sad.

1. Who do you think called Mrs. Sweet?

____

____

2. How do you know that?

____

____

3. Why is Mrs. Sweet sad?

____

____

Name ____________________

Making Inferences

Juniper has three problems to solve. She needs your help.

Directions: Read each problem. Write what you think she should do.

1. Juniper is watching her favorite TV show when the power goes out.

____

____

____

____

2. Juniper is riding her bike to school when the front tire goes flat.

____

____

____

____

3. Juniper loses her father while shopping in the supermarket.

____

____

____

____

Name ______________________________

Making Inferences

Help make a "doggie pizza" for Spotty Dog. The steps to follow are all mixed-up. Three of the steps are not needed.

Directions: Number the steps in order from 1 to 7. Draw a dog bone by the 3 steps that are not needed.

__________ Place the dough on a round pan.

__________ Cover the top with cheese.

__________ Take a nap.

__________ Make the pizza dough.

__________ Run out the door.

__________ Bake it in a hot oven.

__________ Roll the dough out flat.

__________ Play ball with Spotty.

__________ Spread the sauce on the dough.

__________ Sprinkle bits of dog biscuits on top.

Directions: Draw Spotty Dog's pizza in the box.

Name ___________________________

Making Deductions

Dad is cooking dinner tonight. You can find out what day of the week it is.

Directions: Read the clues. Complete the menu. Answer the question.

Menu

Monday ___________________

Tuesday ___________________

Wednesday ___________________

Thursday ___________________

Friday ___________________

Saturday ___________________

Sunday ___________________

1. Mom fixed pizza on Monday.
2. Dad fixed cheese rolls the day before that.
3. Tess made meat pie three days after Mom fixed pizza.
4. Tom fixed corn-on-the-cob the day before Tess made meat pie.
5. Mom fixed hot dogs the day after Tess made meat pie.
6. Tess cooked fish the day before Dad fixed cheese rolls.
7. Dad is making chicken today. What day is it? _______________

Drawing Conclusions: Mrs. Posy's Roses

Directions: Read more about Mrs. Posy, then answer the questions.

Mrs. Posy is working in her rose garden. She is trimming the branches so that the plants will grow better. Mrs. Posy is careful, because rose bushes have thorns on them. "Hello, Mrs. Posy!" calls Ann as she rides her bicycle down the street. "Hi, Ann!" replies Mrs. Posy. Then she yells, "Ouch!" She runs inside the house and stays there for a few minutes. When Mrs. Posy comes back outside, she has a bandage on one finger.

1. Why is Mrs. Posy careful when she works with rose bushes?

   ____

2. Why does Mrs. Posy look up from her work? ____________________

   ____

3. Why did Mrs. Posy yell, "Ouch!"? ____________________

   ____

4. Why did Mrs. Posy run into the house? ____________________

   ____

Drawing Conclusions: Eskimos

Directions: Read about the traditional lives of Eskimos, then answer the questions.

Eskimos live in Alaska. A long time ago, Eskimos lived in houses made of snow, dirt, or animal skins. They moved around from place to place. The Eskimos hunted and fished. They often ate raw meat because they had no way to cook it. When they ate meat raw, they liked it dried or frozen. Eskimos used animal skins for their clothes. They used fat from whales, seals, and other animals to heat their houses.

1. Why did the Eskimos make houses out of snow? ______________________

____

2. How did they prepare their raw meat? ______________________

____

3. How might they use animal fat to heat their houses? ______________________

____

Review

Directions: Read the story. Then answer the questions.

Randa, Emily, Ali, Dave, Liesl, and Deana all love to read. Every Tuesday, they all go to the library together and pick out their favorite books. Randa likes books about fish. Emily likes books about sports and athletes. Ali likes books about art. Dave likes books about wild animals. Liesl likes books with riddles and puzzles. Deanna likes books about cats and dogs.

1. Circle the main idea:

   Randa, Emily, Ali, Dave, Liesl, and Deana are good friends.

   Randa, Emily, Ali, Dave, Liesl, and Deana all like books.

2. Who do you think might grow up to be an artist?

   ____

3. Who do you think might grow up to be an oceanographer (someone who studies the ocean)?

   ____

4. Who do you think might grow up to be a veterinarian (an animal doctor)?

   ____

5. Who do you think might grow up to be a zookeeper (someone who cares for zoo animals)?

   ____

Name ____________________

Cause and Effect

1. Our telephone was not working, so I called the doctor from next door.

2. The police officer began to direct traffic, since the traffic signal was not working.

3. The class will go out to recess when the room is cleaned up.

4. "I can't see you because the room is too dark," said Jordan.

5. He has to wash the dishes alone because his sister is sick.

6. Since the bus had engine trouble, several children were late to school.

7. Monday was a holiday, so Mom and Dad took us to the park.

Name ____________________

Compare and Contrast

To **compare** means to discuss how things are similar. To **contrast** means to discuss how things are different.

Directions: Compare and contrast how people grow gardens. Write at least two answers for each question.

Many people in the country have large gardens. They have a lot of space, so they can plant many kinds of vegetables and flowers. Since the gardens are usually quite large, they use a wheelbarrow to carry the tools they need. Sometimes they even have to carry water or use a garden hose.

People who live in the city do not always have enough room for a garden. Many people in big cities live in apartment buildings. They can put in a window box or use part of their balcony space to grow things. Most of the time, the only garden tools they need are a hand trowel to loosen the dirt and a watering can to make sure the plant gets enough water.

1. Compare gardening in the country with gardening in the city.

____

____

2. Contrast gardening in the country with gardening in the city.

____

____

Name ______________________________

Fiction and Nonfiction

Fiction writing is a story that has been invented. The story might be about things that could really happen (realistic) or about things that couldn't possibly happen (fantasy). **Nonfiction** writing is based on facts. It usually gives information about people, places, or things. A person can often tell while reading whether a story or book is fiction or nonfiction.

Directions: Read the paragraphs below and on page 77. Determine whether each paragraph is fiction or nonfiction. Circle the letter **F** for fiction or the letter **N** for nonfiction.

"Do not be afraid, little flowers," said the oak. "Close your yellow eyes in sleep and trust in me. You have made me glad many a time with your sweetness. Now, I will take care that the winter shall do you no harm." **F N**

The whole team watched as the ball soared over the outfield fence. The game was over! It was hard to walk off the field and face parents, friends, and each other. It had been a long season. Now, they would have to settle for second place. **F N**

Be careful when you remove the dish from the microwave. It will be very hot, so take care not to get burned by the dish or the hot steam. If time permits, leave the dish in the microwave for 2 or 3 minutes to avoid getting burned. It is a good idea to use a potholder, too. **F N**

Name ______________________

Fiction and Nonfiction

Megan and Mariah skipped out to the playground. They enjoyed playing together at recess. Today, it was Mariah's turn to choose what they would do first. To Megan's surprise, Mariah asked, "What do you want to do, Megan? I'm going to let you pick since it's your birthday!" **F N**

It is easy to tell an insect from a spider. An insect has three body parts and six legs. A spider has eight legs and no wings. Of course, if you see the creature spinning a web, you will know what it is. An insect wouldn't want to get too close to the web or it would be stuck. It might become dinner! **F N**

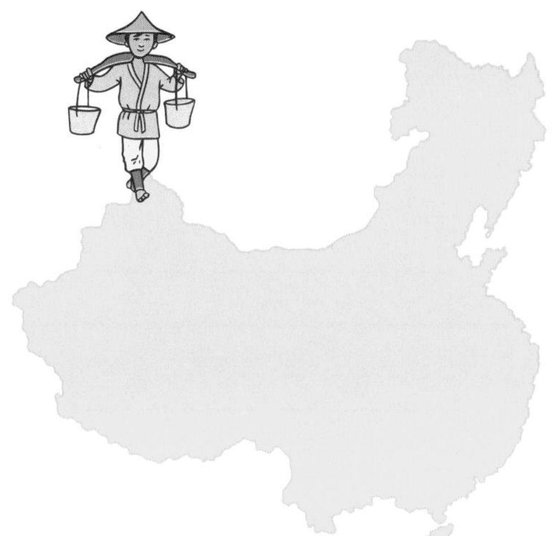

My name is Lee Chang, and I live in a country that you call China. My home is on the other side of the world from yours. When the sun is rising in my country, it is setting in yours. When it is day at your home, it is night at mine. **F N**

Henry washed the dog's foot in cold water from the brook. The dog lay very still, for he knew that the boy was trying to help him. **F N**

Name ____________________

Fantasy and Reality

Something that is **real** could actually happen. Something that is **fantasy** is not real. It could not happen.

Examples: **Real:** Dogs can bark.
Fantasy: Dogs can fly.

Directions: Look at the sentences below. Write **real** or **fantasy** next to each sentence.

1. My cat can talk to me. ____________________
2. Witches ride brooms and cast spells. ____________________
3. Dad can mow the lawn. ____________________
4. I ride a magic carpet to school. ____________________
5. I have a man-eating tree. ____________________
6. My sandbox has toys in it. ____________________
7. Mom can bake chocolate chip cookies. ____________________
8. Mark's garden has tomatoes and corn in it. ____________________
9. Jack grows candy and ice cream in his garden. ____________________
10. I make my bed everyday. ____________________

Write your own **real** sentence. ____________________

____

Write your own **fantasy** sentence. ____________________

____

Name ______________________

Learning Dictionary Skills

A dictionary is a book that gives the meaning of words. It also tells how words sound. Words in a dictionary are in alphabetical order. That makes them easier to find. A picture dictionary lists a word, a picture of the word, and its meaning.

Directions: Look at this page from a picture dictionary, then answer the questions.

baby

A very young child.

band

A group of people who play music.

bank

A place where money is kept.

bark

The sound a dog makes.

berry

A small, juicy fruit.

board

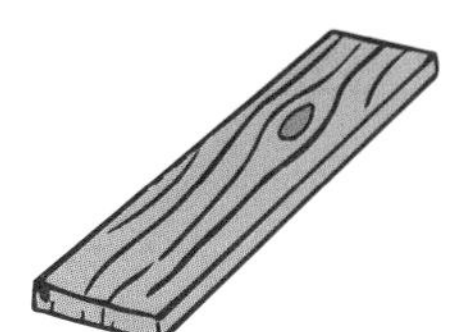

A flat piece of wood.

1. What is a small, juicy fruit? ______________________

2. What is a group of people who play music? ______________________

3. What is the name for a very young child? ______________________

4. What is a flat piece of wood called? ______________________

Name ______________________________

Making Inferences: Dictionary Mystery

Directions: Below are six dictionary entries with pronunciations and definitions. The only things missing are the entry words. Write the correct entry words. Be sure to spell each word correctly.

Entry word:

____

(rōz)
A flower that grows on bushes and vines.

Entry word:

____

(fäks)
A wild animal that lives in the woods.

Entry word:

____

(lāk)
A body of water that is surrounded by land.

Entry word:

____

(ra bət)
A small animal that has long ears.

Entry word:

____

(pē än ō)
A musical instrument that has many keys.

Entry word:

____

(bās bȯl)
A game played with a bat and a ball.

Directions: Now write the entry words in alphabetical order.

1. ______________________________
2. ______________________________
3. ______________________________
4. ______________________________
5. ______________________________
6. ______________________________

Name ______________________________

Reading for Information: Newspapers

A newspaper has many parts. Some of the parts of a newspaper are:

- banner — the name of the paper
- lead story — the top news item
- caption — sentences under the picture which give information about the picture
- sports — scores and information on current sports events
- comics — drawings that tell funny stories
- editorial — an article by the editor expressing an opinion about something
- ads — paid advertisements
- weather — information about the weather
- advice column — letters from readers asking for help with a problem
- movie guides — a list of movies and movie times
- obituary — information about people who have died

Directions: Match the newspaper sections below with their definitions.

banner	an article by the editor
lead story	sentences under pictures
caption	movies and movie times
editorial	the name of the paper
movies	information about people who have died
obituary	the top news item

Library Skills: Alphabetical Order

Ms. Ling, the school librarian, needs help shelving books. Fiction titles are arranged in alphabetical order by the author's last name. Ms. Ling has done the first set for you.

__3__ Silverstein, Shel __1__ Bridwell, Norman __2__ Farley, Walter

Directions: Number the following groups of authors in alphabetical order.

_____ Bemelmans, Ludwig
_____ Stein, R.L.
_____ Sawyer, Ruth
_____ Baum, L. Frank

_____ Perkins, Al
_____ Dobbs, Rose
_____ Baldwin, James
_____ Kipling, Rudyard

The content of some books is also arranged alphabetically.

Directions: Circle the books that are arranged in alphabetical order.

T.V. guide	dictionary	encyclopedia	novel
almanac	science book	Yellow Pages	catalog

Write the books you circled in alphabetical order.

1. ______________________
2. ______________________
3. ______________________

Name ______________________

Periodicals

Libraries also have periodicals such as magazines and newspapers. They are called **periodicals** because they are printed regularly within a set period of time. There are many kinds of magazines. Some discuss the news. Others cover fitness, cats, or other topics of special interest. Almost every city or town has a newspaper. Newspapers usually are printed daily, weekly, or even monthly. Newspapers cover what is happening in your town and in the world. They usually include sections on sports and entertainment. They present a lot of information.

Directions: Follow the instructions.

1. Choose an interesting magazine.

   What is the name of the magazine? ______________________

   List the titles of three articles in the magazine.

   ____

   ____

   ____

2. Now, look at a newspaper.

   What is the name of the newspaper? ______________________

   The title of a newspaper story is called a headline.

   What are some of the headlines in your local newspaper?

   ____

   ____

   ____

Name ______________________

Reading a Schedule

Special Saturday classes are being offered to students of the county schools. They will be given the chance to choose from art, music or gymnastics classes.

Directions: Read the schedule, then answer the questions.

Saturday, November 13

Art	Music	Gymnastics
8:00 A.M.		
Watercolor—Room 350 Clay Sculpting—Room 250	Island Rhythms—Room 54 Orchestra Instruments—Stage	Floor Exercises—W. Gym Parallel Bars—E. Gym
Break (10 minutes)		
10:00 A.M.		
Painting Stills—Room 420 Watercolor—Room 350	Percussion—Room 54 Jazz Sounds—Stage	Uneven Bars—N. Gym ——
Break (10 minutes)		
11:00 A.M.		
Oils on Canvas—Room 258 ——	Island Rhythms—Room 54 Create Your Own Music—Room 40	Uneven Bars—N. Gym Balance Beam—W. Gym

1. Where would you meet to learn about Jazz Sounds? ______________

2. Could a student sign up for Watercolor and Floor Exercises? ______________

   Explain your answer. ______________________________

3. Which music class would a creative person enjoy? ______________

   ____

4. Could a person sign up for an art class at 11:00? ______________

5. What time is the class on clay sculpting offered? ______________

Page 101

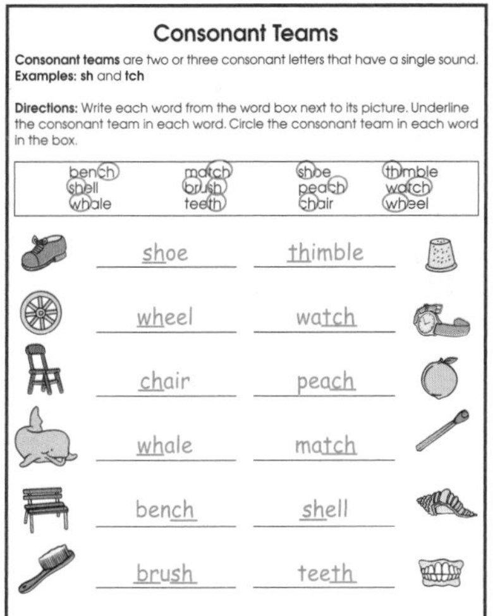

Consonant Teams

Consonant teams are two or three consonant letters that have a single sound. **Examples: sh** and **tch**

Directions: Write each word from the word box next to its picture. Underline the consonant team in each word. Circle the consonant team in each word in the box.

bench	match	shoe	thimble
shell	brush	peach	watch
whale	teeth	chair	wheel

shoe	thimble
wheel	watch
chair	peach
whale	match
bench	shell
brush	teeth

Page 102

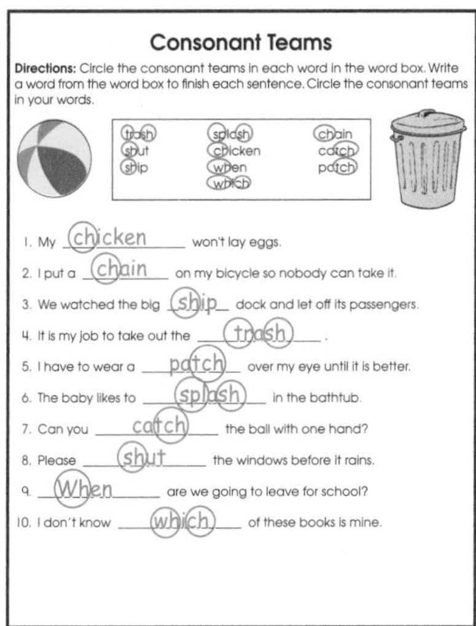

Consonant Teams

Directions: Circle the consonant teams in each word in the word box. Write a word from the word box to finish each sentence. Circle the consonant teams in your words.

trash	splash	chain
shut	chicken	catch
ship	when	patch
	which	

1. My chicken won't lay eggs.
2. I put a chain on my bicycle so nobody can take it.
3. We watched the big ship dock and let off its passengers.
4. It is my job to take out the trash.
5. I have to wear a patch over my eye until it is better.
6. The baby likes to splash in the bathtub.
7. Can you catch the ball with one hand?
8. Please shut the windows before it rains.
9. When are we going to leave for school?
10. I don't know which of these books is mine.

Page 103

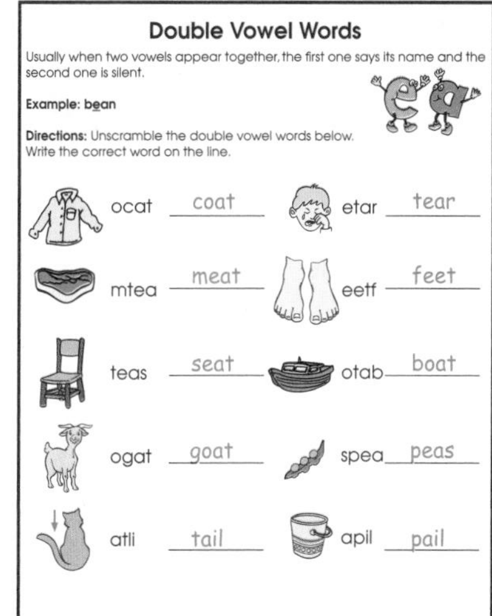

Double Vowel Words

Usually when two vowels appear together, the first one says its name and the second one is silent.

Example: bean

Directions: Unscramble the double vowel words below. Write the correct word on the line.

ocat	coat	etar	tear
mtea	meat	eetf	feet
teas	seat	otab	boat
ogat	goat	spea	peas
atli	tail	apil	pail

Page 104

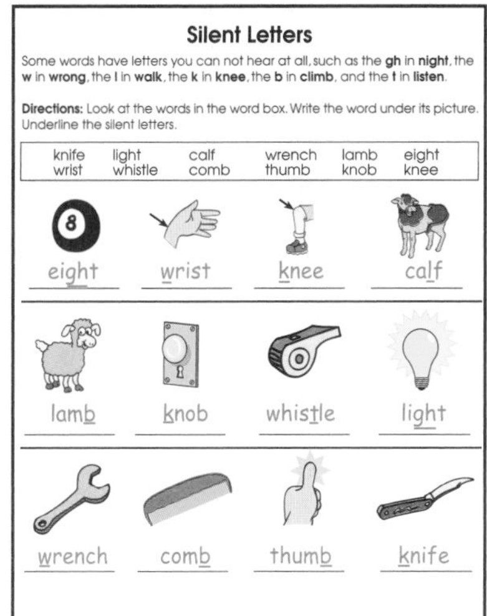

Silent Letters

Some words have letters you can not hear at all, such as the **gh** in **night**, the **w** in **wrong**, the **l** in **walk**, the **k** in **knee**, the **b** in **climb**, and the **t** in **listen**.

Directions: Look at the words in the word box. Write the word under its picture. Underline the silent letters.

knife	light	calf	wrench	lamb	eight
wrist	whistle	comb	thumb	knob	knee

eight	wrist	knee	calf
lamb	knob	whistle	light
wrench	comb	thumb	knife

Page 105

Review

Directions: Read the story. Circle the consonant teams (two or three letters) and silent letters in the underlined words. Be sure to check for more than one team in a word! One has been done for you.

One day last spring, my family went on a picnic. My father picked out a pretty spot next to a stream. While my brother and I climbed a tree, my mother spread out a sheet and placed the food on it. But before we could eat, a skunk walked out of the woods! Mother screamed and scared the skunk. It sprayed us with a terrible smell! Now, we think it is a funny story. But that day, we ran!

Directions: Write the words with three-letter blends on the lines.

Spring stream spread

screamed sprayed

Page 106

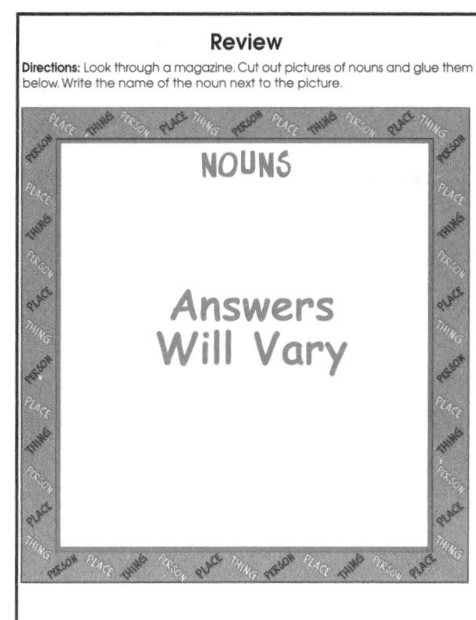

Review

Directions: Look through a magazine. Cut out pictures of nouns and glue them below. Write the name of the noun next to the picture.

NOUNS

Answers Will Vary

Page 107

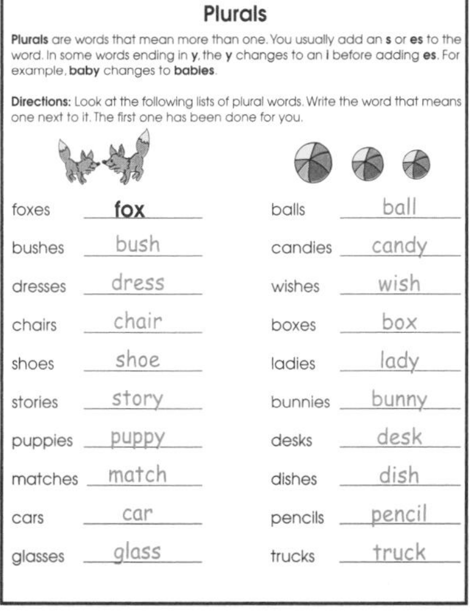

Plurals

Plurals are words that mean more than one. You usually add an **s** or **es** to the word. In some words ending in **y**, the **y** changes to an **i** before adding **es**. For example, **baby** changes to **babies**.

Directions: Look at the following lists of plural words. Write the word that means one next to it. The first one has been done for you.

foxes	fox	balls	ball
bushes	bush	candies	candy
dresses	dress	wishes	wish
chairs	chair	boxes	box
shoes	shoe	ladies	lady
stories	story	bunnies	bunny
puppies	puppy	desks	desk
matches	match	dishes	dish
cars	car	pencils	pencil
glasses	glass	trucks	truck

Page 108

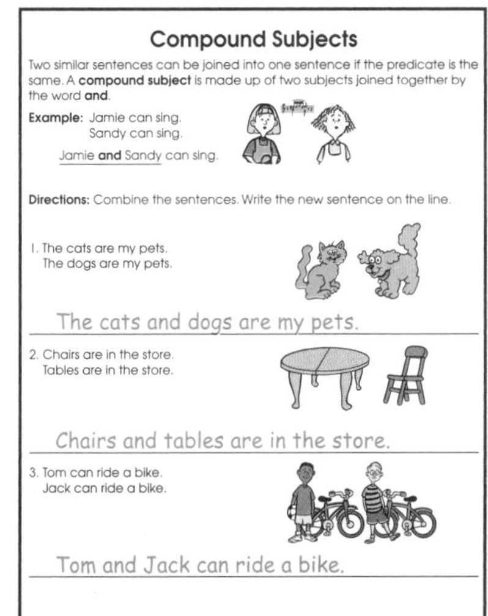

Compound Subjects

Two similar sentences can be joined into one sentence if the predicate is the same. A **compound subject** is made up of two subjects joined together by the word **and**.

Example: Jamie can sing.
Sandy can sing.
Jamie **and** Sandy can sing.

Directions: Combine the sentences. Write the new sentence on the line.

1. The cats are my pets.
The dogs are my pets.
The cats and dogs are my pets.

2. Chairs are in the store.
Tables are in the store.
Chairs and tables are in the store.

3. Tom can ride a bike.
Jack can ride a bike.
Tom and Jack can ride a bike.

Page 109

Verbs

Directions: Write each verb in the correct column.

rake	talked	look	hopped	skip
cooked	fished	call	clean	sewed

Yesterday	Today
cooked	rake
talked	look
fished	call
hopped	clean
sewed	skip

Page 110

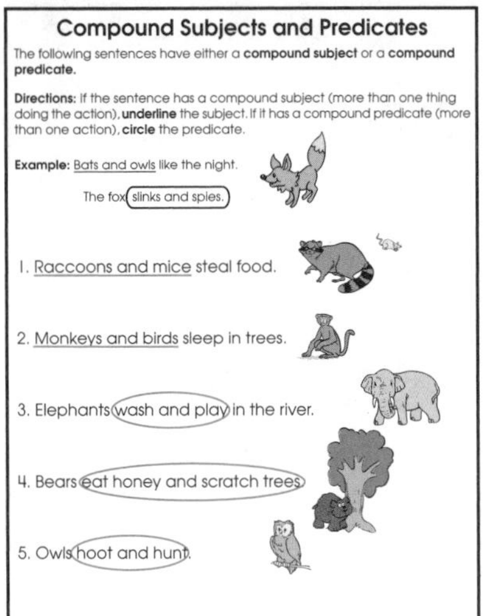

Compound Subjects and Predicates

The following sentences have either a **compound subject** or a **compound predicate.**

Directions: If the sentence has a compound subject (more than one thing doing the action), **underline** the subject. If it has a compound predicate (more than one action), **circle** the predicate.

Example: Bats and owls like the night.

The fox slinks and spies.

1. Raccoons and mice steal food.
2. Monkeys and birds sleep in trees.
3. Elephants wash and play in the river.
4. Bears eat honey and scratch trees.
5. Owls hoot and hunt.

Page 111

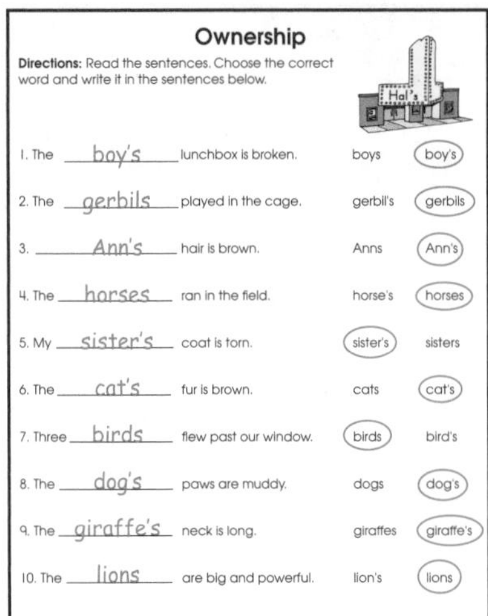

Ownership

Directions: Read the sentences. Choose the correct word and write it in the sentences below.

1. The boy's lunchbox is broken. boys boy's
2. The gerbils played in the cage. gerbil's gerbils
3. Ann's hair is brown. Anns Ann's
4. The horses ran in the field. horse's horses
5. My sister's coat is torn. sister's sisters
6. The cat's fur is brown. cats cat's
7. Three birds flew past our window. birds bird's
8. The dog's paws are muddy. dogs dog's
9. The giraffe's neck is long. giraffes giraffe's
10. The lions are big and powerful. lion's lions

Page 112

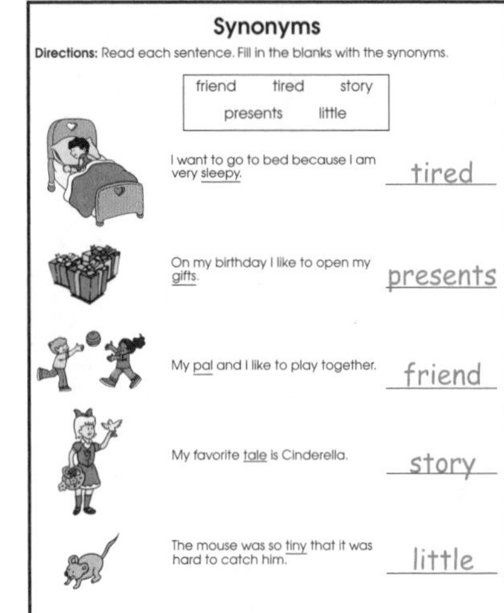

Synonyms

Directions: Read each sentence. Fill in the blanks with the synonyms.

friend tired story presents little

I want to go to bed because I am very sleepy. tired

On my birthday I like to open my gifts. presents

My pal and I like to play together. friend

My favorite tale is Cinderella. story

The mouse was so tiny that it was hard to catch him. little

Page 113

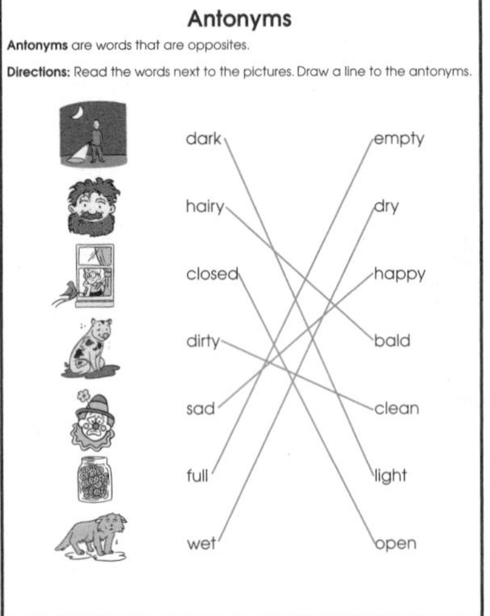

Antonyms

Antonyms are words that are opposites.

Directions: Read the words next to the pictures. Draw a line to the antonyms.

dark	empty
hairy	dry
closed	happy
dirty	bald
sad	clean
full	light
wet	open

Page 114

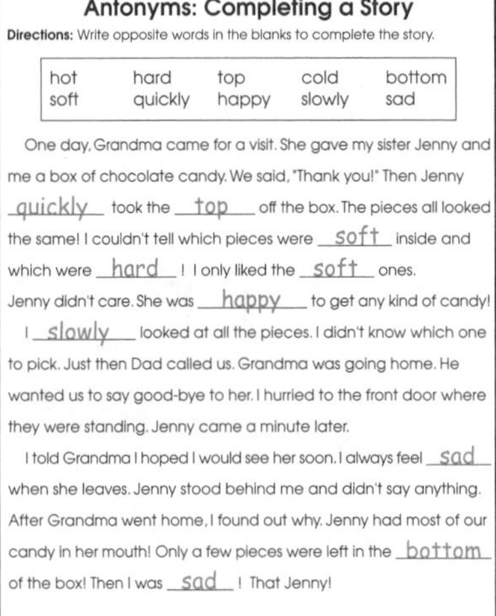

Antonyms: Completing a Story

Directions: Write opposite words in the blanks to complete the story.

hot hard top cold bottom
soft quickly happy slowly sad

One day, Grandma came for a visit. She gave my sister Jenny and me a box of chocolate candy. We said, "Thank you!" Then Jenny quickly took the top off the box. The pieces all looked the same! I couldn't tell which pieces were soft inside and which were hard! I only liked the soft ones. Jenny didn't care. She was happy to get any kind of candy! I slowly looked at all the pieces. I didn't know which one to pick. Just then Dad called us. Grandma was going home. He wanted us to say good-bye to her. I hurried to the front door where they were standing. Jenny came a minute later.

I told Grandma I hoped I would see her soon. I always feel sad when she leaves. Jenny stood behind me and didn't say anything. After Grandma went home, I found out why. Jenny had most of our candy in her mouth! Only a few pieces were left in the bottom of the box! Then I was sad! That Jenny!

Page 115

Homophones

Directions: Read each word. Circle the picture that goes with the word.

1. sun
2. ate
3. buy
4. hi
5. four
6. hear

Page 116

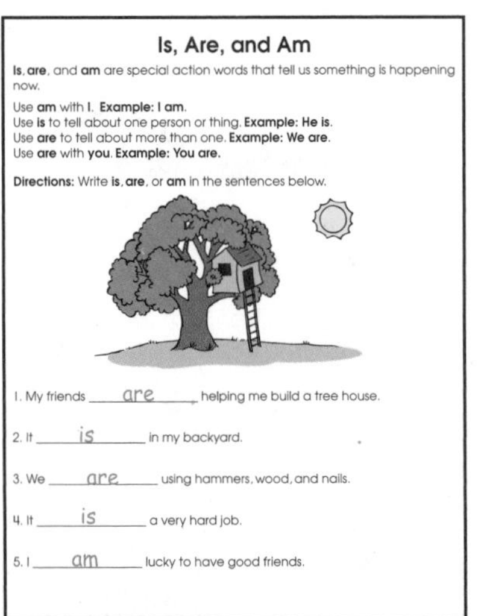

Is, Are, and Am

Is, are, and **am** are special action words that tell us something is happening now.

Use **am** with **I. Example: I am.**
Use **is** to tell about one person or thing. **Example: He is.**
Use **are** to tell about more than one. **Example: We are.**
Use **are** with **you. Example: You are.**

Directions: Write **is, are,** or **am** in the sentences below.

1. My friends are helping me build a tree house.
2. It is in my backyard.
3. We are using hammers, wood, and nails.
4. It is a very hard job.
5. I am lucky to have good friends.

Page 117

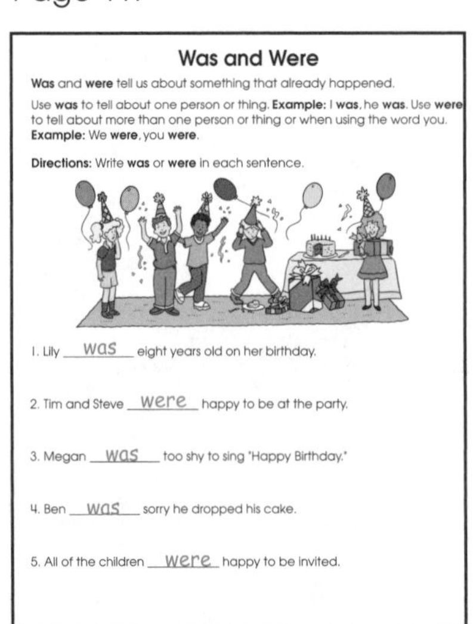

Was and Were

Was and **were** tell us about something that already happened.

Use **was** to tell about one person or thing. **Example: I was,** he **was.** Use **were** to tell about more than one person or thing or when using the word you. **Example:** We **were,** you **were.**

Directions: Write **was** or **were** in each sentence.

1. Lily was eight years old on her birthday.
2. Tim and Steve were happy to be at the party.
3. Megan was too shy to sing "Happy Birthday."
4. Ben was sorry he dropped his cake.
5. All of the children were happy to be invited.

Page 118

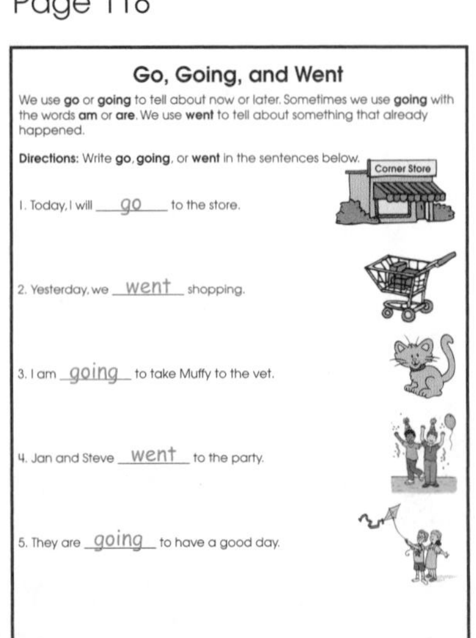

Go, Going, and Went

We use **go** or **going** to tell about now or later. Sometimes we use **going** with the words **am** or **are.** We use **went** to tell about something that already happened.

Directions: Write **go, going,** or **went** in the sentences below.

1. Today, I will go to the store.
2. Yesterday, we went shopping.
3. I am going to take Muffy to the vet.
4. Jan and Steve went to the party.
5. They are going to have a good day.

Page 119

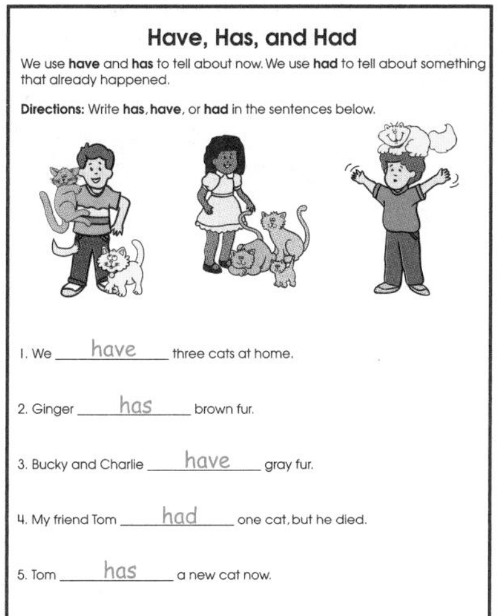

Have, Has, and Had

We use **have** and **has** to tell about now. We use **had** to tell about something that already happened.

Directions: Write **has**, **have**, or **had** in the sentences below.

1. We ___have___ three cats at home.
2. Ginger ___has___ brown fur.
3. Bucky and Charlie ___have___ gray fur.
4. My friend Tom ___had___ one cat, but he died.
5. Tom ___has___ a new cat now.

Page 120

See, Saw, and Sees

We use **see** or **sees** to tell about now. We use **saw** to tell about something that already happened.

Directions: Write **see**, **sees**, or **saw** in the sentences below.

1. Last night, we ___saw___ the stars.
2. John can ___see___ the stars from his window.
3. He ___sees___ them every night.
4. Last week, he ___saw___ the Big Dipper.
5. Can you ___see___ it in the night sky, too?
6. If you ___saw___ it, you would remember it!
7. John ___sees___ it often now.
8. How often do you ___see___ it?

Page 121

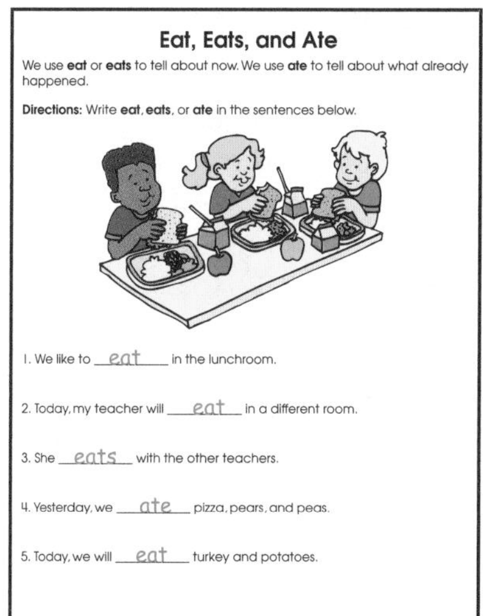

Eat, Eats, and Ate

We use **eat** or **eats** to tell about now. We use **ate** to tell about what already happened.

Directions: Write **eat**, **eats**, or **ate** in the sentences below.

1. We like to ___eat___ in the lunchroom.
2. Today, my teacher will ___eat___ in a different room.
3. She ___eats___ with the other teachers.
4. Yesterday, we ___ate___ pizza, pears, and peas.
5. Today, we will ___eat___ turkey and potatoes.

Page 122

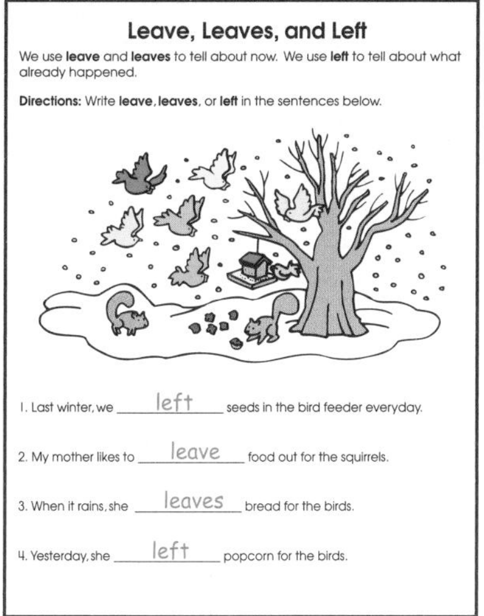

Leave, Leaves, and Left

We use **leave** and **leaves** to tell about now. We use **left** to tell about what already happened.

Directions: Write **leave**, **leaves**, or **left** in the sentences below.

1. Last winter, we ___left___ seeds in the bird feeder everyday.
2. My mother likes to ___leave___ food out for the squirrels.
3. When it rains, she ___leaves___ bread for the birds.
4. Yesterday, she ___left___ popcorn for the birds.

Page 123

Sentences

Directions: Write capital letters where they should appear in the sentences below.

Example: joe can play in january.

1. we celebrate thanksgiving on the third thursday in november.

We celebrate Thanksgiving on the third Thursday in November.

2. in june, michelle and mark will go camping every friday.

In June, Michelle and Mark will go camping every Friday.

3. on mondays in october, i will take piano lessons.

On Mondays in October, I will take piano lessons.

Page 124

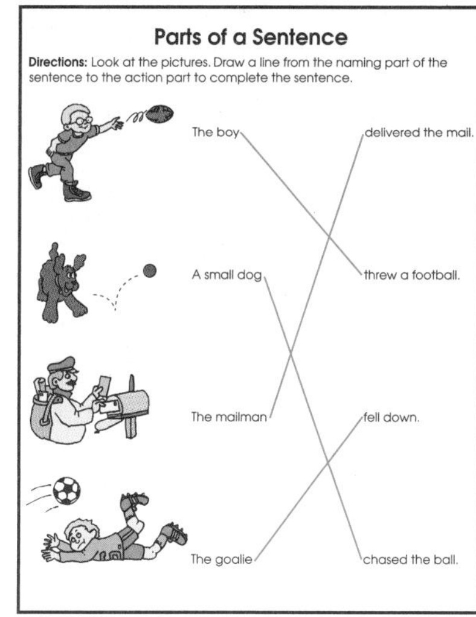

Parts of a Sentence

Directions: Look at the pictures. Draw a line from the naming part of the sentence to the action part to complete the sentence.

The boy	delivered the mail.
A small dog	threw a football.
The mailman	fell down.
The goalie	chased the ball.

Page 125

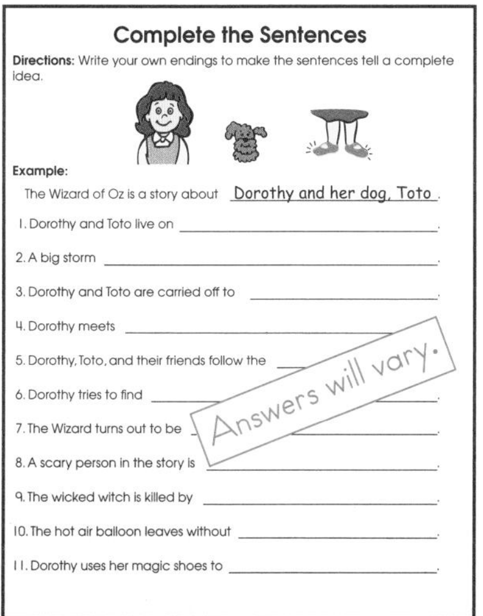

Complete the Sentences

Directions: Write your own endings to make the sentences tell a complete idea.

Example:
The Wizard of Oz is a story about Dorothy and her dog, Toto.

1. Dorothy and Toto live on ________.
2. A big storm ________.
3. Dorothy and Toto are carried off to ________.
4. Dorothy meets ________.
5. Dorothy, Toto, and their friends follow the ________.
6. Dorothy tries to find ________.
7. The Wizard turns out to be ________.
8. A scary person in the story is ________.
9. The wicked witch is killed by ________.
10. The hot air balloon leaves without ________.
11. Dorothy uses her magic shoes to ________.

Answers will vary.

Page 126

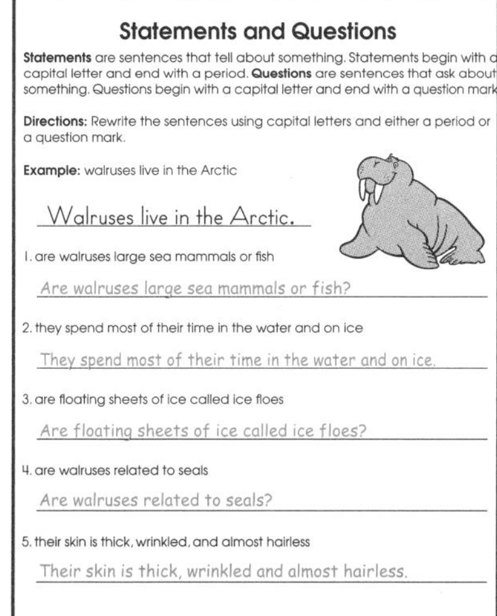

Statements and Questions

Statements are sentences that tell about something. Statements begin with a capital letter and end with a period. **Questions** are sentences that ask about something. Questions begin with a capital letter and end with a question mark.

Directions: Rewrite the sentences using capital letters and either a period or a question mark.

Example: walruses live in the Arctic

Walruses live in the Arctic.

1. are walruses large sea mammals or fish

Are walruses large sea mammals or fish?

2. they spend most of their time in the water and on ice

They spend most of their time in the water and on ice.

3. are floating sheets of ice called ice floes

Are floating sheets of ice called ice floes?

4. are walruses related to seals

Are walruses related to seals?

5. their skin is thick, wrinkled, and almost hairless

Their skin is thick, wrinkled and almost hairless.

Page 127

Commands

Commands tell someone to do something. **Example: "Be careful."** It can also be written as "Be careful!" if it tells a strong feeling.

Directions: Put a period at the end of the command sentences. Use an exclamation point if the sentence tells a strong feeling. Write your own commands on the lines below.

1. Clean your room.
2. Now!
3. Be careful with your goldfish.
4. Watch out!
5. Be a little more careful.

Answers will vary.

Page 128

Questions

Questions are sentences that ask something. They begin with a capital letter and end with a question mark.

Directions: Write the questions on the lines below. Begin each sentence with a capital letter and end it with a question mark.

1. will you be my friend
   Will you be my friend?
2. what is your name
   What is your name?
3. are you eight years old
   Are you eight years old?
4. do you like rainbows
   Do you like rainbows?

Page 129

Main Idea

Directions: Circle the sentence in each paragraph that does not support the main idea.

The school picnic was so much fun! When we arrived, we each made a name tag. Then we signed up for the contests we wanted to enter. My best friend was my partner for every contest. (The hen laid so many eggs that I needed a basket to carry them.) All that exercise made us very hungry. We were glad to see those tables full of food.

The storm howled outside, so we stayed in for an evening of fun. (The colorful rainbow stretched across the sky.) The dining room table was stacked with games and puzzles. The delightful smell of popcorn led us into the kitchen where Dad led a parade around the kitchen table. Then we carried our bowls of popcorn into the dining room. We laughed so hard and ate so much, we didn't care who won the games. It was a great evening!

The city championship game would be played on Saturday at Brookside Park. Coach Metzger called an extra practice Friday evening. He said he knew we were good, because we had made it this far. He didn't want us to get nervous and forget everything we knew. (School starts on Monday, but I'm not ready to go back yet.) After working on some drills, Coach told us to relax, get lots of rest, and come back ready to play.

Page 130

Main Idea: Chewing Gum

Directions: Read about chewing gum, then answer the questions.

Thomas Adams was an American inventor. In 1870, he was looking for a substitute for rubber. He was working with **chicle** (chick-ul), a substance that comes from a certain kind of tree in Mexico. Years ago, Mexicans chewed chicle. Thomas Adams decided to try it for himself. He liked it so much he started selling it. Twenty years later, he owned a large factory that produced chewing gum.

1. Who was the American inventor who started selling chewing gum? Thomas Adams
2. What was he hoping to invent? a substitute for rubber
3. When did he invent chewing gum? in 1870
4. Where does the chicle come from? a tree in Mexico
5. Why did Thomas Adams start selling chewing gum? He liked it so much.
6. How long was it until Adams owned a large factory that produced chewing gum? 20 years

Page 131

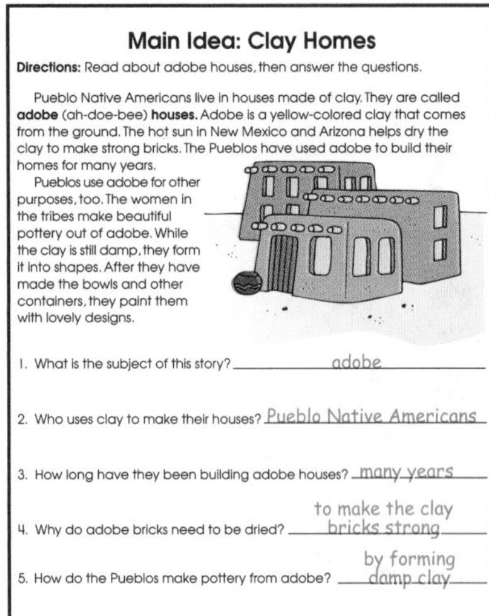

Main Idea: Clay Homes

Directions: Read about adobe houses, then answer the questions.

Pueblo Native Americans live in houses made of clay. They are called **adobe** (ah-doe-bee) **houses.** Adobe is a yellow-colored clay that comes from the ground. The hot sun in New Mexico and Arizona helps dry the clay to make strong bricks. The Pueblos have used adobe to build their homes for many years.

Pueblos use adobe for other purposes, too. The women in the tribes make beautiful pottery out of adobe. While the clay is still damp, they form it into shapes. After they have made the bowls and other containers, they paint them with lovely designs.

1. What is the subject of this story? adobe
2. Who uses clay to make their houses? Pueblo Native Americans
3. How long have they been building adobe houses? many years
4. Why do adobe bricks need to be dried? to make the clay bricks strong
5. How do the Pueblos make pottery from adobe? by forming damp clay

Page 132

Noting Details

Directions: Read the story. Then answer the questions.

The giant panda is much smaller than a brown bear or a polar bear. In fact, a horse weighs about four times as much as a giant panda. So why is it called "giant"? It is giant next to another kind of panda called the red panda.

The red panda also lives in China. The red panda is about the size of a fox. It has a long, fluffy, striped tail and beautiful reddish fur. It looks very much like a raccoon.

Many people think the giant pandas are bears. They look like bears. Even the word panda is Chinese for "white bear." But because of its relationship to the red panda, many scientists now believe that the panda is really more like a raccoon!

1. Why is the giant panda called "giant"?
   It is larger than the red panda.
2. Where does the red panda live?
   in China
3. How big is the red panda?
   about the size of a fox
4. What animal does the red panda look like?
   a raccoon
5. What does the word panda mean?
   "white bear"

Page 133

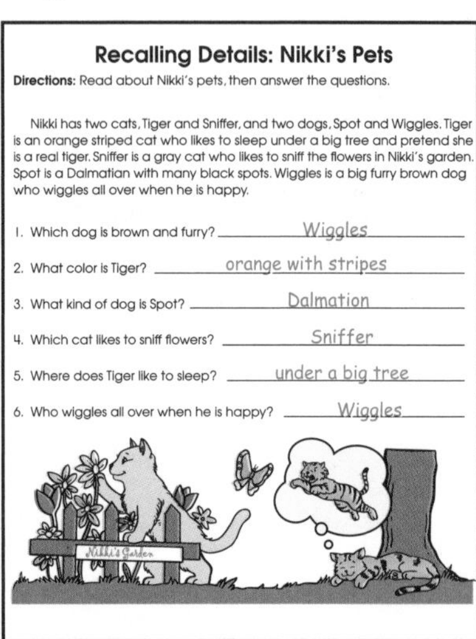

Recalling Details: Nikki's Pets

Directions: Read about Nikki's pets, then answer the questions.

Nikki has two cats, Tiger and Sniffer, and two dogs, Spot and Wiggles. Tiger is an orange striped cat who likes to sleep under a big tree and pretend she is a real tiger. Sniffer is a gray cat who likes to sniff the flowers in Nikki's garden. Spot is a Dalmatian with many black spots. Wiggles is a big furry brown dog who wiggles all over when he is happy.

1. Which dog is brown and furry? Wiggles
2. What color is Tiger? orange with stripes
3. What kind of dog is Spot? Dalmation
4. Which cat likes to sniff flowers? Sniffer
5. Where does Tiger like to sleep? under a big tree
6. Who wiggles all over when he is happy? Wiggles

Page 134

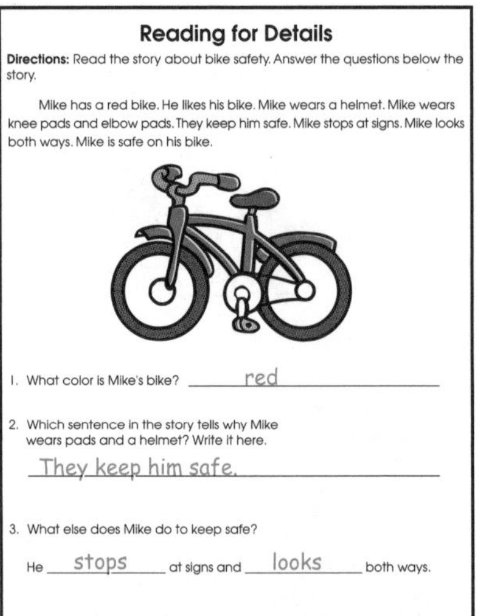

Reading for Details

Directions: Read the story about bike safety. Answer the questions below the story.

Mike has a red bike. He likes his bike. Mike wears a helmet. Mike wears knee pads and elbow pads. They keep him safe. Mike stops at signs. Mike looks both ways. Mike is safe on his bike.

1. What color is Mike's bike? red
2. Which sentence in the story tells why Mike wears pads and a helmet? Write it here.
   They keep him safe.
3. What else does Mike do to keep safe?
   He stops at signs and looks both ways.

Page 135

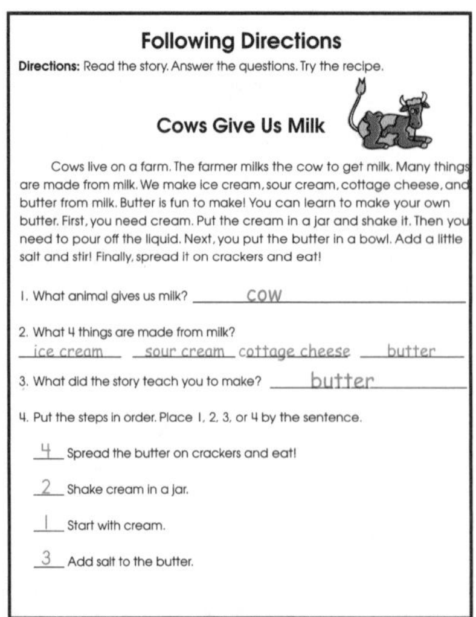

Following Directions

Directions: Read the story. Answer the questions. Try the recipe.

Cows Give Us Milk

Cows live on a farm. The farmer milks the cow to get milk. Many things are made from milk. We make ice cream, sour cream, cottage cheese, and butter from milk. Butter is fun to make! You can learn to make your own butter. First, you need cream. Put the cream in a jar and shake it. Then you need to pour off the liquid. Next, you put the butter in a bowl. Add a little salt and stir! Finally, spread it on crackers and eat!

1. What animal gives us milk? cow
2. What 4 things are made from milk?
   ice cream, sour cream, cottage cheese, butter
3. What did the story teach you to make? butter
4. Put the steps in order. Place 1, 2, 3, or 4 by the sentence.
   - 4 Spread the butter on crackers and eat!
   - 2 Shake cream in a jar.
   - 1 Start with cream.
   - 3 Add salt to the butter.

Page 136

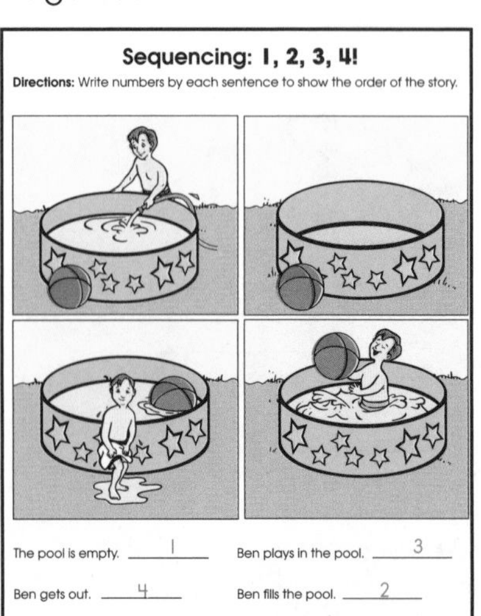

Sequencing: 1, 2, 3, 4!

Directions: Write numbers by each sentence to show the order of the story.

The pool is empty. 1

Ben plays in the pool. 3

Ben gets out. 4

Ben fills the pool. 2

Page 137

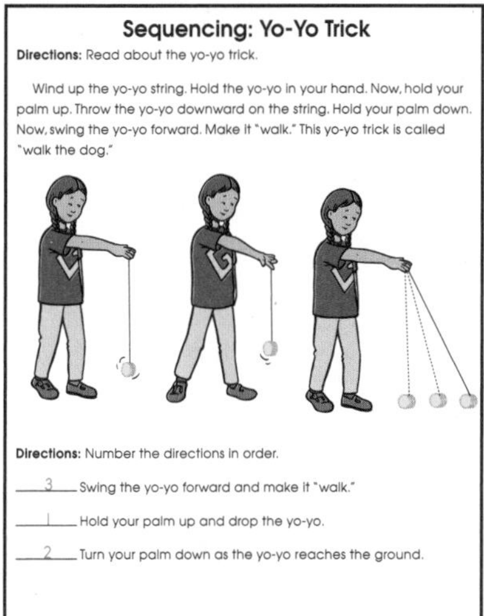

Sequencing: Yo-Yo Trick

Directions: Read about the yo-yo trick.

Wind up the yo-yo string. Hold the yo-yo in your hand. Now, hold your palm up. Throw the yo-yo downward on the string. Hold your palm down. Now, swing the yo-yo forward. Make it "walk." This yo-yo trick is called "walk the dog."

Directions: Number the directions in order.

3 Swing the yo-yo forward and make it "walk."

1 Hold your palm up and drop the yo-yo.

2 Turn your palm down as the yo-yo reaches the ground.

Page 138

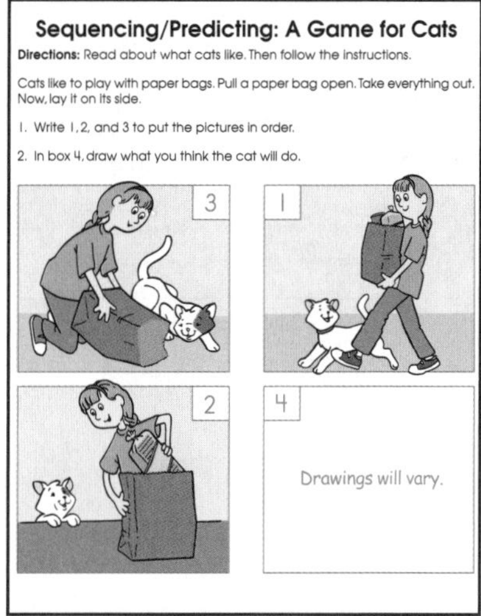

Sequencing/Predicting: A Game for Cats

Directions: Read about what cats like. Then follow the instructions.

Cats like to play with paper bags. Pull a paper bag open. Take everything out. Now, lay it on its side.

1. Write 1, 2, and 3 to put the pictures in order.
2. In box 4, draw what you think the cat will do.

3 | 1 | 2 | 4

Drawings will vary.

Page 139

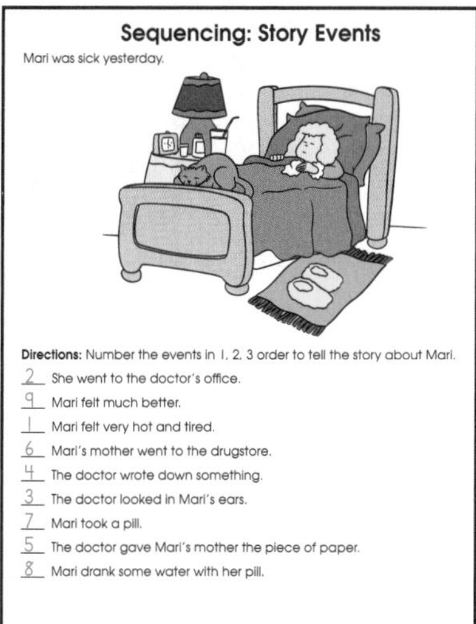

Sequencing: Story Events

Mari was sick yesterday.

Directions: Number the events in 1, 2, 3 order to tell the story about Mari.

2 She went to the doctor's office.

9 Mari felt much better.

1 Mari felt very hot and tired.

6 Mari's mother went to the drugstore.

4 The doctor wrote down something.

3 The doctor looked in Mari's ears.

7 Mari took a pill.

5 The doctor gave Mari's mother the piece of paper.

8 Mari drank some water with her pill.

Page 140

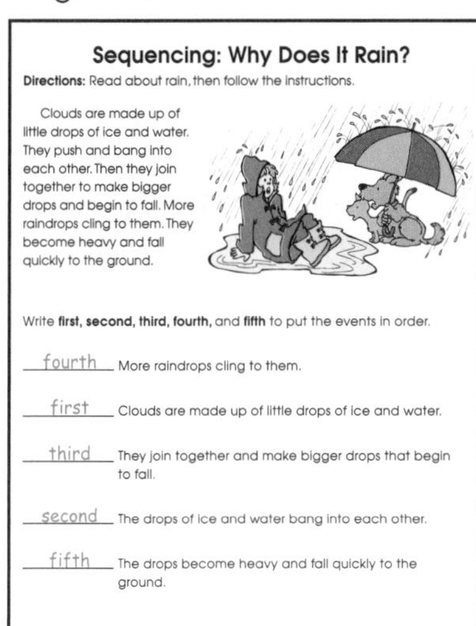

Sequencing: Why Does It Rain?

Directions: Read about rain, then follow the instructions.

Clouds are made up of little drops of ice and water. They push and bang into each other. Then they join together to make bigger drops and begin to fall. More raindrops cling to them. They become heavy and fall quickly to the ground.

Write **first, second, third, fourth,** and **fifth** to put the events in order.

fourth More raindrops cling to them.

first Clouds are made up of little drops of ice and water.

third They join together and make bigger drops that begin to fall.

second The drops of ice and water bang into each other.

fifth The drops become heavy and fall quickly to the ground.

Page 142

Sequencing: A Story

The Crow and the Robin

The robin flew to another tree and kept on singing, but the crow sat still and made himself very unhappy. "The wind is so cold," he said. "It always blows the wrong way for me."

Very soon the sun came out, warm and bright, and the clouds went away, but the crow was as cross as ever.

The grass began to spring up in the meadows. Green leaves and flowers were seen in the woods. Birds and bees flew here and there in the glad sunshine. The crow sat and croaked on the branch of the old oak tree.

"It is always too warm or too cold," said he. "To be sure, it is a little pleasant just now, but I know that the sun will soon shine warm enough to burn me up. Then before night, it will be colder than ever. I do not see how anyone can sing at such a time as this."

Just then the robin came back to the tree with a straw in her mouth for her nest. "Well, my friend," asked she, "where is your snow?"

"Don't talk about that," croaked the crow. "It will snow all the harder for this sunshine."

"And snow or shine," said the robin, "you will keep on croaking. For my part, I shall always look on the bright side of things and have a song for every day in the year."

Which will you be like—the crow or the robin? Answers will vary.

Page 143

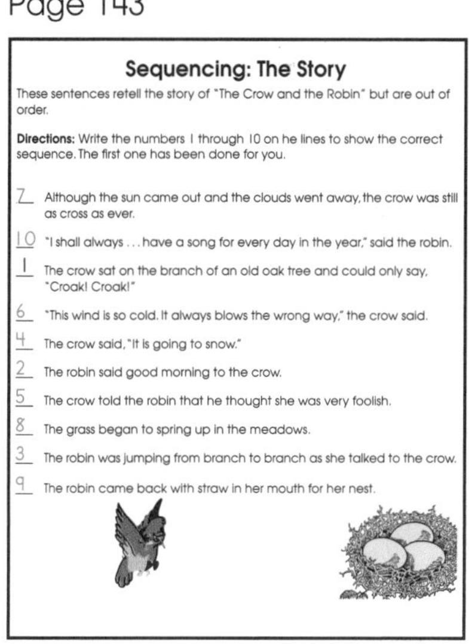

Sequencing: The Story

These sentences retell the story of "The Crow and the Robin" but are out of order.

Directions: Write the numbers 1 through 10 on he lines to show the correct sequence. The first one has been done for you.

7 Although the sun came out and the clouds went away, the crow was still as cross as ever.

10 "I shall always . . . have a song for every day in the year," said the robin.

1 The crow sat on the branch of an old oak tree and could only say, "Croak! Croak!"

6 "This wind is so cold. It always blows the wrong way," the crow said.

4 The crow said, "It is going to snow."

2 The robin said good morning to the crow.

5 The crow told the robin that he thought she was very foolish.

8 The grass began to spring up in the meadows.

3 The robin was jumping from branch to branch as she talked to the crow.

9 The robin came back with straw in her mouth for her nest.

Page 144

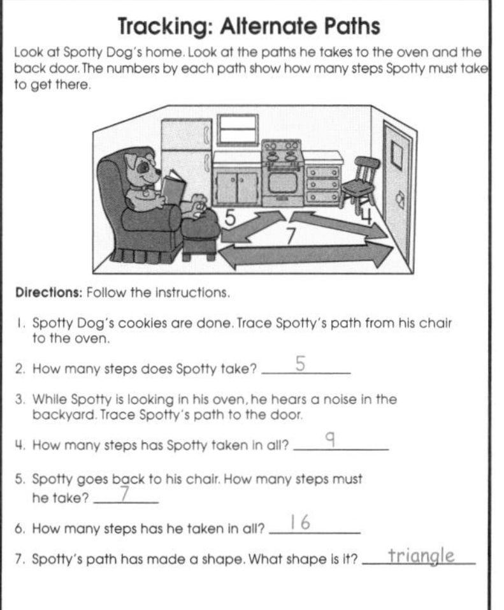

Tracking: Alternate Paths

Look at Spotty Dog's home. Look at the paths he takes to the oven and the back door. The numbers by each path show how many steps Spotty must take to get there.

5 4 7

Directions: Follow the instructions.

1. Spotty Dog's cookies are done. Trace Spotty's path from his chair to the oven.
2. How many steps does Spotty take? 5
3. While Spotty is looking in his oven, he hears a noise in the backyard. Trace Spotty's path to the door.
4. How many steps has Spotty taken in all? 9
5. Spotty goes back to his chair. How many steps must he take? 7
6. How many steps has he taken in all? 16
7. Spotty's path has made a shape. What shape is it? triangle

Page 145

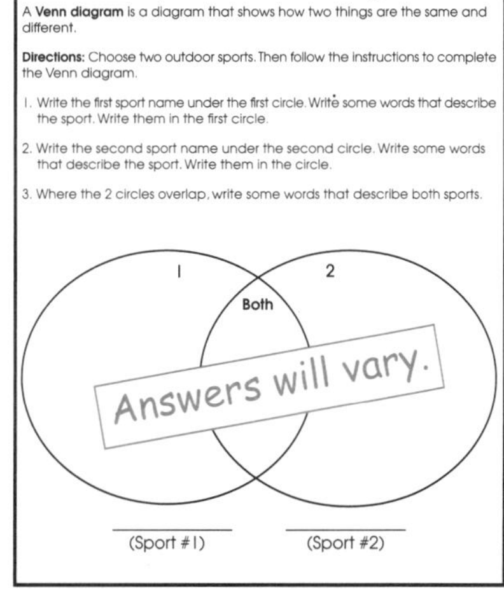

Same/Different: Venn Diagram

A **Venn diagram** is a diagram that shows how two things are the same and different.

Directions: Choose two outdoor sports. Then follow the instructions to complete the Venn diagram.

1. Write the first sport name under the first circle. Write some words that describe the sport. Write them in the first circle.
2. Write the second sport name under the second circle. Write some words that describe the sport. Write them in the circle.
3. Where the 2 circles overlap, write some words that describe both sports.

1 | Both | 2

Answers will vary.

(Sport #1) (Sport #2)

Page 146

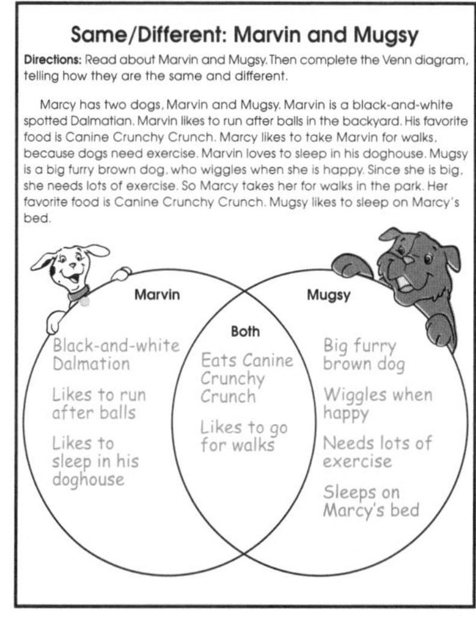

Same/Different: Marvin and Mugsy

Directions: Read about Marvin and Mugsy. Then complete the Venn diagram, telling how they are the same and different.

Marcy has two dogs, Marvin and Mugsy. Marvin is a black-and-white spotted Dalmatian. Marvin likes to run after balls in the backyard. His favorite food is Canine Crunchy Crunch. Marcy likes to take Marvin for walks, because dogs need exercise. Marvin loves to sleep in his doghouse. Mugsy is a big furry brown dog, who wiggles when she is happy. Since she is big, she needs lots of exercise. So Marcy takes her for walks in the park. Her favorite food is Canine Crunchy Crunch. Mugsy likes to sleep on Marcy's bed.

Marvin: Black-and-white Dalmation; Likes to run after balls; Likes to sleep in his doghouse

Both: Eats Canine Crunchy Crunch; Likes to go for walks

Mugsy: Big furry brown dog; Wiggles when happy; Needs lots of exercise; Sleeps on Marcy's bed

Page 147

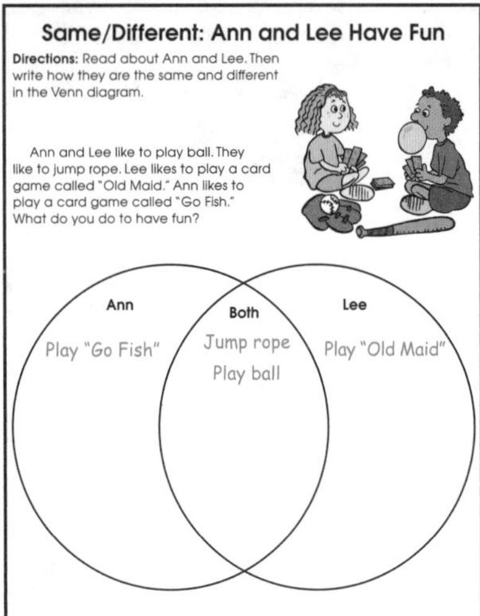

Same/Different: Ann and Lee Have Fun

Directions: Read about Ann and Lee. Then write how they are the same and different in the Venn diagram.

Ann and Lee like to play ball. They like to jump rope. Lee likes to play a card game called "Old Maid." Ann likes to play a card game called "Go Fish." What do you do to have fun?

Page 148

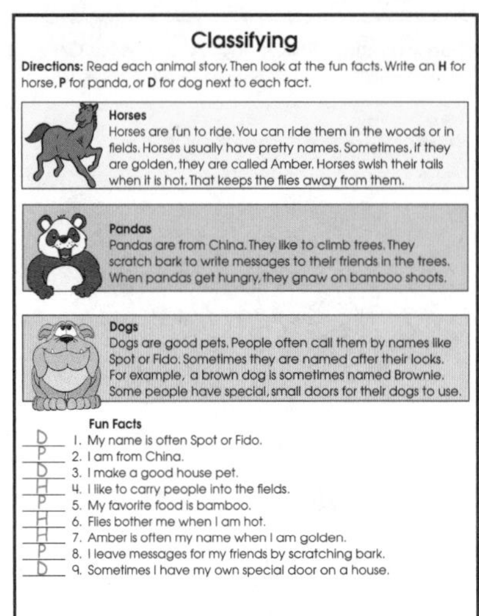

Classifying

Directions: Read each animal story. Then look at the fun facts. Write an **H** for horse, **P** for panda, or **D** for dog next to each fact.

Horses
Horses are fun to ride. You can ride them in the woods or in fields. Horses usually have pretty names. Sometimes, if they are golden, they are called Amber. Horses swish their tails when it is hot. That keeps the flies away from them.

Pandas
Pandas are from China. They like to climb trees. They scratch bark to write messages to their friends in the trees. When pandas get hungry, they gnaw on bamboo shoots.

Dogs
Dogs are good pets. People often call them by names like Spot or Fido. Sometimes they are named after their looks. For example, a brown dog is sometimes named Brownie. Some people have special, small doors for their dogs to use.

Fun Facts
D 1. My name is often Spot or Fido.
P 2. I am from China.
D 3. I make a good house pet.
H 4. I like to carry people into the fields.
P 5. My favorite food is bamboo.
H 6. Flies bother me when I am hot.
H 7. Amber is often my name when I am golden.
P 8. I leave messages for my friends by scratching bark.
D 9. Sometimes I have my own special door on a house.

Page 149

Classifying

Classifying is putting similar things into groups.

Directions: Write each word from the word box on the correct line.

baby	donkey	whale	family	fox
uncle	goose	grandfather	kangaroo	policeman

people	animal
baby	goose
family	whale
grandfather	fox
policeman	kangaroo
uncle	donkey

Page 150

Classifying: Watch Out for Poison Ivy!

Poison ivy is not safe. If you touch it, it can make your skin red and itchy. It can hurt. It grows on the ground. It has three leaves. It can be green or red. Watch out, Jay! There is poison ivy in these woods.

Directions: Color the poison ivy leaves red. Then color the "safe" leaves other colors.

Page 151

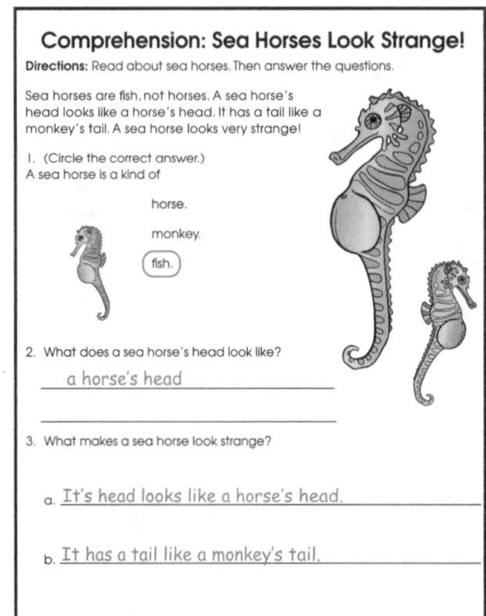

Comprehension: Sea Horses Look Strange!

Directions: Read about sea horses. Then answer the questions.

Sea horses are fish, not horses. A sea horse's head looks like a horse's head. It has a tail like a monkey's tail. A sea horse looks very strange!

1. (Circle the correct answer.)
A sea horse is a kind of
horse.
monkey.
(fish.)

2. What does a sea horse's head look like?
a horse's head

3. What makes a sea horse look strange?
a. It's head looks like a horse's head.
b. It has a tail like a monkey's tail.

Page 152

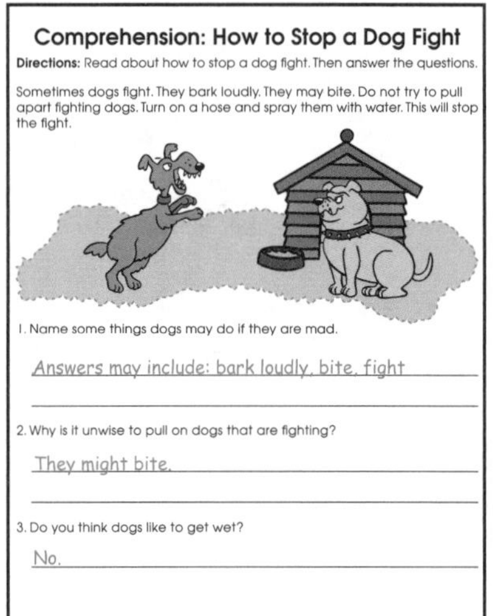

Comprehension: How to Stop a Dog Fight

Directions: Read about how to stop a dog fight. Then answer the questions.

Sometimes dogs fight. They bark loudly. They may bite. Do not try to pull apart fighting dogs. Turn on a hose and spray them with water. This will stop the fight.

1. Name some things dogs may do if they are mad.
Answers may include: bark loudly, bite, fight

2. Why is it unwise to pull on dogs that are fighting?
They might bite.

3. Do you think dogs like to get wet?
No.

Page 153

Comprehension: A Winter Story

Directions: Read about winter. Then follow the instructions.

It is cold in winter. Snow falls. Water freezes. Most kids like to play outdoors. Some kids make a snowman. Some kids skate. What do you do in winter?

1. Circle the main idea:
Snow falls in winter.
(In winter, there are many things to do outside.)

2. Write two things about winter weather.
1)
2)

3. Write what you like to do in winter.

Answers will vary.

Page 154

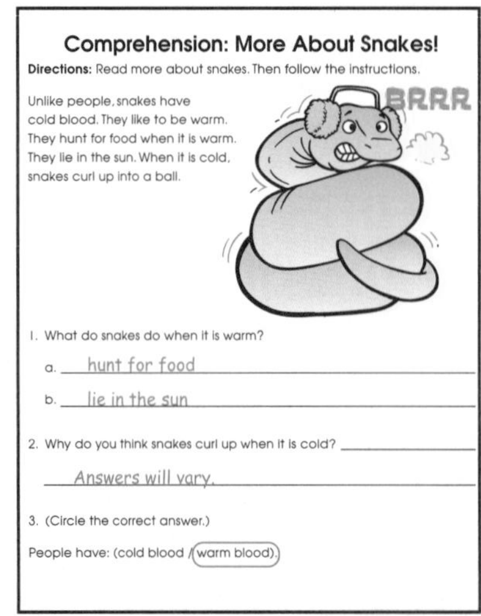

Comprehension: More About Snakes!

Directions: Read more about snakes. Then follow the instructions.

Unlike people, snakes have cold blood. They like to be warm. They hunt for food when it is warm. They lie in the sun. When it is cold, snakes curl up into a ball.

1. What do snakes do when it is warm?
a. hunt for food
b. lie in the sun

2. Why do you think snakes curl up when it is cold?
Answers will vary.

3. (Circle the correct answer.)
People have: (cold blood / (warm blood))

Page 155

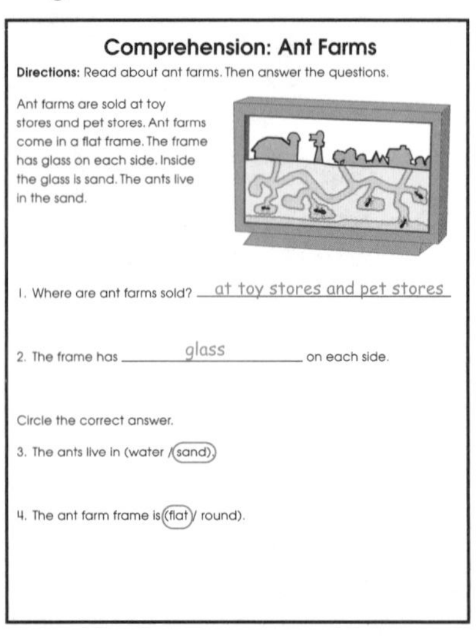

Comprehension: Ant Farms

Directions: Read about ant farms. Then answer the questions.

Ant farms are sold at toy stores and pet stores. Ant farms come in a flat frame. The frame has glass on each side. Inside the glass is sand. The ants live in the sand.

1. Where are ant farms sold? at toy stores and pet stores

2. The frame has glass on each side.

Circle the correct answer.

3. The ants live in (water / (sand)).

4. The ant farm frame is ((flat) / round).

Page 156

Comprehension: Sharks Are Fish, Too!

Directions: Read the story. Then follow the instructions.

Angela learned a lot about sharks when her class visited the city aquarium. She learned that sharks are fish. Some sharks are as big as an elephant, and some can fit into a small paper bag. Sharks have no bones. They have hundreds of teeth, and when they lose them, they grow new ones. They eat animals of any kind. Whale sharks are the largest of all fish.

1. Circle the main idea:

(Angela learned a lot about sharks at the aquarium.)

Some sharks are as big as elephants.

2. When sharks lose teeth, they grow new ones

3. Whale sharks are the largest of all fish.

4. Sharks have bones. (Circle the answer.)

Yes (No)

Page 157

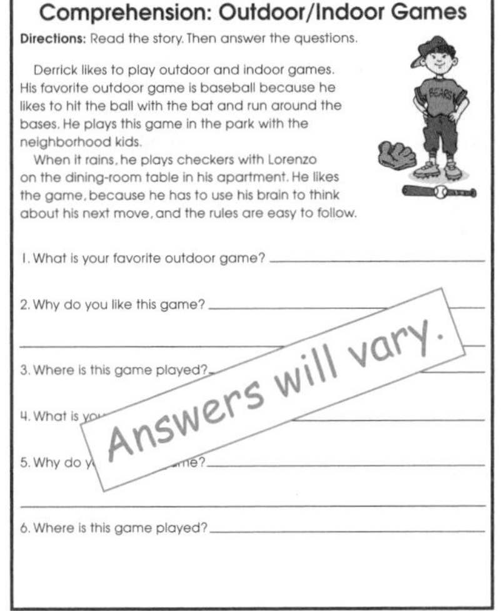

Comprehension: Outdoor/Indoor Games

Directions: Read the story. Then answer the questions.

Derrick likes to play outdoor and indoor games. His favorite outdoor game is baseball because he likes to hit the ball with the bat and run around the bases. He plays this game in the park with the neighborhood kids.

When it rains, he plays checkers with Lorenzo on the dining-room table in his apartment. He likes the game, because he has to use his brain to think about his next move, and the rules are easy to follow.

1. What is your favorite outdoor game?
2. Why do you like this game?
3. Where is this game played?
4. What is yo...
5. Why do y... ...me?
6. Where is this game played?

Answers will vary.

Page 158

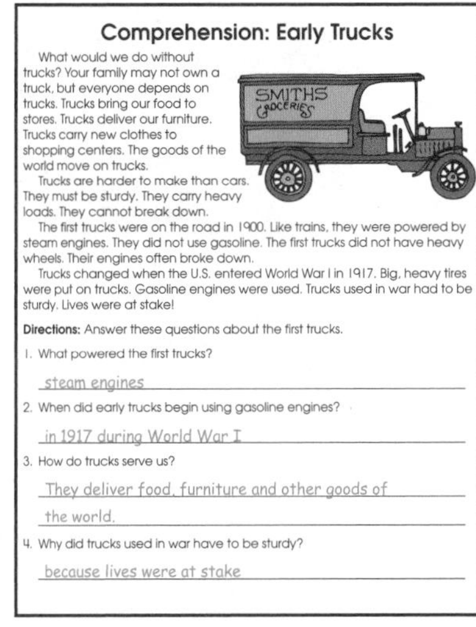

Comprehension: Early Trucks

What would we do without trucks? Your family may not own a truck, but everyone depends on trucks. Trucks bring our food to stores. Trucks deliver our furniture. Trucks carry new clothes to shopping centers. The goods of the world move on trucks.

Trucks are harder to make than cars. They must be sturdy. They carry heavy loads. They cannot break down.

The first trucks were on the road in 1900. Like trains, they were powered by steam engines. They did not use gasoline. The first trucks did not have heavy wheels. Their engines often broke down.

Trucks changed when the U.S. entered World War I in 1917. Big, heavy tires were put on trucks. Gasoline engines were used. Trucks used in war had to be sturdy. Lives were at stake!

Directions: Answer these questions about the first trucks.

1. What powered the first trucks?

steam engines

2. When did early trucks begin using gasoline engines?

in 1917 during World War I

3. How do trucks serve us?

They deliver food, furniture and other goods of the world.

4. Why did trucks used in war have to be sturdy?

because lives were at stake

Page 159

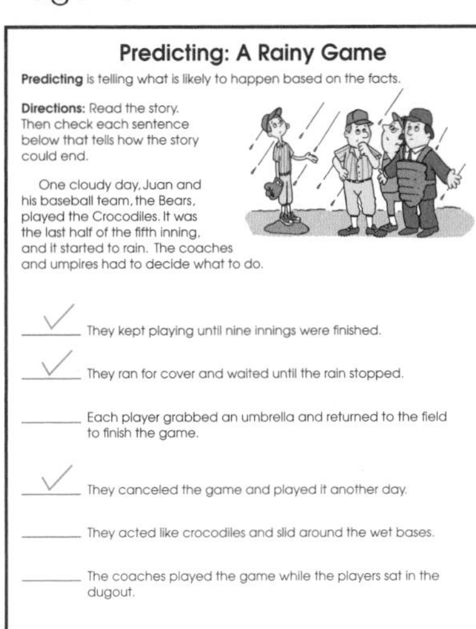

Predicting: A Rainy Game

Predicting is telling what is likely to happen based on the facts.

Directions: Read the story. Then check each sentence below that tells how the story could end.

One cloudy day, Juan and his baseball team, the Bears, played the Crocodiles. It was the last half of the fifth inning, and it started to rain. The coaches and umpires had to decide what to do.

✓ They kept playing until nine innings were finished.

✓ They ran for cover and waited until the rain stopped.

____ Each player grabbed an umbrella and returned to the field to finish the game.

✓ They canceled the game and played it another day.

____ They acted like crocodiles and slid around the wet bases.

____ The coaches played the game while the players sat in the dugout.

Page 160

Predicting Outcome

Directions: Read the story. Complete the story in the last box.

1. "Look at that elephant! He sure is big!"
2. "I'm hungry." "I bet that elephant is, too."
3. "Stop, Amy! Look at that sign!"
4. Answers will vary.

Drawings will vary.

Page 161

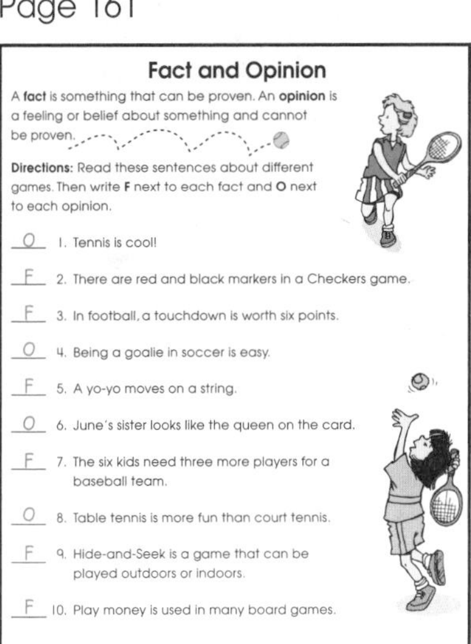

Fact and Opinion

A **fact** is something that can be proven. An **opinion** is a feeling or belief about something and cannot be proven.

Directions: Read these sentences about different games. Then write **F** next to each fact and **O** next to each opinion.

O 1. Tennis is cool!

F 2. There are red and black markers in a Checkers game.

F 3. In football, a touchdown is worth six points.

O 4. Being a goalie in soccer is easy.

F 5. A yo-yo moves on a string.

O 6. June's sister looks like the queen on the card.

F 7. The six kids need three more players for a baseball team.

O 8. Table tennis is more fun than court tennis.

F 9. Hide-and-Seek is a game that can be played outdoors or indoors.

F 10. Play money is used in many board games.

Page 162

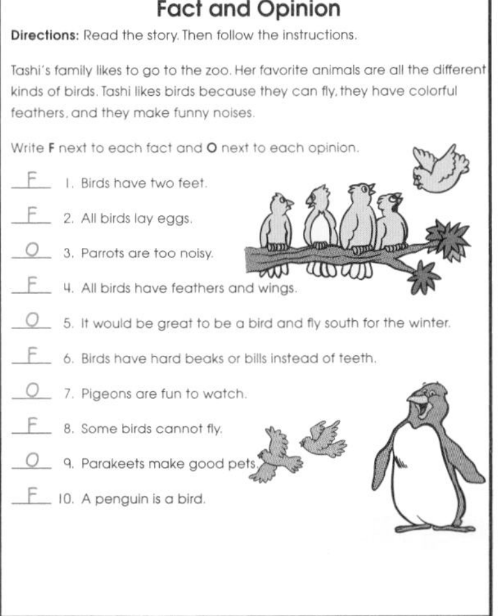

Fact and Opinion

Directions: Read the story. Then follow the instructions.

Tashi's family likes to go to the zoo. Her favorite animals are all the different kinds of birds. Tashi likes birds because they can fly, they have colorful feathers, and they make funny noises.

Write **F** next to each fact and **O** next to each opinion.

F 1. Birds have two feet.

F 2. All birds lay eggs.

O 3. Parrots are too noisy.

F 4. All birds have feathers and wings.

O 5. It would be great to be a bird and fly south for the winter.

F 6. Birds have hard beaks or bills instead of teeth.

O 7. Pigeons are fun to watch.

F 8. Some birds cannot fly.

O 9. Parakeets make good pets.

F 10. A penguin is a bird.

Page 163

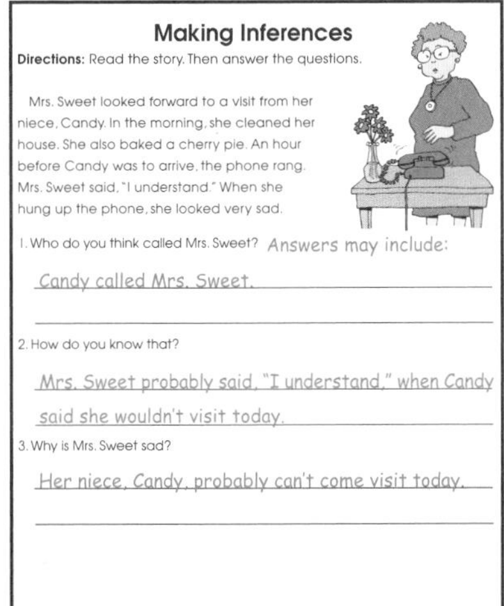

Making Inferences

Directions: Read the story. Then answer the questions.

Mrs. Sweet looked forward to a visit from her niece, Candy. In the morning, she cleaned her house. She also baked a cherry pie. An hour before Candy was to arrive, the phone rang. Mrs. Sweet said, "I understand." When she hung up the phone, she looked very sad.

1. Who do you think called Mrs. Sweet? Answers may include:

Candy called Mrs. Sweet.

2. How do you know that?

Mrs. Sweet probably said, "I understand," when Candy said she wouldn't visit today.

3. Why is Mrs. Sweet sad?

Her niece, Candy, probably can't come visit today.

Page 164

Making Inferences

Juniper has three problems to solve. She needs your help.

Directions: Read each problem. Write what you think she should do.

HELP!

1. Juniper is watching her favorite TV show when the power goes out.

2. Juniper is riding her bike to school...

3. Juniper loses her father while shopping in the supermarket.

Answers will vary.

Page 165

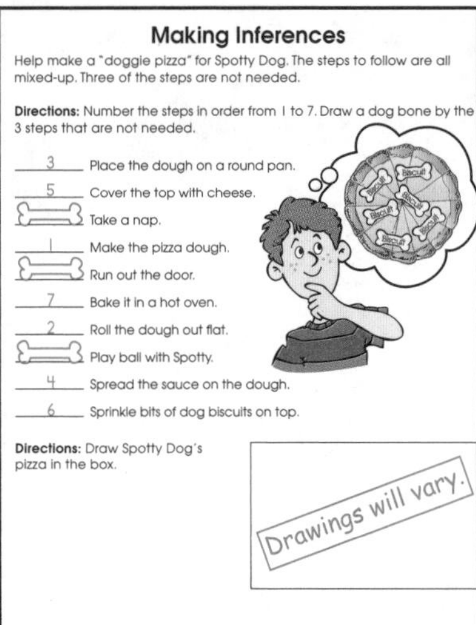

Making Inferences

Help make a "doggie pizza" for Spotty Dog. The steps to follow are all mixed-up. Three of the steps are not needed.

Directions: Number the steps in order from 1 to 7. Draw a dog bone by the 3 steps that are not needed.

3 Place the dough on a round pan.
5 Cover the top with cheese.
[bone] Take a nap.
1 Make the pizza dough.
[bone] Run out the door.
7 Bake it in a hot oven.
2 Roll the dough out flat.
[bone] Play ball with Spotty.
4 Spread the sauce on the dough.
6 Sprinkle bits of dog biscuits on top.

Directions: Draw Spotty Dog's pizza in the box.

Drawings will vary.

Page 166

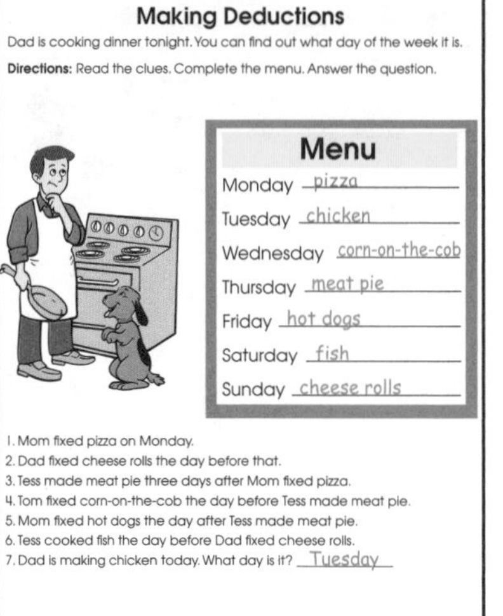

Making Deductions

Dad is cooking dinner tonight. You can find out what day of the week it is.

Directions: Read the clues. Complete the menu. Answer the question.

Menu

Monday pizza
Tuesday chicken
Wednesday corn-on-the-cob
Thursday meat pie
Friday hot dogs
Saturday fish
Sunday cheese rolls

1. Mom fixed pizza on Monday.
2. Dad fixed cheese rolls the day before that.
3. Tess made meat pie three days after Mom fixed pizza.
4. Tom fixed corn-on-the-cob the day before Tess made meat pie.
5. Mom fixed hot dogs the day after Tess made meat pie.
6. Tess cooked fish the day before Dad fixed cheese rolls.
7. Dad is making chicken today. What day is it? Tuesday

Page 167

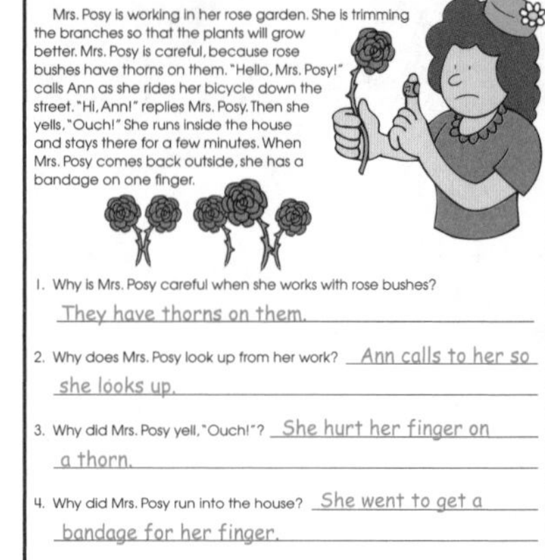

Drawing Conclusions: Mrs. Posy's Roses

Directions: Read more about Mrs. Posy, then answer the questions.

Mrs. Posy is working in her rose garden. She is trimming the branches so that the plants will grow better. Mrs. Posy is careful, because rose bushes have thorns on them. "Hello, Mrs. Posy!" calls Ann as she rides her bicycle down the street. "Hi, Ann!" replies Mrs. Posy. Then she yells, "Ouch!" She runs inside the house and stays there for a few minutes. When Mrs. Posy comes back outside, she has a bandage on one finger.

1. Why is Mrs. Posy careful when she works with rose bushes? They have thorns on them.
2. Why does Mrs. Posy look up from her work? Ann calls to her so she looks up.
3. Why did Mrs. Posy yell, "Ouch!"? She hurt her finger on a thorn.
4. Why did Mrs. Posy run into the house? She went to get a bandage for her finger.

Page 168

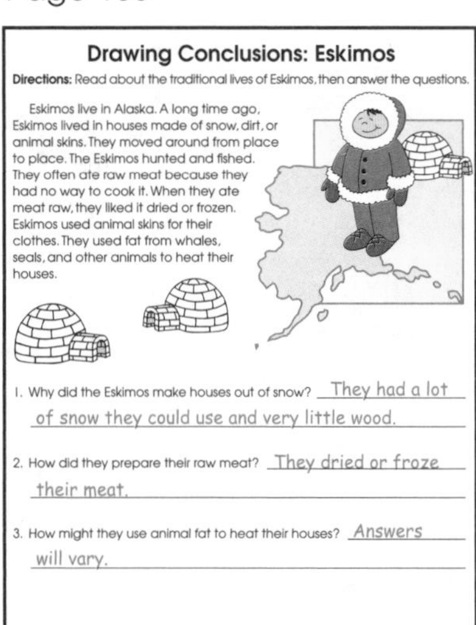

Drawing Conclusions: Eskimos

Directions: Read about the traditional lives of Eskimos, then answer the questions.

Eskimos live in Alaska. A long time ago, Eskimos lived in houses made of snow, dirt, or animal skins. They moved around from place to place. The Eskimos hunted and fished. They often ate raw meat because they had no way to cook it. When they ate meat raw, they liked it dried or frozen. Eskimos used animal skins for their clothes. They used fat from whales, seals, and other animals to heat their houses.

1. Why did the Eskimos make houses out of snow? They had a lot of snow they could use and very little wood.
2. How did they prepare their raw meat? They dried or froze their meat.
3. How might they use animal fat to heat their houses? Answers will vary.

Page 169

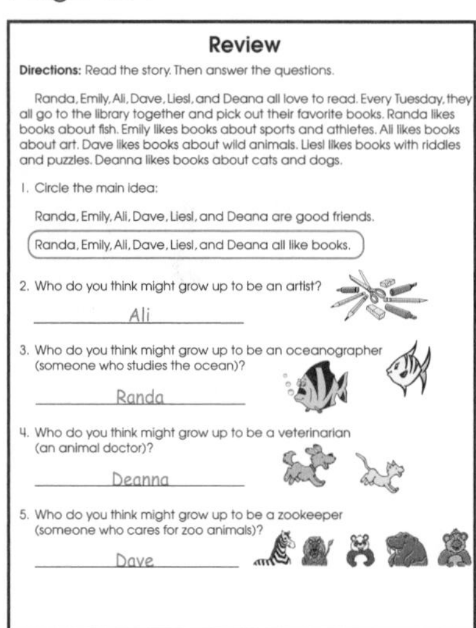

Review

Directions: Read the story. Then answer the questions.

Randa, Emily, Ali, Dave, Liesl, and Deana all love to read. Every Tuesday, they all go to the library together and pick out their favorite books. Randa likes books about fish. Emily likes books about sports and athletes. Ali likes books about art. Dave likes books about wild animals. Liesl likes books with riddles and puzzles. Deanna likes books about cats and dogs.

1. Circle the main idea:
   Randa, Emily, Ali, Dave, Liesl, and Deana are good friends.
   (Randa, Emily, Ali, Dave, Liesl, and Deana all like books.)
2. Who do you think might grow up to be an artist? Ali
3. Who do you think might grow up to be an oceanographer (someone who studies the ocean)? Randa
4. Who do you think might grow up to be a veterinarian (an animal doctor)? Deanna
5. Who do you think might grow up to be a zookeeper (someone who cares for zoo animals)? Dave

Page 170

Cause and Effect

1. Our telephone was not working (so) I called the doctor from next door.
2. The police officer began to direct traffic (since) the traffic signal was not working.
3. The class will go out to recess (when) the room is cleaned up.
4. "I can't see you (because) the room is too dark," said Jordan.
5. He has to wash the dishes alone (because) his sister is sick.
6. (Since) the bus had engine trouble, several children were late to school.
7. Monday was a holiday (so) Mom and Dad took us to the park.

Page 171

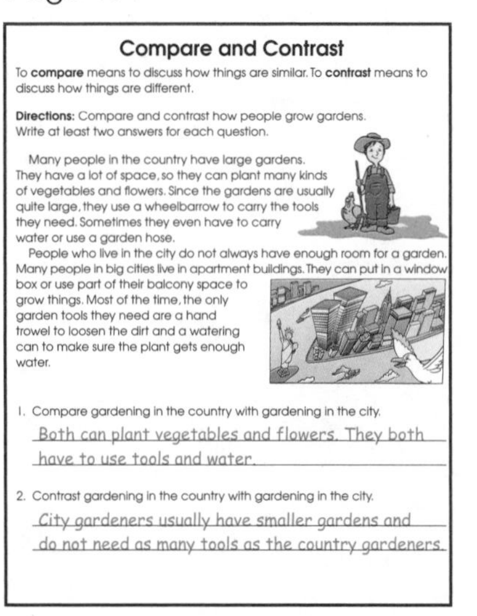

Compare and Contrast

To **compare** means to discuss how things are similar. To **contrast** means to discuss how things are different.

Directions: Compare and contrast how people grow gardens. Write at least two answers for each question.

Many people in the country have large gardens. They have a lot of space, so they can plant many kinds of vegetables and flowers. Since the gardens are usually quite large, they use a wheelbarrow to carry the tools they need. Sometimes they even have to carry water or use a garden hose.

People who live in the city do not always have enough room for a garden. Many people in big cities live in apartment buildings. They can put in a window box or use part of their balcony space to grow things. Most of the time, the only garden tools they need are a hand trowel to loosen the dirt and a watering can to make sure the plant gets enough water.

1. Compare gardening in the country with gardening in the city. Both can plant vegetables and flowers. They both have to use tools and water.
2. Contrast gardening in the country with gardening in the city. City gardeners usually have smaller gardens and do not need as many tools as the country gardeners.

Page 172

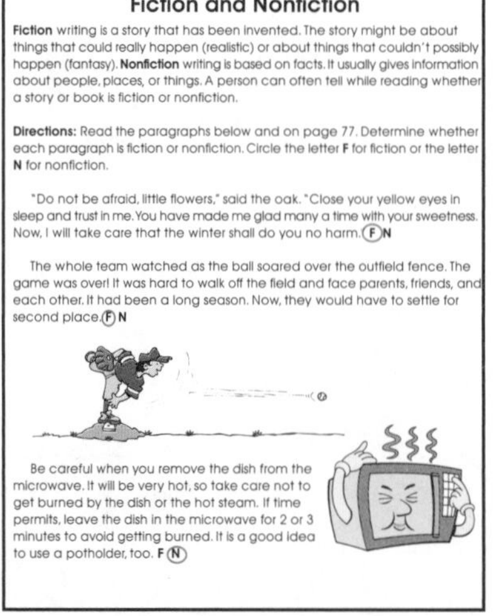

Fiction and Nonfiction

Fiction writing is a story that has been invented. The story might be about things that could really happen (realistic) or about things that couldn't possibly happen (fantasy). **Nonfiction** writing is based on facts. It usually gives information about people, places, or things. A person can often tell while reading whether a story or book is fiction or nonfiction.

Directions: Read the paragraphs below and on page 77. Determine whether each paragraph is fiction or nonfiction. Circle the letter **F** for fiction or the letter **N** for nonfiction.

"Do not be afraid, little flowers," said the oak. "Close your yellow eyes in sleep and trust in me. You have made me glad many a time with your sweetness. Now, I will take care that the winter shall do you no harm. (F) N

The whole team watched as the ball soared over the outfield fence. The game was over! It was hard to walk off the field and face parents, friends, and each other. It had been a long season. Now, they would have to settle for second place. (F) N

Be careful when you remove the dish from the microwave. It will be very hot, so take care not to get burned by the dish or the hot steam. If time permits, leave the dish in the microwave for 2 or 3 minutes to avoid getting burned. It is a good idea to use a potholder, too. F (N)

Page 173

Fiction and Nonfiction

Megan and Mariah skipped out to the playground. They enjoyed playing together at recess. Today, it was Mariah's turn to choose what they would do first. To Megan's surprise, Mariah asked, "What do you want to do, Megan? I'm going to let you pick since it's your birthday!" (F) N

It is easy to tell an insect from a spider. An insect has three body parts and six legs. A spider has eight legs and no wings. Of course, if you see the creature spinning a web, you will know what it is. An insect wouldn't want to get too close to the web or it would be stuck. It might become dinner! F (N)

My name is Lee Chang, and I live in a country that you call China. My home is on the other side of the world from yours. When the sun is rising in my country, it is setting in yours. When it is day at your home, it is night at mine. F (N)

Henry washed the dog's foot in cold water from the brook. The dog lay very still, for he knew that the boy was trying to help him. (F) N

Page 174

Fantasy and Reality

Something that is **real** could actually happen. Something that is **fantasy** is not real. It could not happen.

Examples: **Real:** Dogs can bark.
Fantasy: Dogs can fly.

Directions: Look at the sentences below. Write **real** or **fantasy** next to each sentence.

1. My cat can talk to me. fantasy
2. Witches ride brooms and cast spells. fantasy
3. Dad can mow the lawn. real
4. I ride a magic carpet to school. fantasy
5. I have a man-eating tree. fantasy
6. My sandbox has toys in it. real
7. Mom can bake chocolate chip cookies. real
8. Mark's garden has tomatoes and corn in it. real
9. Jack grows candy and ice cream in his garden. fantasy
10. I make my bed everyday. real

Write your own **real** sentence. Answers will vary.

Write your own **fantasy** sentence. Answers will vary.

Page 175

Learning Dictionary Skills

A dictionary is a book that gives the meaning of words. It also tells how words sound. Words in a dictionary are in alphabetical order. That makes them easier to find. A picture dictionary lists a word, a picture of the word, and its meaning.

Directions: Look at this page from a picture dictionary, then answer the questions.

baby — A very young child.
band — A group of people who play music.
bank — A place where money is kept.
bark — The sound a dog makes.
berry — A small, juicy fruit.
board — A flat piece of wood.

1. What is a small, juicy fruit? berry
2. What is a group of people who play music? band
3. What is the name for a very young child? baby
4. What is a flat piece of wood called? board

Page 176

Making Inferences: Dictionary Mystery

Directions: Below are six dictionary entries with pronunciations and definitions. The only things missing are the entry words. Write the correct entry words. Be sure to spell each word correctly.

Entry word: rose
(rōz)
A flower that grows on bushes and vines.

Entry word: rabbit
(ra bet)
A small animal that has long ears.

Entry word: fox
(fäks)
A wild animal that lives in the woods.

Entry word: piano
(pē ăn ō)
A musical instrument that has many keys.

Entry word: lake
(lāk)
A body of water that is surrounded by land.

Entry word: baseball
(bās bôl)
A game played with a bat and a ball.

Directions: Now write the entry words in alphabetical order.

1. baseball
2. fox
3. lake
4. piano
5. rabbit
6. rose

Page 177

Reading for Information: Newspapers

A newspaper has many parts. Some of the parts of a newspaper are:

- banner — the name of the paper
- lead story — the top news item
- caption — sentences under the picture which give information about the picture
- sports — scores and information on current sports events
- comics — drawings that tell funny stories
- editorial — an article by the editor expressing an opinion about something
- ads — paid advertisements
- weather — information about the weather
- advice column — letters from readers asking for help with a problem
- movie guides — a list of movies and movie times
- obituary — information about people who have died

Directions: Match the newspaper sections below with their definitions.

banner	an article by the editor
lead story	sentences under pictures
caption	movies and movie times
editorial	the name of the paper
movies	information about people who have died
obituary	the top news item

Page 178

Library Skills: Alphabetical Order

Ms. Ling, the school librarian, needs help shelving books. Fiction titles are arranged in alphabetical order by the author's last name. Ms. Ling has done the first set for you.

3 Silverstein, Shel 1 Bridwell, Norman 2 Farley, Walter

Directions: Number the following groups of authors in alphabetical order.

2 Bemelmans, Ludwig
4 Stein, R.L.
3 Sawyer, Ruth
1 Baum, L. Frank

4 Perkins, Al
2 Dobbs, Rose
1 Baldwin, James
3 Kipling, Rudyard

The content of some books is also arranged alphabetically.

Directions: Circle the books that are arranged in alphabetical order.

T.V. guide (dictionary) (encyclopedia) novel
almanac science book (Yellow Pages) catalog

Write the books you circled in alphabetical order.

1. dictionary
2. encyclopedia
3. Yellow Pages

Page 179

Periodicals

Libraries also have periodicals such as magazines and newspapers. They are called **periodicals** because they are printed regularly within a set period of time. There are many kinds of magazines. Some discuss the news. Others cover fitness, cats, or other topics of special interest. Almost every city or town has a newspaper. Newspapers usually are printed daily, weekly, or even monthly. Newspapers cover what is happening in your town and in the world. They usually include sections on sports and entertainment. They present a lot of information.

Directions: Follow the instructions.

1. Choose an interesting magazine.
What is the name of the magazine?
List the titles of three articles in the magazine.

Answers will vary.

2. Now, look at a newspaper.
What is the name of the newspaper?
The title of a newspaper story is called a headline.
What are some of the headlines in your local newspaper?

Page 180

Reading a Schedule

Special Saturday classes are being offered to students of the county schools. They will be given the chance to choose from art, music or gymnastics classes.

Directions: Read the schedule, then answer the questions.

Saturday, November 13

Art	Music	Gymnastics
8:00 A.M.		
Watercolor—Room 350 Clay Sculpting—Room 250	Island Rhythms—Room 54 Orchestra Instruments—Stage	Floor Exercises—W. Gym Parallel Bars—E. Gym
Break (10 minutes)		
10:00 A.M.		
Painting Stills—Room 420 Watercolor—Room 350	Percussion—Room 54 Jazz Sounds—Stage	Uneven Bars—N. Gym
Break (10 minutes)		
11:00 A.M.		
Oils on Canvas—Room 258	Island Rhythms—Room 54 Create Your Own Music—Room 40	Uneven Bars—N. Gym Balance Beam—W. Gym

1. Where would you meet to learn about Jazz Sounds? on the stage
2. Could a student sign up for Watercolor and Floor Exercises? yes
Explain your answer. They are offered at different times.
3. Which music class would a creative person enjoy? Create Your Own Music
4. Could a person sign up for an art class at 11:00? yes
5. What time is the class on clay sculpting offered? 8:00 A.M.

Developmental Skills for Third Grade Reading Success

Parents and educators alike know that the School Specialty name ensures outstanding educational experience and content. Summer Link Reading was designed to help your child retain those skills learned during the past school year. With Summer Link Reading, your child will be ready to review and take on new material with confidence when he or she returns to school in the fall. The skills reviewed here will help your child be prepared for proficiency testing.

You can use this checklist to evaluate your child's progress. Place a check mark in the box if the appropriate skill has been mastered. If your child needs more work with a particular skill, place an "R" in the box and come back to it for review.

Language Arts Skills

- ☐ Recognizes uppercase letters
- ☐ Recognizes lowercase letters
- ☐ Knows difference between consonants and vowels
- ☐ Knows the single letter sounds
- ☐ Knows digraphs ch, sh, th, wh
- ☐ Knows consonant and vowel blends
- ☐ Knows beginning, ending, and middle sounds of words
- ☐ Recognizes compound words
- ☐ Discriminates between antonyms and synonyms
- ☐ Discriminates between homophones and other words

Recognizes parts of speech:

- ☐ nouns and proper nouns
- ☐ verbs
- ☐ adjectives
- ☐ pronouns
- ☐ articles

- ☐ Knows how to create contractions
- ☐ Recognizes controlled vowels: er, ar, ir, ur, or
- ☐ Can break words into syllables
- ☐ Can look up words in a dictionary
- ☐ Correctly writes upper- and lowercase letters

Language Arts Skills, continued

Uses writing strategies:

- ☐ Uses knowledge of letter sounds to create words
- ☐ Copies or traces words
- ☐ Writing shows a sequence of events or clear ideas
- ☐ Ability to use rhymes

☐ Identifies types of sentences

☐ Can identify prefixes and suffixes

☐ Recognizes meaning and use of possessives

☐ Recognizes various tenses of verbs

☐ Identifies types of sentences

☐ Recognizes subject/predicate of a sentence

☐ Recognizes complete and incomplete sentences

☐ Uses correction punctuation: .,?,!

☐ Recognizes misspelled words

Reading Skills

Uses reading strategies:

- ☐ Uses pictures to tell a story
- ☐ Follows text from left to right
- ☐ Uses story content and pattern to predict
- ☐ Uses grammar to help decipher words
- ☐ Sounds out words

☐ Can interpret characters in a story

☐ Recalls main events in a story

☐ Recalls conflict of a story

☐ Recalls setting of a story

☐ Recalls conclusion of a story

☐ Recalls or predicts a simple sequence of events

☐ Recognizes causes and effects of situations

☐ Recognizes forms of literature (poetry, nonfiction, etc.)

Name ______________________

Cursive Handwriting

Directions: Practice by tracing the letter. Then write the letter.

Name ______________________________

Cursive Handwriting

Directions: Practice by tracing the letter. Then write the letter.

Name ______________________

Cursive Handwriting

Directions: Practice by tracing the letter. Then write the letter.

Name ______________________________

Cursive Handwriting

Directions: Practice by tracing the letter. Then write the letter.

Name ______________________

Cursive Handwriting

Directions: Practice by tracing the letter. Then write the letter.

Name ___

Cursive Handwriting

Directions: Practice by tracing the letter. Then write the letter.

Name ______________________

Cursive Handwriting

Directions: Practice by tracing the letter. Then write the letter.

Name ___________________________

Cursive Handwriting

Directions: Practice by tracing the letter. Then write the letter.

Name ______________________________

Cursive Handwriting

Directions: Practice by tracing the letter. Then write the letter.

Name ____________________

Cursive Handwriting

Directions: Practice by tracing the letter. Then write the letter.

Name ______________________

Cursive Handwriting

Directions: Practice by tracing the letter. Then write the letter.

K K K K K

k k k k k

Name ____________________

Cursive Handwriting

Directions: Practice by tracing the letter. Then write the letter.

Name ______________________

Cursive Handwriting

Directions: Practice by tracing the letter. Then write the letter.

Name ______________________

Cursive Handwriting

Directions: Practice by tracing the letter. Then write the letter.

Name ______________________

Cursive Handwriting

Directions: Practice by tracing the letter. Then write the letter.

Name ______________________________

Cursive Handwriting

Directions: Practice by tracing the letter. Then write the letter.

Name ____________________

Cursive Handwriting

Directions: Practice by tracing the letter. Then write the letter.

Name ______________________

Cursive Handwriting

Directions: Practice by tracing the letter. Then write the letter.

Name ______________________

Cursive Handwriting

Directions: Practice by tracing the letter. Then write the letter.

Name ______________________

Cursive Handwriting

Directions: Practice by tracing the letter. Then write the letter.

Name ______________________________

Cursive Handwriting

Directions: Practice by tracing the letter. Then write the letter.

Name ____________________

Cursive Handwriting

Directions: Practice by tracing the letter. Then write the letter.

Name ____________________

Cursive Handwriting

Directions: Practice by tracing the letter. Then write the letter.

W W W W W

w w w w w

Name ______________________________

Cursive Handwriting

Directions: Practice by tracing the letter. Then write the letter.

Name ______________________

Cursive Handwriting

Directions: Practice by tracing the letter. Then write the letter.

Name ____________________

Cursive Handwriting

Directions: Practice by tracing the letter. Then write the letter.

This page intentionally left blank.

Test Prep Table of Contents

Just for Parents

For All Students

Practice Test

Final Test

About the Tests

What Are Standardized Achievement Tests?

Achievement tests measure what children know in particular subject areas such as reading, language arts, and mathematics. They do not measure your child's intelligence or ability to learn.

When tests are standardized, or *normed*, children's test results are compared with those of a specific group who have taken the test, usually at the same age or grade.

Standardized achievement tests measure what children around the country are learning. The test makers survey popular textbook series, as well as state curriculum frameworks and other professional sources, to determine what content is covered widely.

Because of variations in state frameworks and textbook series, as well as grade ranges on some test levels, the tests may cover some material that children have not yet learned. This is especially true if the test is offered early in the school year. However, test scores are compared to those of other children who take the test at the same time of year, so your child will not be at a disadvantage if his or her class has not covered specific material yet.

Different School Districts, Different Tests

There are many flexible options for districts when offering standardized tests. Many school districts choose not to give the full test battery, but select certain content and scoring options. For example, many schools may test only in the areas of reading and mathematics. Similarly, a state or district may use one test for certain grades and another test for other grades. These decisions are often based on the amount of time and money a district wishes to spend on test administration. Some states choose to develop their own statewide assessment tests.

On pages 222 and 223 you will find information about these five widely used standardized achievement tests:

- California Achievement Test (CAT)
- Terra Nova/CTBS
- Iowa Test of Basic Skills (ITBS)
- Stanford Achievement Test (SAT9)
- Metropolitan Achievement Test (MAT)

However, this book contains strategies and practice questions for use with a variety of tests. Even if your state does not give one of the five tests listed above, your child will benefit from doing the practice questions in this book. If you're unsure about which test your child takes, contact your local school district to find out which tests are given.

Types of Test Questions

Traditionally, standardized achievement tests have used only multiple-choice questions. Today, many tests may include constructed response (short answer) and extended response (essay) questions as well.

In addition, many tests include questions that tap students' higher-order thinking skills. Instead of simple recall questions, such as identifying a date in history, questions may require students to make comparisons and contrasts or analyze results, among other skills.

What the Tests Measure

These tests do not measure your child's level of intelligence, but they do show how well your child knows material that he or she has learned and that is also covered on the tests. It's important to remember

that some tests cover content that is not taught in your child's school or grade. In other instances, depending on when in the year the test is given, your child may not yet have covered the material.

If the test reports you receive show that your child needs improvement in one or more skill areas, you may want to seek help from your child's teacher and find out how you can work with your child to improve his or her skills.

California Achievement Test (CAT/5)

What Is the California Achievement Test?

The *California Achievement Test* is a standardized achievement test battery that is widely used with elementary through high school students.

Parts of the Test

The *CAT* includes tests in the following content areas:

Reading
- Word Analysis
- Vocabulary
- Comprehension

Spelling

Language Arts
- Language Mechanics
- Language Usage

Mathematics

Science

Social Studies

Your child may take some or all of these subtests if your district uses the *California Achievement Test*.

Terra Nova/CTBS (Comprehensive Tests of Basic Skills)

What Is the Terra Nova/CTBS?

The *Terra Nova/Comprehensive Tests of Basic Skills* is a standardized achievement test battery used in elementary through high school grades.

While many of the test questions on the T*erra Nova* are in the traditional multiple choice form, your child may take parts of the *Terra Nova* that include some open-ended questions (constructed-response items).

Parts of the Test

Your child may take some or all of the following subtests if your district uses the *Terra Nova/CTBS*:

Reading/Language Arts

Mathematics

Science

Social Studies

Supplementary tests include:
- Word Analysis
- Vocabulary
- Language Mechanics
- Spelling
- Mathematics Computation

Critical thinking skills may also be tested.

Iowa Test of Basic Skills (ITBS)

What Is the ITBS?

The *Iowa Test of Basic Skills* is a standardized achievement test battery used in elementary through high school grades.

Parts of the Test

Your child may take some or all of these subtests if your district uses the *ITBS*, also known as the *Iowa*:

Reading
- Vocabulary
- Reading Comprehension

Language Arts
- Spelling
- Capitalization
- Punctuation
- Usage and Expression

Math
- Concepts/Estimate
- Problems/Data Interpretation

Social Studies

Science

Sources of Information

Stanford Achievement Test (SAT9)

What Is the Stanford Achievement Test?

The *Stanford Achievement Test, Ninth Edition (SAT9)* is a standardized achievement test battery used in elementary through high school grades.

Note that the *Stanford Achievement Test (SAT9)* is a different test from the *SAT* used by high school students for college admissions.

While many of the test questions on the *SAT9* are in traditional multiple choice form, your child may take parts of *the SAT9* that include some open-ended questions (constructed-response items).

Parts of the Test

Your child may take some or all of these subtests if your district uses the *Stanford Achievement Test*:

Reading
- Vocabulary
- Reading Comprehension

Mathematics
- Problem Solving
- Procedures

Language Arts

Spelling

Study Skills

Listening

Critical thinking skills may also be tested.

Metropolitan Achievement Test (MAT7 and MAT8)

What Is the Metropolitan Achievement Test?

The *Metropolitan Achievement Test* is a standardized achievement test battery used in elementary through high school grades.

Parts of the Test

Your child may take some or all of these subtests if your district uses the *Metropolitan Achievement Test*:

Reading
- Vocabulary
- Reading Comprehension

Math
- Concepts and Problem Solving
- Computation

Language Arts
- Pre-writing
- Composing
- Editing

Science

Social Studies

Research Skills

Thinking Skills

Spelling

Statewide Assessments

Today the majority of states give statewide assessments. In some cases these tests are known as *high-stakes assessments.* This means that students must score at a certain level in order to be promoted. Some states use minimum competency or proficiency tests. Often these tests measure more basic skills than other types of statewide assessments.

Statewide assessments are generally linked to state curriculum frameworks. Frameworks provide a blueprint, or outline, to ensure that teachers are covering the same curriculum topics as other teachers in the same grade level in the state. In some states, standardized achievement tests (such as the five described in this book) are used in connection with statewide assessments.

When Statewide Assessments Are Given

Statewide assessments may not be given at every grade level. Generally, they are offered at one or more grades in elementary school, middle school, and high school. Many states test at grades 4, 8, and 10.

State-by-State Information

You can find information about statewide assessments and curriculum frameworks at your state Department of Education Web site. To find the address for your individual state, go to www.ed.gov, click on Topics A–Z, and then click on State Departments of Education. You will find a list of all the state departments of education, mailing addresses, and Web sites.

How to Help Your Child Prepare for Standardized Testing

Preparing All Year Round

Perhaps the most valuable way you can help your child prepare for standardized achievement tests is by providing enriching experiences. Keep in mind also that test results for younger children are not as reliable as for older students. If a child is hungry, tired, or upset, this may result in a poor test score. Here are some tips on how you can help your child do his or her best on standardized tests.

Read aloud with your child. Reading aloud helps develop vocabulary and fosters a positive attitude toward reading. Reading together is one of the most effective ways you can help your child succeed in school.

Share experiences. Baking cookies together, planting a garden, or making a map of your neighborhood are examples of activities that help build skills that are measured on the tests, such as sequencing and following directions.

Become informed about your state's testing procedures. Ask about or watch for announcements of meetings that explain about standardized tests and statewide assessments in your school district. Talk to your child's teacher about your child's individual performance on these state tests during a parent-teacher conference.

Help your child know what to expect. Read and discuss with your child the test-taking tips in this book. Your child can prepare by working through a couple of strategies a day so that no practice session takes too long.

Help your child with his or her regular school assignments. Set up a quiet study area for homework. Supply this area with pencils, paper, markers, a calculator, a ruler, a dictionary, scissors, glue, and so on. Check your child's homework and offer to help if he or she gets stuck. But remember, it's your child's homework, not yours. If you help too much, your child will not benefit from the activity.

Keep in regular contact with your child's teacher. Attend parent-teacher conferences, school functions, PTA or PTO meetings, and school board meetings. This will help you get to know the educators in your district and the families of your child's classmates.

Learn to use computers as an educational resource. If you do not have a computer and Internet access at home, try your local library.

Remember—simply getting your child comfortable with testing procedures and helping him or her know what to expect can improve test scores!

Getting Ready for the Big Day

There are lots of things you can do on or immediately before test day to improve your child's chances of testing success. What's more, these strategies will help your child prepare him-or herself for school tests, too, and promote general study skills that can last a lifetime.

Provide a good breakfast on test day. Instead of sugar cereal, which provides immediate but not long-term energy, have your child eat a breakfast with protein or complex carbohydrates, such as an egg, whole grain cereal or toast, or a banana-yogurt shake.

Promote a good night's sleep. A good night's sleep before the test is essential. Try not to overstress the importance of the test. This may cause your child to lose sleep because of anxiety. Doing some exercise after school and having a quiet evening routine will help your child sleep well the night before the test.

Assure your child that he or she is not expected to know all of the answers on the test. Explain that other children in higher grades may take the same test, and that the test may measure things your child has not yet learned in school. Help your child understand that you expect him or her to put forth a good effort—and that this is enough. Your child should not try to cram for these tests. Also avoid threats or bribes; these put undue pressure on children and may interfere with their best performance.

Keep the mood light and offer encouragement. To provide a break on test days, do something fun and special after school—take a walk around the neighborhood, play a game, read a favorite book, or prepare a special snack together. These activities keep your child's mood light—even if the testing sessions have been difficult—and show how much you appreciate your child's effort.

Taking Standardized Tests

What You Need to Know About Taking Tests

You can get better at taking tests. Here are some tips.

Do your schoolwork. Study in school. Do your homework all the time. These things will help you in school and on any tests you take. Learn new things a little at a time. Then you will remember them better when you see them on a test.

Feel your best. One way you can do your best on tests and in school is to make sure your body is ready. Get a good night's sleep. Eat a healthy breakfast.

One more thing: Wear comfortable clothes. You can also wear your lucky shirt or your favorite color on test day. It can't hurt. It may even make you feel better about the test.

Be ready for the test. Do practice questions. Learn about the different kinds of questions. Books like this one will help you.

Follow the test directions. Listen carefully to the directions your teacher gives. Read all instructions carefully. Watch out for words such as *not*, *none*, *never*, *all*, and *always*. These words can change the meaning of the directions. You may want to circle words like these. This will help you keep them in mind as you answer the questions.

Look carefully at each page before you start. Do reading tests in a special order. First, read the directions. Read the questions next. This way you will know what to look for as you read. Then read the story. Last, read the story again quickly. Skim it to find the best answer.

On math tests, look at the labels on graphs and charts. Think about what the graph or chart shows. You will often need to draw conclusions about the information to answer some questions.

Use your time wisely. Many tests have time limits. Look at the clock when the test starts. Figure out when you need to stop. When you begin, look over the whole thing. Do the easy parts first. Go back and do the hard parts last. Make sure you do not spend too much time on any one part. This way, if you run out of time, you still have completed much of the test.

Fill in the answer circles the right way. Fill in the whole circle. Make your pencil mark dark, but not so dark that it goes through the paper! Be sure you pick just one answer for each question. If you pick two answers, both will be marked as wrong.

Use context clues to figure out hard questions. You may come across a word or an idea you don't understand. First, try to say it in your own words. Then use context clues—the words in the sentences nearby— to help you figure out its meaning.

Sometimes it's good to guess. Here's what to do. Each question may have four or five answer choices. You may know that two answers are wrong, but you are not sure about the rest. Then make your best guess. If you are not sure about any of the answers, skip it. Do not guess. Tests like these take away extra points for wrong answers. So it is better to leave them blank.

Check your work. You may finish the test before the time is up. Then you can go back and check your answers. Make sure you answered each question you could. Also, make sure that you filled in only one answer circle for each question. Erase any extra marks on the page.

Finally—stay calm! Take time to relax before the test. One good way to relax is to get some exercise. Stretch, shake out your fingers, and wiggle your toes. Take a few slow, deep breaths. Then picture yourself doing a great job!

Skills Checklists

In which subjects do you need more practice? Find out. Use the checklists below. These are skills you should have mastered in Grade 2. Read each sentence. Is it true for you? Put a check next to it. Then look at the unchecked sentences. These are the skills you need to review.

Reading, Language Arts, and Writing: Grade 2

Reading

- ☐ I can find the main idea.
- ☐ I can note details.
- ☐ I can understand characters' feelings.
- ☐ I can figure out the author's purpose for writing.
- ☐ I use information from a story and what I already know to make inferences and draw conclusions.
- ☐ I understand similes.
- ☐ I can compare and contrast.
- ☐ I can find what happens first, next, and last.
- ☐ I can predict what will happen next in a story.
- ☐ I can choose the best title for a story.

Language Arts

- ☐ I can identify and use the different parts of speech
- ☐ common and proper nouns
- ☐ plural nouns
- ☐ pronouns
- ☐ verbs
- ☐ adjectives
- ☐ I can tell the difference between a complete sentence and an incomplete sentence.
- ☐ I can tell the difference between a correctly written sentence and an incorrectly written one.
- ☐ I use end punctuation correctly.
- ☐ I use capital letters correctly.
- ☐ I can tell the difference between a correctly spelled word and an incorrectly spelled one.

Writing

Before I write

- ❑ I think about who will read my work.
- ❑ I think about my purpose for writing (to inform or entertain).

When I write a draft

- ❑ It has a main idea and supporting details.
- ❑ I use words and actions that tell about my characters.
- ❑ I use words that tell about the setting.

As I revise my work

- ❑ I check for spelling, capitalization, punctuation, and grammar mistakes.
- ❑ I take out parts that are not necessary.
- ❑ I add words and sentences to make my work more interesting.
- ❑ I neatly write or type my final copy.
- ❑ I include my name and a title on the finished work.

Word Analysis/Phonics

- ❑ I can find root words.
- ❑ I understand prefixes and suffixes.

I can match

- ❑ beginning sounds
- ❑ ending sounds
- ❑ vowel sounds

Vocabulary

- ❑ I can use context clues to figure out hard words.
- ❑ I know what synonyms are.
- ❑ I can find antonyms.
- ❑ I can find compound words.
- ❑ I can define words that have more than one meaning.
- ❑ I can form contractions for words.

Mathematics: Grade 2

Numeration

- ❑ I can read numbers to 1000.
- ❑ I can count objects to 1000.
- ❑ I can compare numbers.
- ❑ I can count on by 2s, 3s, 4s, 5s, and 10s.
- ❑ I understand place value to the hundreds place.
- ❑ I can put numbers in order.
- ❑ I can complete number patterns.

Addition, Subtraction, and Multiplication

- ❑ I know addition and subtraction facts to 18.
- ❑ I can add and subtract two- and three-digit numbers with regrouping.
- ❑ I can multiply one-digit numbers by 2, 3, 4, 5, and 10.
- ❑ I can write and solve number sentences.

Problem Solving

- ❑ When I do number problems, I read the directions carefully.
- ❑ When I do word problems, I read the problem carefully.
- ❑ I look for words that tell whether I must add or subtract to solve the problem.

Time, Measurement, Money, and Geometry

- ❑ I can use charts and graphs.
- ❑ I can understand a calendar.
- ❑ I can tell time on both kinds of clocks.
- ❑ I can use basic measuring tools.
- ❑ I can compare and measure lengths.
- ❑ I understand how much coins are worth.
- ❑ I know the basic shapes.
- ❑ I can match and complete shape patterns.
- ❑ I can find lines of symmetry.
- ❑ I understand basic fractions.

Getting Ready All Year

You can do better in school and on tests if you know how to study and make good use of your time. Here are some tips.

Make it easy to get your homework done. Set up a place in which to do it each day. Choose a place that is quiet. Get the things you need, such as pencils, paper, and markers. Put them in your homework place.

Homework Log and Weekly Calendar Make your own homework log. Or copy the one on pages 234–235 of this book. Write down your homework each day. Also list other things you have to do, such as sports practice or music lessons. Then you won't forget easily.

Do your homework right away. Do it soon after you get home from school. Give yourself a lot of time. Then you won't be too tired to do it later on.

Get help if you need it. If you need help, just ask. Call a friend. Or ask a family member. If they cannot help you, ask your teacher the next day.

Figure out how you learn best. Some people learn best by listening, others by looking. Some learn best by doing something with their hands or moving around. Some children like to work in groups. And some are very happy working alone.

Think about your favorite parts of school. Are you good in art, mathematics, or maybe gym? Your favorite class maybe a clue to how you learn best. Try to figure it out. Then use it to study and learn better.

Practice, practice, practice! The best way to get better is by practicing a lot. You may have trouble in a school subject. Do some extra work in that subject. It can give you just the boost you need.

	MONDAY	TUESDAY	WEDNESDAY
MATHEMATICS			
READING			
LANGUAGE ARTS			
OTHER			

THURSDAY	FRIDAY	SATURDAY/SUNDAY	
			MATHEMATICS
			READING
			LANGUAGE ARTS
			OTHER

What's Ahead in This Book?

Everyone in school has to take tests. This book will help you get ready for them. Ask a family member to help you.

The best way to get ready for tests is to do your best in school. You can also learn about the kinds of questions that will be on them. That is what this book is about. It will help you know what to do on the day of the test.

You will learn about the questions that will be on the test. You will get questions on which to practice. You will get hints for how to answer the questions.

In the last part of this book, there is a Practice Test and Final Test for Grade 1. These tests look like the ones you take in school. There is also a list of answers to help you check your answers.

If you practice, you will be all ready on test day.

Multiple Choice Questions

A multiple choice question has 3 or 4 answer choices.
You must choose the right answer.

EXAMPLE **Which word does *not* fit in this group?**

dog, cat, _____

○ hamster

○ goldfish

○ bike

Sometimes you will know the answer right away. Other times you won't. To answer multiple choice questions on a test, do the following:

- Always read or listen to the directions.
- Look at each answer first. Then mark which one you think is right.
- Answer easy questions first.
- Skip hard questions. Come back to them later. Circle the question to remember which ones you still need to do.

Testing It Out

Now look at the sample question more closely.

Think: Dogs and cats are both pets. I see the word *not*. I need a word that is not a kind of pet. Hamsters and goldfish are pets. I know that a bike is not a pet. I will choose bike.

Multiple Choice Practice

Directions: Find the word that means the same thing, or almost the same thing, as the underlined word. Fill in the circle next to your answer.

1 **<u>delicious</u> pizza**

○ boring

○ hungry

○ tasty

2 **<u>below</u> the desk**

○ above

○ behind

○ under

Directions: Find the word that rhymes with the underlined word. Fill in the circle next to your answer.

3 **I am afraid of <u>mice</u>.**

○ bears

○ rice

○ moose

4 **I like to eat spaghetti <u>dinner</u>.**

○ winner

○ supper

○ finger

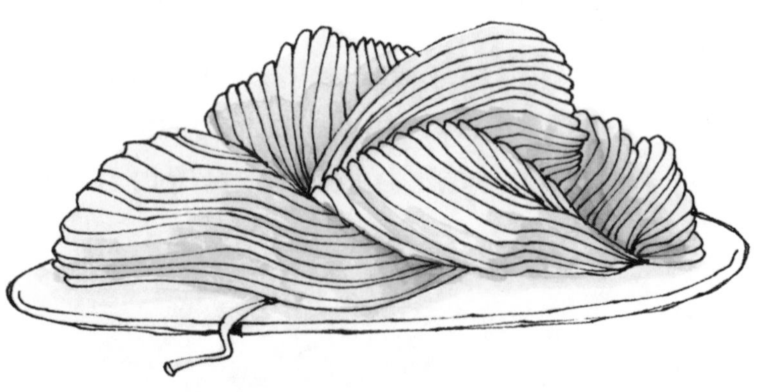

Fill-in-the-Blank Questions

On some tests you must find a word that is missing from a sentence.

EXAMPLE **__________ your teeth before you go to bed.**

○ Smile

○ Brush

○ Buy

To answer fill-in-the-blank questions:

- Try to think of the answer before you look at the choices.
- See if one of the choices matches your answer.
- Always check the other choices. There may be a better answer.

Testing It Out

Now look at the sample question above more closely.

Think: *Smile* reminds me of teeth. But it does not make sense. *Brush* seems right. I will look at all the choices. *Buy* starts with the same letter as *Brush*. But it does not make sense. I will mark *Brush*.

Fill-in-the-Blank Practice

Directions: Find the word that best completes the sentence. Fill in the circle next to your answer.

1 The cereal is ____________.

- ○ in the bowl
- ○ at a movie
- ○ in the attic

2 The ____________ is full of apples.

- ○ tall tree
- ○ blue sea
- ○ big building

3 When I am thirsty, I ____________.

- ○ chop wood
- ○ sing songs
- ○ drink water

4 We had cake at my birthday ____________.

- ○ hike
- ○ party
- ○ flower

5 Be ____________ not to touch the oven.

- ○ careful
- ○ happy
- ○ silly

Oral Questions

On some tests you will listen to your teacher read a word. Then you will answer a question about the sounds. Ask an adult to read you the questions.

EXAMPLE **Which word starts with the same sound as *dish*?**

○ plate

○ door

○ bath

To answer oral questions:

- Listen to the directions.
- Say each answer to yourself. Listen to the sounds.
- Look at all the words. Then mark the one you think is correct.

Testing It Out

Now look at the sample question more closely.

Think: *Plate* means the same thing as *dish.* But it does not start with the same sound. *Door* starts with the same sound as *dish. Bath* does not start with the same sound. *Door* must be the right answer.

Oral Questions Practice

Directions: Listen to an adult say the word.
Fill in the circle next to the word that starts with same sound.

1 desk

○ chair ○ bat ○ den

Directions: Listen to an adult say the word. Fill in the circle next to the word that ends with same sound.

2 make

○ man ○ nose ○ rock

Directions: Listen to an adult say the word. Fill in the circle next to the word that rhymes.

3 find

○ left ○ fun ○ kind

Short Answer Questions

Some questions do not give you answers to choose from. You must write short answers in your own words.

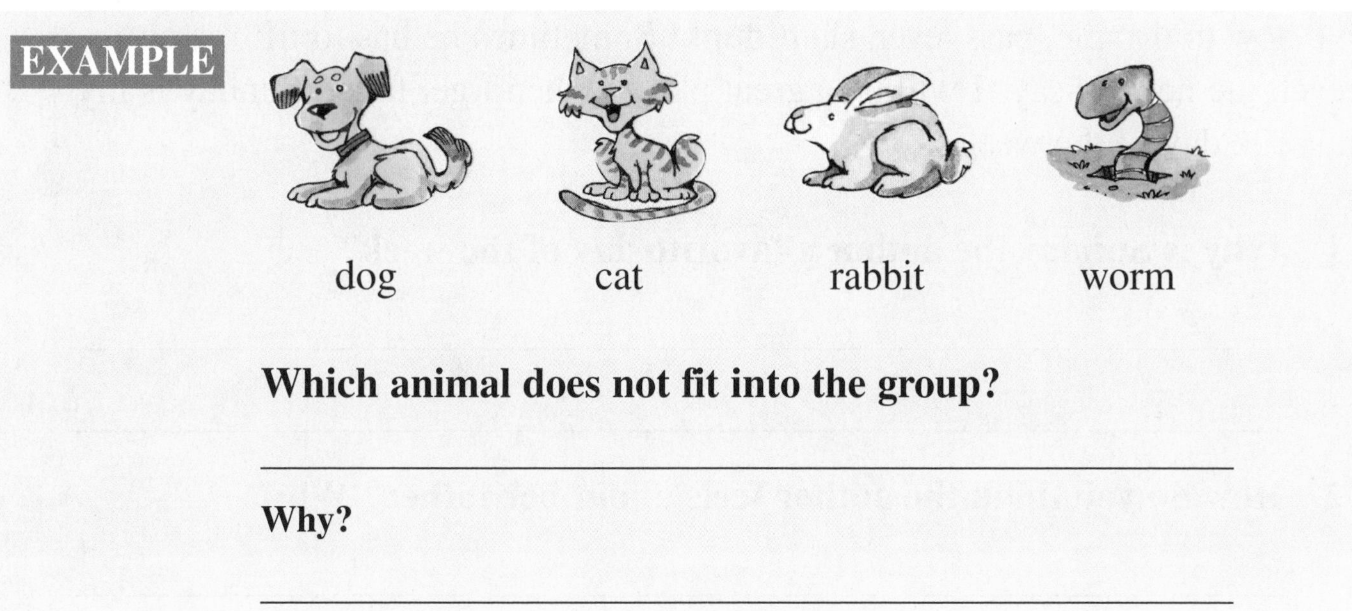

Which animal does not fit into the group?

____

Why?

____

When you write short answers to questions on a test:

- Read each question. Make sure you answer the question. Do not write other things about the words or pictures.
- Your answer should be short. But make sure you answer the whole question.
- Write complete sentences.

Testing It Out

Now look at the sample question more closely.

Think: Dogs, cats, and rabbits have four legs and fur. But worms do not have legs or fur. So *worm* is the answer.

Which animal does not fit into the group?

The worm does not fit into the group.

Why?

The other animals have four legs and fur. A worm does not.

Short Answer Practice

Directions: Read the story. Then answer the questions.

Every Sunday I go with my dad to play basketball in the park. He teaches me how to dribble, pass, even slam-dunk! Sometimes he has to lift me up to reach the net. He says I will be a great player when I get taller. Sunday is my favorite day of the week.

1 **Why is Sunday the author's favorite day of the week?**

____

____

2 **How do you think the author feels about her father? Why?**

____

____

Directions: Look at the pictures to decide which one does not belong. Write your answers on the lines.

3

cup plate book

Which picture does not belong?

____

Why?

____

Choosing a Picture to Answer a Question

Sometimes your teacher will read you a story and ask you a question about it. You will choose the picture that best answers the question. Ask an adult to read this story to you.

EXAMPLE Carly and Mike were best friends. One day they were playing hide and seek in Mike's back yard. Carly could not find Mike anywhere. Carly gave up and went into their tree house. She was very surprised when Mike popped out and said "boo!"

Where was Mike hiding?

○

○

○

When you choose a picture to answer a question on a test:

- Listen to the story carefully.
- Try to imagine what is happening. Choose the picture that is closest to what you imagine.
- Mark your answer as soon as you know which one is right. Then get ready for the next question.
- Change your answer only if you are sure it is wrong and another one is right.

Testing It Out

Now look at the sample question more closely.Where was Mike hiding?

Think: Mike did not hide *behind* a tree in the story. He did not hide *under* a bed. They were playing in the back yard. Mike was hiding in a tree house. The third picture is right.

Choosing a Picture to Answer a Question Practice

Directions: Listen to the story. Then choose the picture that best answers the question.

Wendy was Tanya's baby sister. Wendy wanted to do everything Tanya did. Tanya was going to eat the last piece of cake. Wendy wanted a piece too. Tanya got an idea. She cut the piece of cake in half. They ate their snack together.

1 Which picture shows Wendy?

○ ○ ○

2 What did Wendy want to eat?

○

Math Questions

On some tests, you will have to answer math questions. Some of these questions will tell a story or show pictures.

EXAMPLE

Look at the picture. Which number sentence shows how many treats there are in all?

1 + 2 + 1 ○

4 + 6 ○

3 + 2 + 1 ○

When you answer math questions on a test:

- Look at the picture. Read all the choices. Then mark your answer.
- Look for important words and numbers.
- Draw pictures or write numbers on scratch paper.
- Look for clue words like *in all, more, less, left,* and *equal.*

Testing It Out

Look at the sample question more closely.

Think: I see 3 groups of treats. The number sentence should have 3 numbers. The first sentence has 3 numbers. But it does not match the pictures. The next sentence only has 2 numbers. They are also too big. The last sentence matches the picture. There are 3 cookies, 2 lollipops, and 1 candy bar.

Math Questions Practice

Directions: Fill in the circle next to the answer that matches the picture.

1

- ○ 39 cents
- ○ 40 cents
- ○ 50 cents

2

- ○ 13 books
- ○ 11 books
- ○ 14 books

Directions: Use scratch paper to work out your answer. Then fill in the circle next to the right number.

3

$$\begin{array}{r} 26 \\ +\ 7 \\ \hline \end{array}$$

- ○ 33
- ○ 36
- ○ 39

4

$$\begin{array}{r} 11 \\ 21 \\ +\ 32 \\ \hline \end{array}$$

- ○ 34
- ○ 54
- ○ 64

Using a Graph

You will have to read a graph to answer some questions.

EXAMPLE

Who read the same amount of books?

○ Barbara and Tom

○ Sue and Barbara

○ Sammy and Sue

When answering graph questions:

- Read the question carefully.
- Look for clue words such as *most, least, same, more*, and *less.*
- You don't always need to count. Try to see how much of each column or row is filled in.

Testing It Out

Now look at the sample question more closely.

Think: Barbara read 2 books and Tom only read 1. Sue read 2 books and Barbara read 2 books. That is the same number. Sammy read 3 books and Sue read 2. The answer is Sue and Barbara.

Using a Graph Practice

Directions: The graph shows how many children get to school by bus, car, train, bike, and walking. Look at the graph. Then fill in the circle next to your answer.

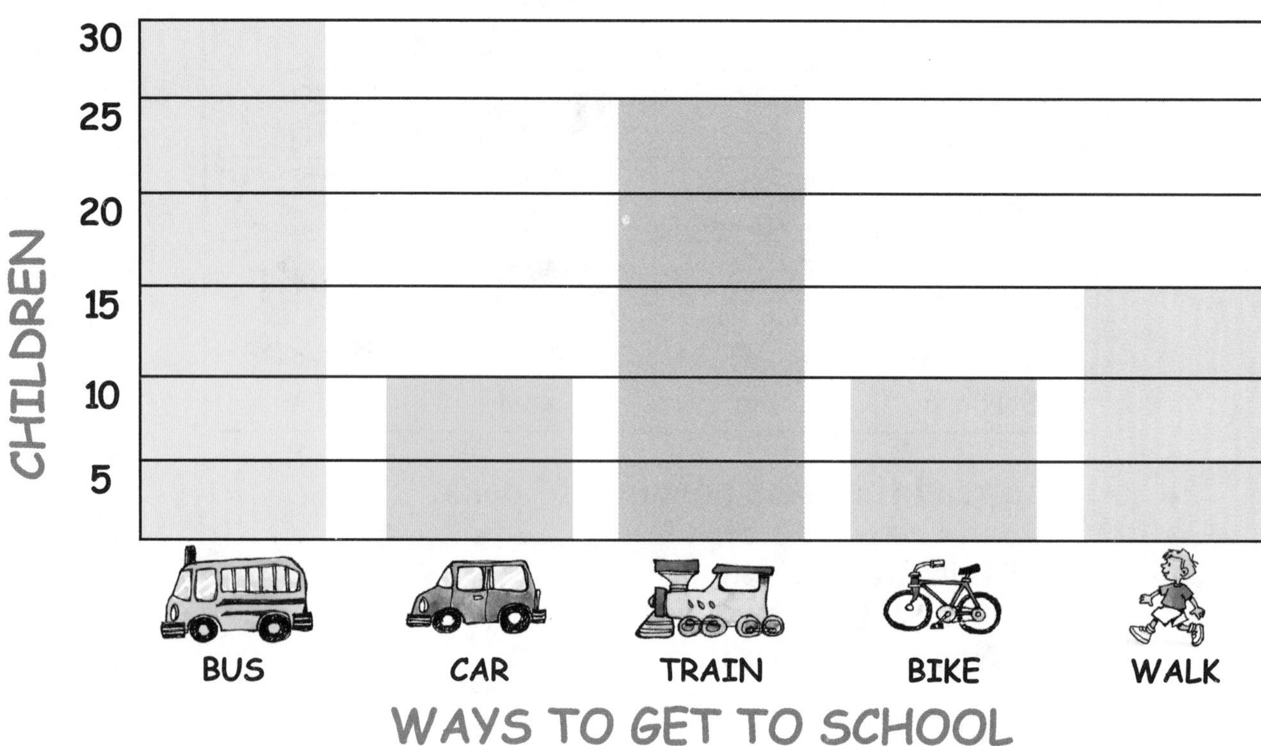

1 **How do most children get to school?**

○ Bus

○ Car

○ Train

○ Bike

○ Walk

2 **How many children walk to school?**

○ 10

○ 15

○ 20

3 **Do more children ride in cars or on the train?**

○ Car

○ Train

Writing

On some tests you will have to write a long answer to a question. The question is called a writing prompt. Sometimes you may have to write a paragraph or a story.

EXAMPLE **Think of one thing that you do outside that you enjoy. Tell what you enjoy doing outside and why.**

When answering writing prompts:

- Write about something you know.
- Read the prompt carefully. Answer every part of the question.
- Plan your time. Leave enough time to check for spelling, punctuation, and grammar mistakes when you are finished.

Testing It Out

Look at the sample prompt more closely.

Think: I want to write about something I really like to do. Let's see, what is my favorite thing to do? I like to play drums. But I do not do that outside. What is my favorite thing to do outside? I love to climb trees. I am a very good climber.

When I am outside, I like to climb trees. I know how to climb every tree in my backyard. I like climbing trees because when I get to the top, I can see down our whole street. Sometimes I see my friends and wave to them. Sometimes I feel like a bird looking down from the sky. Climbing trees makes me happy.

Writing Practice

Directions: Think of one thing you want to learn to do. What is it? Why do you want to learn how to do it? How can you learn it? Write your answers on the lines.

Grade 2 Introduction to Practice Test and Final Test

The rest of this book is made up of two tests. On page 255, you will find Grade 2 Practice Test. On page 291, you will find Grade 2 Final Test. These tests will give you a chance to put the tips you have learned to work. It will also give you an idea about what skills you need to review to be ready for Grade 3.

Here are some things to remember as you take these tests:

- Read and listen carefully to all the directions.
- Be sure you understand all the directions before you begin.
- Ask an adult questions about the directions if you do not understand them.
- Work as quickly as you can during each test.
- Using a pencil, make sure to fill in only one little answer circle for each question. Don't mark outside the circle. If you change an answer, be sure to erase your first mark completely.
- If you're not sure about an answer, you can guess.
- Use the tips you have learned whenever you can.
- It is OK to be a little nervous. You may even do better.
- When you complete all the lessons in this book, you will be on your way to test success!

Grade 2 Table of Contents

Practice Test

Unit 1: Reading and Language Arts

Unit 2: Basic Skills

Unit 3: Mathematics

Final Test

Reading and Language Arts

Lesson 1 Story Reading

The wind was blowing hard and it was snowing. Because of the storm, school was closed. Pedro and Juanita could play outside.

in shorts	in a sweater	in warm clothes
○	○	○

SAMPLE B **Find the words that best complete the sentence.**

The _____ has lots of apples.

big tree	small bush	green lawn
○	○	○

Listen carefully to the directions.
Look at each answer before marking the one you think is right.

Do you like to try things that are new and different? Turn the page to read some stories and a poem about new experiences.

GO

Directions: This is a story about a family looking for something. Read the whole story and answer numbers 1–4.

The Surprise Kitten

Mrs. Jennings heard a noise.
She looked and looked around the house.
She couldn't find anything.

GO 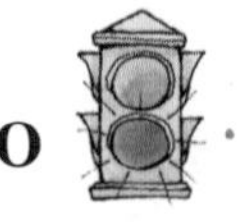

Just then, Mr. Jennings came outside.
"Do you hear something?" asked Mrs. Jennings.
"Why, yes I do," answered Mr. Jennings.
Both of them looked and looked but still couldn't find anything.

While they were looking, Jared came outside.
"What are you looking for?" he asked.
"We don't know," said his parents.
"How will you know if you find it?" asked Jared.
Everyone laughed, then Jared heard the sound.

GO

They were all searching in the bushes when Lettie stuck her head through an open window. "What are you doing?" she wondered out loud. "We are looking for something that is making a strange noise," said the three of them at once.

"Hmm," replied Lettie, "I think you are all in for a surprise. Look behind you." There on the lawn was a kitten. It said "meow" and walked up to the three of them. It wound its way among their legs and said "meow" again and again. Everyone laughed because they hadn't found the sound. It had found them.

GO

Name ______________________

1 **Who said, "How will you know if you find it?"**

Mrs. Jennings

○

Jared

○

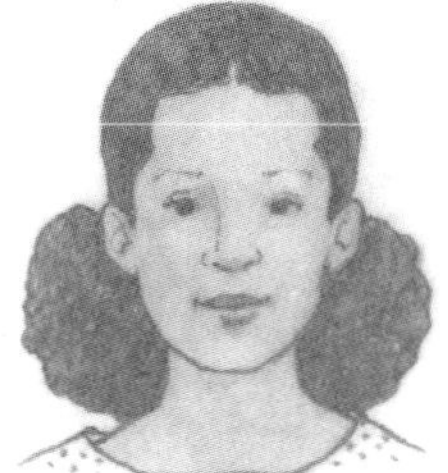

Lettie

○

---

2 **The kitten in this story**

- ○ is Jared's.
- ○ is sleepy.
- ○ is lost.

---

3 **Find the picture that shows where the Jennings family lives.**

○

○

○

GO

Name ____________________

4 **Find the picture of what probably happened next.**

○

○

Directions: For numbers 5 and 6, find the sentence that fits best in the blank.

5 **Mr. Jennings went shopping. He bought food for dinner.**

____________________.

○ Then he came home.

○ Then he stayed at the store.

○ Then he sold the food.

6 **The kitten is hungry. Lettie knows what to do.**

____________________.

○ The kitten runs away.

○ She gives it a bath.

○ She feeds the kitten.

Directions: For numbers 7 and 8, find the word that can take the place of the underlined word or words.

7 **<u>Ned and I</u> visited Jared.**

○ He

○ We

○ They

8 **Where is <u>Lettie</u>?**

○ he

○ her

○ she

STOP

Name ______________________

Lesson 2 Reading a Poem

A friend is someone you can trust
And ask a favor, if you must.

The writer thinks a friend is someone you can

- ○ play with.
- ○ depend on.
- ○ complain to.

Look back at the poem to find the answer.

Directions: Here is a poem about a child who flies in a plane for the first time. Read the poem and then do numbers 1–9.

Up and Away

I fasten my belt
And close my eyes;
The next time I look
We're up in the skies!

My very first chance
To soar like a bird
We're flying so high
I can't say a word.

Blue sky above;
White clouds below;
In a window seat
I enjoy the show.

Then the plane lands
And I head for the door.
I'm going to ask Mom
When I can fly more.

GO

Name ______________________

1 **How is this child traveling?**

boat
○

car
○

plane
○

2 **What does the child do first?**

fix belt
○

eat food
○

read book
○

3 **What does the child see below?**

birds
○

clouds
○

stars
○

4 **Look at your answer for number 3. Where must the child be sitting?**

○

○

○

GO

Name ______________________________

5 **If the child added a sentence to the poem about traveling with a relative, it might be**

Beside me sat
______________ .

My best friend, Nat.	My sister, Pat.	A man with a hat.
○	○	○

---

6 **The child in the poem says**

To soar like a bird.

To soar like a bird is to

step.	land.	fly.
○	○	○

---

7 **The child in the poem says**

The next time I look
We're up in the skies!

What does the child mean?

○ The plane rose quickly.
○ She saw the plane fly.
○ The plane is landing.

GO

Name ____________________

8 **In the poem, what is soaring?**

train	plane	car
○	○	○

---

9 In this poem, the child fastens a belt. **What is the opposite of fasten?**

tighten	unfasten	attach	move
○	○	○	○

Directions: For numbers 10 and 11, find the sentence that best fits the blank.

10 People need clothes when they travel. ______________. The suitcase is stored in the plane.

○ Planes are faster than cars.

○ An airport is a large building.

○ They put clothes in a suitcase.

11 An airport is a busy place. ________________ . Planes take off and land all day.

○ You drive to get to the airport.

○ Many people come and go.

○ Sometimes a plane ride is long.

Directions: For numbers 12 and 13, choose the sentence that is written correctly.

12

○ You need a ticket to fly in a plane.

○ Some people for a plane.

○ A seat belt for a bumpy plane ride.

13

○ This is my seat.

○ Ticket in my pocket.

○ With my sister.

STOP

Name ______________________

Lesson 3 Writing

Directions: Read the letter that one boy wrote to his grandmother.

37 Pierce Avenue
Spring Lake, NJ 07762
March 15, 2002

Dear Gram,

There was a spelling bee at school. Guess what. I won! I spelled the word caramel. It was very exciting.

Love,
Pete

Directions: Think about what you would say in a friendly letter. Write it on the lines below.

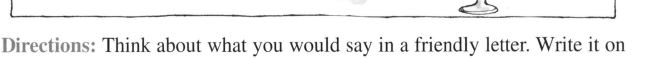

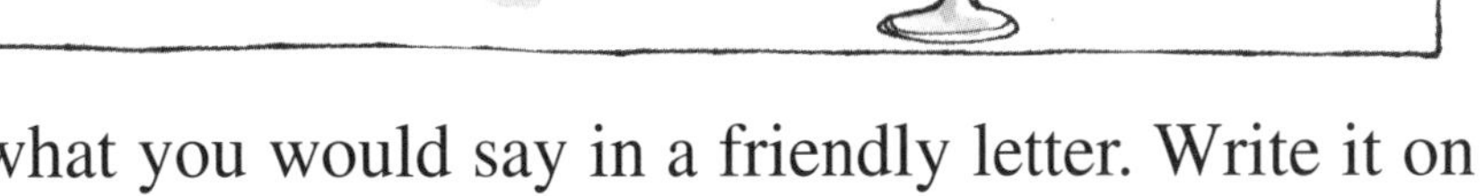

GO

Name ______________________

Directions: Read the story one child wrote.

One morning Chris couldn't find his homework. He looked in his folder. But it wasn't there. He looked in the kitchen. It wasn't there, either. Chris looked every place he could think of. Then he looked at his dog Ruff and had a hunch. Ruff liked to hide things in his dog bed. Chris's hunch was right. Under a dog pillow was his homework. Chris looked at Ruff and just shook his head. The next time, Chris thought, he would make sure his homework was in a safe place.

Directions: Think about a story you would like to write. Fill in the story map.

Beginning
Who?
When and where?
What is the problem?

Middle
What is the problem?

Ending
What is the problem?

Directions: Use your story map to write your story.

____

____

____

STOP 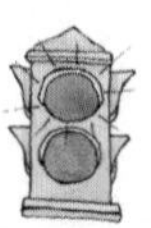

Name ___________________________

Lesson 4 Review

Directions: Mark the circle for the answer you think is correct.

Our neighbor is a gardener. One of her trees recently died. She said it was because of a bug.

From the story, you know that the neighbor's hobby is

gardening. ○ insects. ○ wood. ○

Directions: A new boy named Raj, who is deaf, came to Patsy's school. Raj was born in India, and he knows Sign Language, English, and Hindi, his family's language in India. This story is about Patsy's first experience with Raj. Read the story and then do numbers 1–7.

    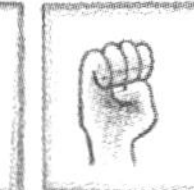

A New Friend

"Can I sit here?" asked Raj in an unusual voice. He signed while he talked, and it was a little difficult to understand him.

"Sure," answered Patsy. She was very nervous, and her words barely came out. "What am I supposed to do?" she asked herself. "I've never met a deaf person before."

All that morning, Patsy kept looking over at Raj. He seemed to be able to understand what was going on in class. "How does he do that?" she wondered to herself.

That afternoon, Mrs. Martin took some time to let Raj and the other students get to know each other better. Patsy was surprised to find that her friend, Kyle, actually knew Sign Language. Soon, Patsy found she could understand most of what Raj was saying.

That afternoon, Raj and Patsy walked home together. Patsy learned some signs and told Raj about her family. By the time they reached Raj's house, she was able to sign "good-bye."

Name ______________________________

1 Patsy said she was nervous.

Which of these words means the opposite of nervous?

- ○ calm
- ○ annoyed
- ○ frightened

2 Kyle actually knew Sign Language.

Which of these words means the same as actually?

- ○ rarely
- ○ really
- ○ seldom

3 **From the story, you know that Raj is**

- ○ embarrassed.
- ○ pleasant.
- ○ unfriendly.

4 **What did Patsy do at the end of the story?**

read a book

○

shake hands

○

sign "good-bye"

○

5 **In a few weeks, Patsy will probably**

- ○ forget Sign Language.
- ○ look for some other friends.
- ○ know more Sign Language.

GO

Name ____________________

6 In the story, Raj has an unusual voice.

Which of these words means the opposite of unusual?

loud	regular	soft
○	○	○

---

7 **People would probably agree that Raj**

○ makes new friends easily.

○ has a hard time learning languages.

○ was more frightened than Patsy.

---

8 **Find the word that has the same vowel, or middle, sound as found.**

road	flood	clown
○	○	○

---

9 **Which of these is the root, or base, word of trying?**

try	ing	ryin
○	○	○

* A base word is a word from which other words are made.

---

10 **Which of these is the root, or base, word of reached?**

each	ched	reach
○	○	○

GO

Name ____________________

11 **Choose the sentence that uses capital letters and end marks correctly.**

- ○ Raj was born in India.
- ○ he came to the United States last year.
- ○ His Family visits him often?

---

12 **Did Leo and Elaine finish the project?**

he	they	them
○	○	○

Directions: For numbers 13–15, find the answer choices with the correct capital letters and end marks for each missing part.

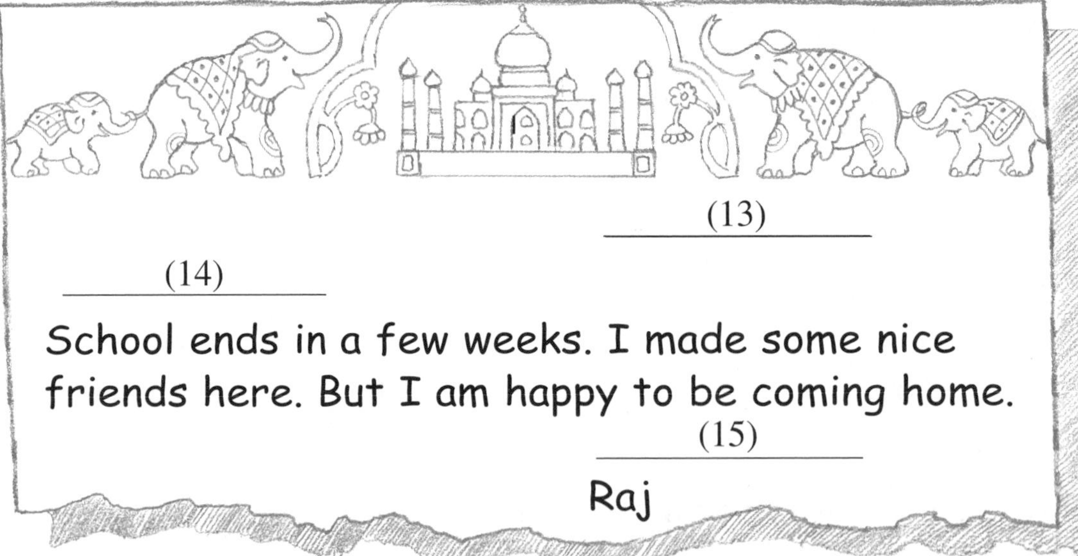

(13)
(14)
School ends in a few weeks. I made some nice friends here. But I am happy to be coming home.
(15)
Raj

13
- ○ May 5, 2001
- ○ May, 5, 2001
- ○ may 5, 2001

14
- ○ Dear Mom
- ○ dear Mom,
- ○ Dear Mom,

15
- ○ Your son,
- ○ your son
- ○ your Son,

STOP

Directions: Read the paragraph that describes an animal.

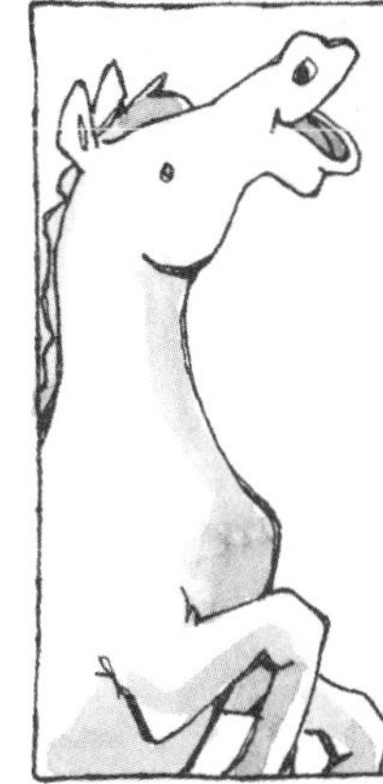

Horses are beautiful animals. Most horses have smooth, shiny coats and long manes and tails. Their hair may be brown, black, white, yellow, or even spotted. Sometimes horses neigh, or make a loud, long cry. Horses need to be brushed every day. This keeps them clean. Dirty horses may smell.

Directions: Think about an animal. Write words in the web that describe it.

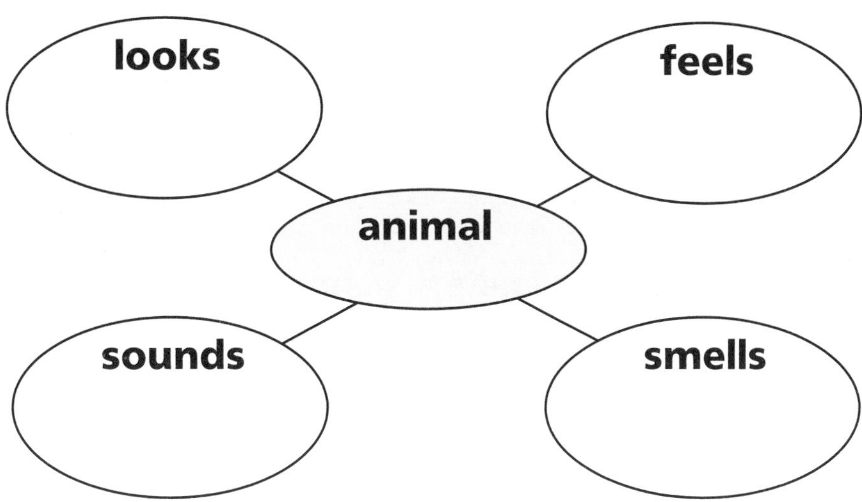

Directions: Write a paragraph that describes the animal. Use the ideas in your web.

____

____

____

____

STOP 

Name ____________________

Basic Skills

Lesson 1 Word Analysis

Directions: Find the word that has the same beginning sound as drink.

SAMPLE A

desk ○ dry ○ done ○

Listen to the directions while you look at the answer choices.

1 Which word has the same beginning sound as block?

box ○ breeze ○ blink ○

2 Which word has the same ending sound as build?

bell ○ cold ○ hard ○

3 Which word has the same vowel sound as rock?

hop ○ rode ○ stick ○ rake ○

4 Which word has the same vowel sound as join?

spoil ○ joke ○ grin ○ tool ○

5 Find the words that say what don't means.

did it ○ drive in ○ do think ○ do not ○

STOP

Name ______________________

Lesson 2 Vocabulary

Directions: Which word means <u>by yourself</u>?

SAMPLE A
- ○ young
- ○ busy
- ○ alone
- ○ tired

Directions: Which answer means about the same as the underlined word?

SAMPLE B **<u>large</u> room**
- ○ pretty
- ○ big
- ○ cold
- ○ noisy

1 Which word means <u>choose</u>?
- ○ decide
- ○ sell
- ○ separate
- ○ fix

2 Find the word that means <u>lift up</u>.
- ○ find
- ○ raise
- ○ release
- ○ haul

3 Find the word that means <u>talk about</u>.
- ○ write
- ○ chase
- ○ enjoy
- ○ discuss

4 Find the word that means <u>bend toward</u>.
- ○ lean
- ○ fall
- ○ sleep
- ○ turn

Directions: For numbers 5–8, mark the circle for the answer that means about the same as the underlined word.

5 <u>muddy</u> clothes
- ○ loose
- ○ cheap
- ○ baggy
- ○ dirty

6 <u>normal</u> day
- ○ strange
- ○ long
- ○ usual
- ○ funny

7 full <u>bag</u>
- ○ sack
- ○ barrel
- ○ can
- ○ box

8 <u>hidden</u> place
- ○ open
- ○ secret
- ○ known
- ○ friendly

Stay with your first answer.

GO

Name ______________________

Directions: Which word fits best in the blank?

SAMPLE C **The boat began to _____ .**

climb	wait	sink	talk
○	○	○	○

Directions: For numbers 9 and 10, find the words that best complete the story.

The (9) was easy to enter. All you had to do was show up at the park. To win, you had to (10) how many jelly beans were in a jar.

9 ○ door ○ tunnel ○ contest ○ room

10 ○ play ○ guess ○ read ○ count

Directions: For Sample D and numbers 11 and 12, which word fits best in both blanks?

SAMPLE D **It was a _____ day. The speeder paid a _____ .**

nice	fine	ticket	great
○	○	○	○

11 **_____ the light over here.**
The _____ on this pencil broke.

○ point ○ shine ○ eraser ○ top

12 **The puppy began to _____ .**
The car needs a new _____ .

○ sleep ○ light ○ run ○ tire

Use the meaning of the sentence to find the answer.

STOP 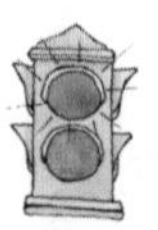

Name ____________________________

Lesson 3 Language Mechanics

Directions: For Sample A and number 1, decide which part needs a capital letter. If no capital letter is missing, choose "None."

SAMPLE A

Football practice	will start	on monday.	None
○	○	○	○

1

when did	you buy	that bike?	None
○	○	○	○

Directions: For Sample B and number 2, decide which punctuation mark is needed. If no punctuation mark is needed, write "None."

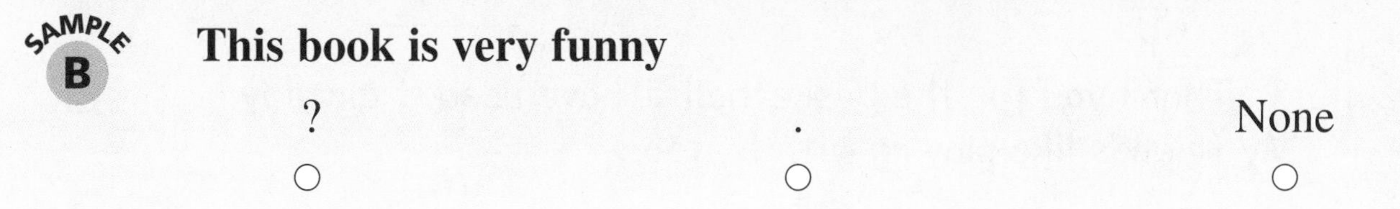

SAMPLE B **This book is very funny**

○ ?　　○ .　　○ None

2 **The phone is ringing**

○ .　　○ ?　　○ None

Directions: For Sample C and number 3, find the sentence that has correct capitalization and punctuation.

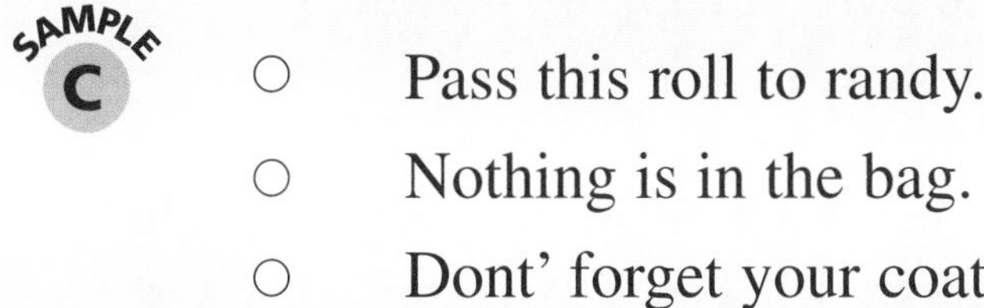

SAMPLE C

○ Pass this roll to randy.
○ Nothing is in the bag.
○ Dont' forget your coat.

3

○ Lennie isn't home
○ She is upstairs.
○ Who just called.

GO

Name ______________________

Directions: Which answer choice fits best in the blank?

Call _____ before you go.

○ Jan miller
○ Jan Miller
○ jan Miller

Directions: Which answer choice shows the correct capitalization and punctuation, or is it "Best as it is"?

The bus is late today.

○ late Today
○ Late today
○ Best as it is

Directions: For numbers 4–6, choose the answer that fits best in the blank.

(4) ______

(5) ______

Thank you for the basketball. I have used it already. My friends like playing with it, too.

(6) ______

Sarah

4
○ January 5, 2001
○ january 5, 2001
○ january 5 2001

5
○ dear dad
○ Dear dad
○ Dear Dad,

6
○ with love
○ With love,
○ with love,

Directions: Choose the answer that shows the correct capitalization and punctuation. If it's already correct, choose "Best as it is."

The window was open When it started to rain, I ran to close it. I got there just in time. The same thing happened when it rained on Tuesday.

7
○ open when
○ open. When
○ Best as it is

8
○ On Tuesday
○ on tuesday
○ Best as it is

STOP

Name ______________________

Lesson 4 Spelling

Directions: For Sample A and numbers 1–3, which word is spelled correctly and fits best in the blank?

Directions: For Sample B and numbers 4–6, find the word that is not spelled correctly. If all are spelled correctly, choose "All correct."

SAMPLE A

Did you_____ who was there?

- ○ notise
- ○ notisce
- ○ notice
- ○ notis

SAMPLE B

- ○ look around
- ○ hidden prize
- ○ never mind
- ○ All correct

1 Our _____ run is about two miles.

- ○ dailly
- ○ daley
- ○ dailey
- ○ daily

2 The _____ is open.

- ○ wendow
- ○ window
- ○ windo
- ○ windowe

3 The _____ is on the table.

- ○ butter
- ○ butterr
- ○ buter
- ○ budder

4

- ○ drop a spoon
- ○ fly a plain
- ○ bunch of flowers
- ○ All correct

5

- ○ floating log
- ○ windy day
- ○ many birds
- ○ All correct

6

- ○ hot paivment
- ○ strong branch
- ○ right answer
- ○ All correct

If an item is difficult, skip it and come back to it later.

STOP

Name ______________________

Lesson 5 Computation

Directions: For Sample A and numbers 1–3, solve the addition problems.

SAMPLE A

$$\begin{array}{r} 4 \\ +\ 6 \\ \hline \end{array}$$

○ 2
○ 10
○ 24
○ 46

Directions: For Sample B and numbers 4–6, solve the subtraction or multiplication problems.

SAMPLE B

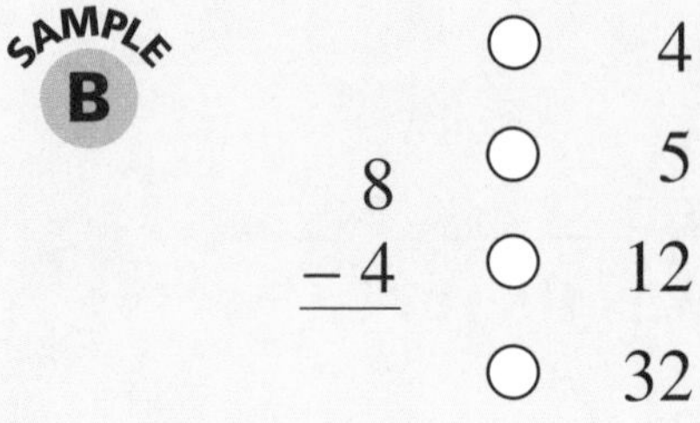

$$\begin{array}{r} 8 \\ -\ 4 \\ \hline \end{array}$$

○ 4
○ 5
○ 12
○ 32

Pay attention to the operation sign so you know what to do.

1 $40 + 10 =$

○ 30
○ 40
○ 50
○ 60

2

$$\begin{array}{r} 28¢ \\ +\ 23¢ \\ \hline \end{array}$$

○ 51¢
○ 55¢
○ 45¢
○ 50¢

3 $38 + 9 =$

○ 31
○ 47
○ 49
○ 57

4

$$\begin{array}{r} 7 \\ -\ 5 \\ \hline \end{array}$$

○ 15
○ 4
○ 12
○ 2

5

$$\begin{array}{r} 44¢ \\ -\ 26¢ \\ \hline \end{array}$$

○ 22¢
○ 18¢
○ 28¢
○ 12¢

6

$$\begin{array}{r} 3 \\ \times\ 2 \\ \hline \end{array}$$

○ 1
○ 5
○ 6
○ 23

STOP

Name ______________________

Lesson 6 Review

Directions: Find the word that has the same beginning sound as cry.

SAMPLE A

crush ○ climb ○ chew ○

Directions: Find the word that has the same vowel sound as home.

SAMPLE B

young ○ alone ○ busy ○ tired ○

1 **Which word has the same beginning sound as from?**

float ○ farm ○ fry ○

2 **Which word has the same vowel sound as read?**

round ○ rest ○ meet ○ late ○

3 **Look at the underlined word. Find the answer that tells what the contraction means.**

they're

they rest ○ they care ○ they run ○ they are ○

4 **Which word is a compound word?**

outside ○ repeat ○ follow ○ shopping ○

5 **Which word is a root word of faster?**

fas ○ fast ○ aster ○ ster ○

6 **Which answer choice is the suffix of rested?**

ted ○ rest ○ ed ○ sted ○

GO

Name ______________________________

Directions: Which word is something hot?

SAMPLE C

○ long ○ poor
○ fire ○ small

7 **Find the word that means something that flies.**

○ bird ○ worm
○ fish ○ dog

8 **Find the word that means part of a tree.**

○ shade ○ cool
○ leaf ○ moist

Directions: For Sample D and number 9, which answer means about the same as the underlined word?

SAMPLE D

hard riddle

○ job ○ puzzle
○ race ○ portion

9 **to be certain**

○ late ○ absent
○ worried ○ sure

10 **Find the word that best completes both sentences.**

Hit the _____ with the hammer.
The _____ on my little finger is broken.

○ tack ○ nail
○ skin ○ wood

Directions: For numbers 11 and 12, find the words that best complete the story.

Each house on the block had a __(11)__ backyard. There were small patches of lawn, flowers, and even some __(12)__ gardens.

11 ○ sloppy ○ lost
○ neat ○ loose

12 ○ sand ○ vegetable
○ recent ○ unlikely

GO

Directions: For Sample E and number 13, which part of the sentence needs a capital letter? If no capital letter is missing, choose "None."

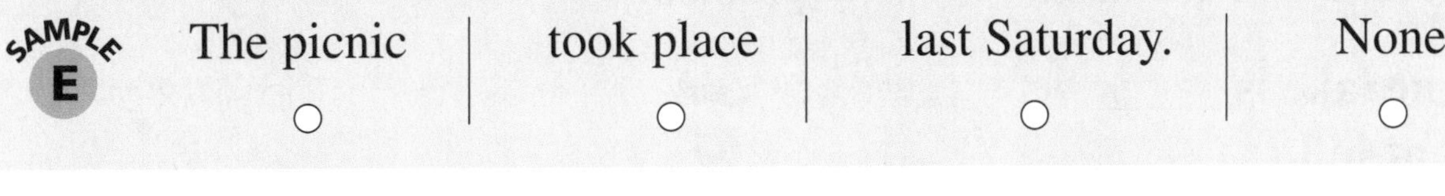

SAMPLE E The picnic ○ | took place ○ | last Saturday. ○ | None ○

13 My friends ○ | will visit us ○ | on thanksgiving. ○ | None ○

Monty Nelson
368 King Street

(14)

14 Choose the answer with correct capitalization and punctuation.

○ Wilson Pennsylvania 18302

○ Wilson, Pennsylvania 18302

○ Wilson, pennsylvania 18302

○ wilson, Pennsylvania 18302

Directions: For numbers 15 and 16, choose the answer that shows the correct capitalization and punctuation for each underlined part. If it's already correct, choose "Best as it is."

One holiday is special to our
(15) family. It is Labor day. We volunteer
at a local hospital so some of the
(16) workers can take the day off. It doesnt
bother us to work on this holiday.

15
○ labor day
○ Labor Day
○ labor Day
○ Best as it is

16
○ doesn't
○ does'nt
○ doesnt'
○ Best as it is

GO

Name ______________________

Directions: For Sample F and numbers 17 and 18, choose the correctly spelled word that best fits in the blank.

SAMPLE F **The lake is _____ that hill.**

- ○ beayond
- ○ beyon
- ○ beyond
- ○ beyont

17 **We _____ arrive around two o'clock.**

- ○ usully
- ○ usuwally
- ○ usuelly
- ○ usually

18 **A _____ blocked the sun.**

- ○ clowd
- ○ cloud
- ○ clawd
- ○ claud

Directions: For number 19 choose the underlined word that is not spelled correctly. If all the words in the group are spelled correctly, choose "All correct."

19

- ○ nice <u>chare</u>
- ○ apple <u>tree</u>
- ○ <u>subtract</u> numbers
- ○ All correct

Directions: For Sample G and numbers 20–23, solve each problem.

SAMPLE G

$$\begin{array}{r} 6 \\ +\ 32 \\ \hline \end{array}$$

- ○ 38
- ○ 39
- ○ 56
- ○ 92

20 $415 + 25 =$

- ○ 390
- ○ 430
- ○ 440
- ○ 467

21

$$\begin{array}{r} 11 \\ 21 \\ +\ 32 \\ \hline \end{array}$$

- ○ 34
- ○ 53
- ○ 54
- ○ 64

22

$$\begin{array}{r} 54¢ \\ -\ 16¢ \\ \hline \end{array}$$

- ○ 42¢
- ○ 38¢
- ○ 60¢
- ○ 28¢

23 $3 \times 5 =$

- ○ 31
- ○ 2
- ○ 8
- ○ 15

STOP

Mathematics

Lesson 1 Mathematics Skills

Directions: Choose the longest bug.

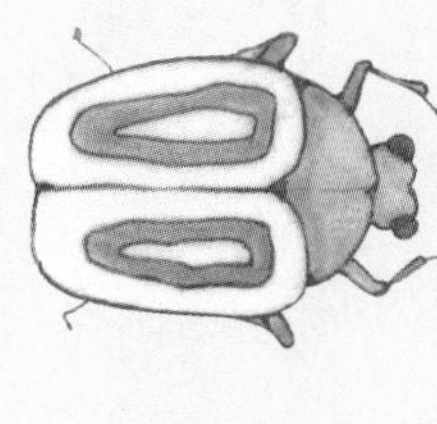 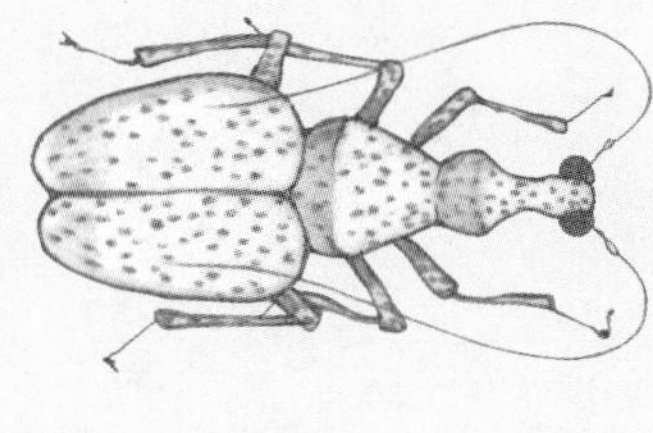  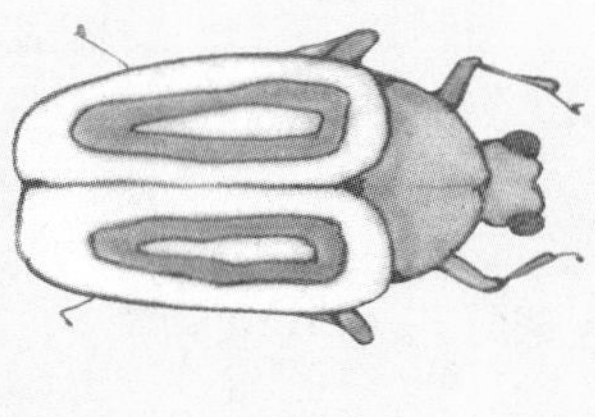

○ ○ ○ ○

Listen carefully while you look at the problem and all the answer choices.

Listen for key words and numbers.

Mark the right answer as soon as you know which one it is. Then get ready for the next item.

GO

Name ______________________________

1 **What number is shown on the place value chart?**

36	360	306	63
○	○	○	○

---

2 **Find the shape that is one-third shaded.**

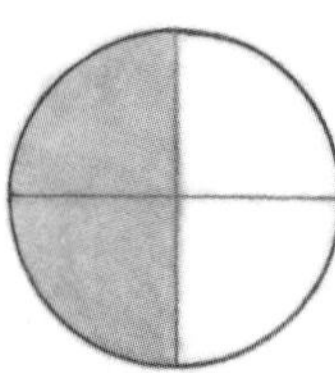

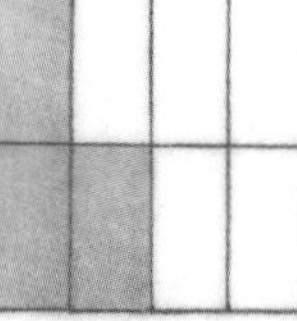

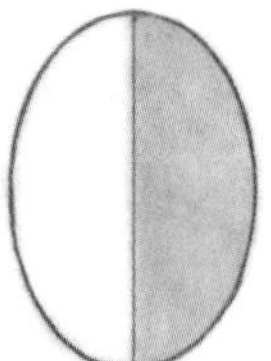
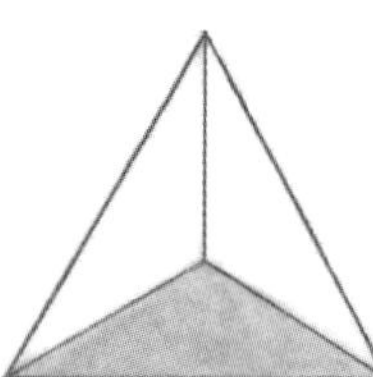

Shape 1	Shape 2	Shape 3	Shape 4
○	○	○	○

---

3 **Which number sentence can be used to show the total number of books?**

○ 4 + 2 = ☐ ○ 2 + 2 + 2 + 2 =☐

○ 4 + 4 + 4 + 4 =☐ ○ 4 + 4 = ☐

GO

4 **Which tool would students use to measure a pint of water from the stream?**

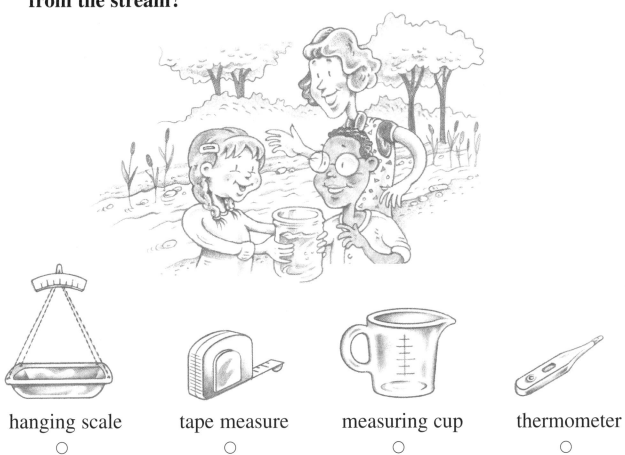

hanging scale	tape measure	measuring cup	thermometer
○	○	○	○

---

5 **Pablo has two quarters, one dime, and three nickels. How much money does he have in all?**

75¢	65¢	60¢	70¢
○	○	○	○

GO

Name ____________________

6 **Which child is third from the lifeguard?**

Ann	Tom	Reg	Beth
○	○	○	○

---

7 **Which squares contain numbers that are all less than 19?**

○ 7 15 10 18

○ 18 6 23 65

○ 91 20 32 57

○ 12 81 17 44

---

8 **Which answer choice names a shape not in the circle?**

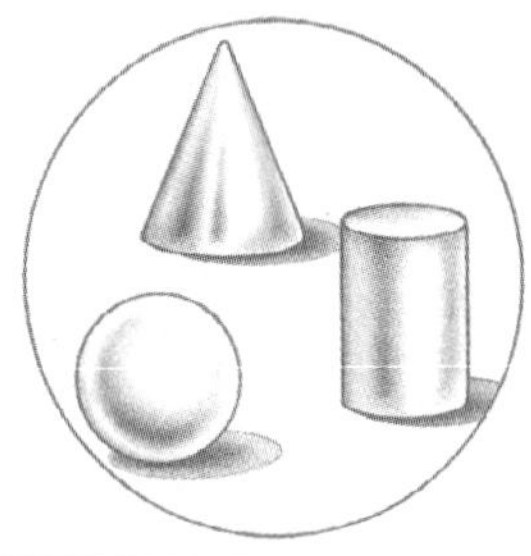

○ cone

○ box

○ can

○ ball

---

9 **Which number is missing from the pattern?**

6	8	9	10
○	○	○	○

GO

Name ______________________

Directions: The students in Mr. Naldo's class are having a Math Fair. One of the games is a number wheel. The chart shows how many times the spinner landed on each number after 20 spins. Use the chart to do numbers 10 and 11.

10 How many times did the spinner land on the number 3?

3	5	7	12
○	○	○	○

---

11 Which spinner looks most like the one the students are using?

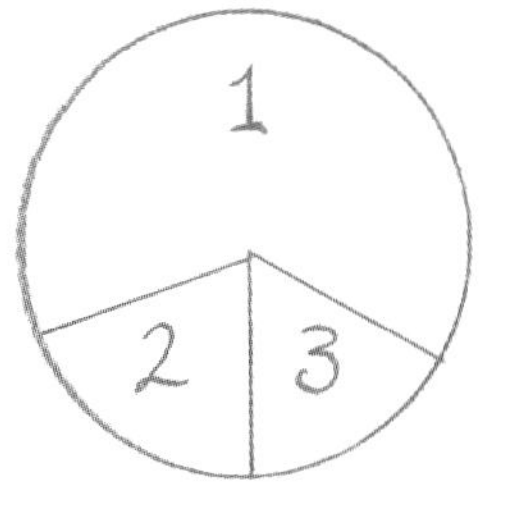

spinner 1

○

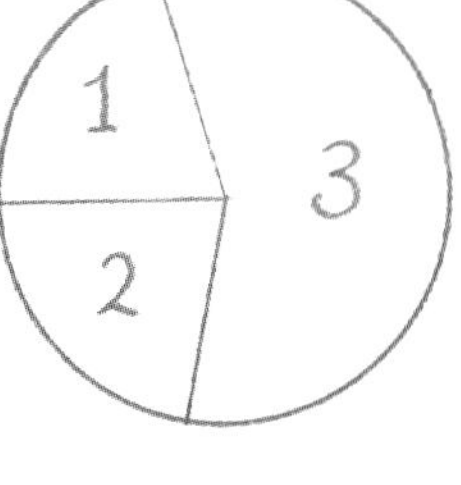

spinner 2

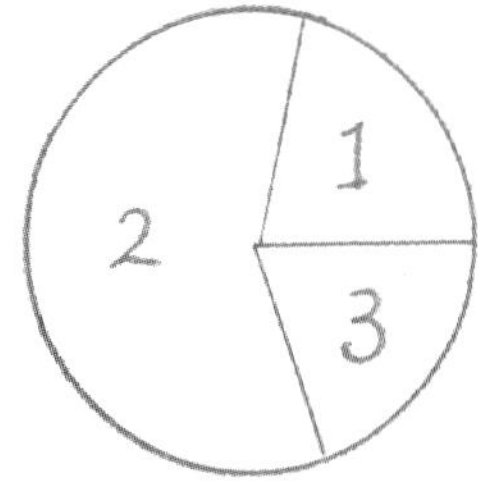

spinner 3

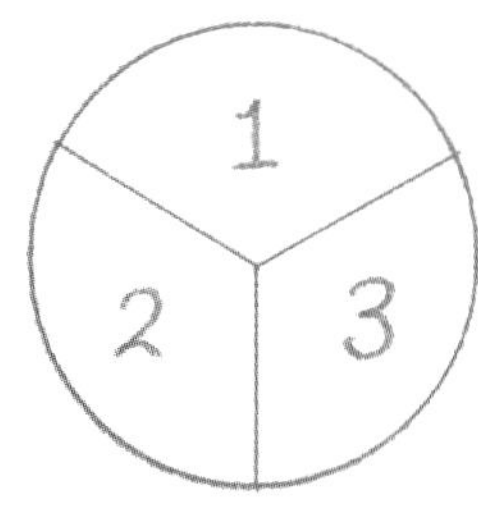

spinner 4

○

STOP 

Name ____________________

Lesson 2 Review

SAMPLE A **Directions:** A train left the station at 9:30. It arrived in Sharon Hill twenty minutes later. Which clock shows the time the train arrived?

○ ○ ○ ○

1 **Four planes are on the ground at the airport. Two more planes land. How many planes are on the ground all together?**

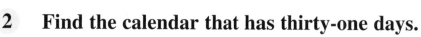

○ 8
○ 6
○ 7
○ 2

2 **Find the calendar that has thirty-one days.**

June

S	M	T	W	T	F	S
				1	2	3
4	5	6	7	8	9	10
11	12	13	14	15	16	17
18	19	20	21	22	23	24
25	26	27	28	29	30	

June
○

September

S	M	T	W	T	F	S
					1	2
3	4	5	6	7	8	9
10	11	12	13	14	15	16
17	18	19	20	21	22	23
24	25	26	27	28	29	30

September
○

October

S	M	T	W	T	F	S
1	2	3	4	5	6	7
8	9	10	11	12	13	14
15	16	17	18	19	20	21
22	23	24	25	26	27	28
29	30	31				

October
○

November

S	M	T	W	T	F	S
			1	2	3	4
5	6	7	8	9	10	11
12	13	14	15	16	17	18
19	20	21	22	23	24	25
26	27	28	29	30		

November
○

GO 

Name ______________________________

Directions: The bar graph shows how many fish are in a pond at a school's nature center. Use the graph to do numbers 3–5 on the next page.

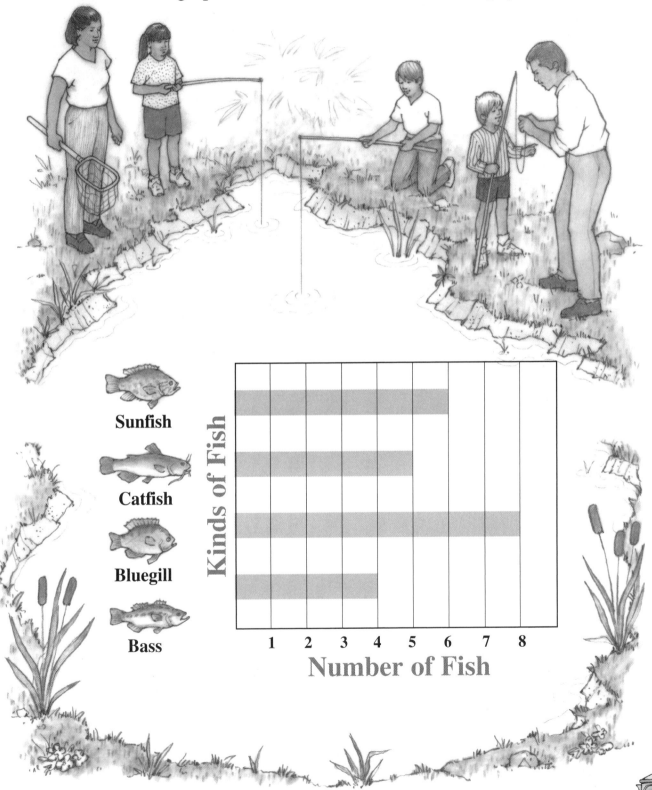

Sunfish

Catfish

Bluegill

Bass

Kinds of Fish

1 2 3 4 5 6 7 8

Number of Fish

GO

Name ____________________

3 **Look at the graph. What kind of fish are there fewest of in the pond?**

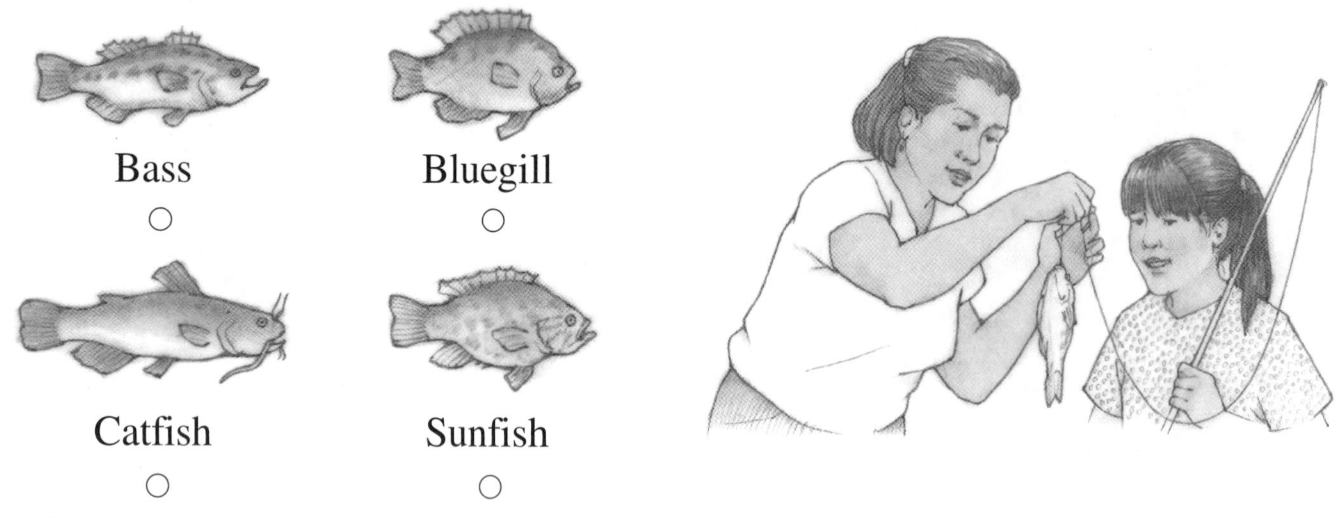

4 **The average weight of the sunfish in the pond is six ounces. How much do the sunfish in the pond weigh all together?**

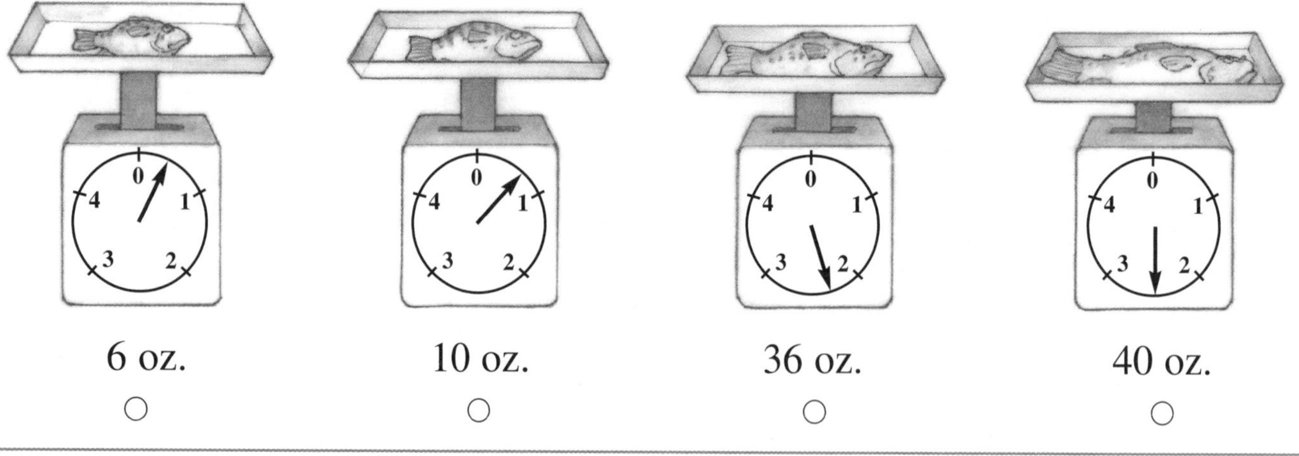

5 **Nadia counted eight of this kind of fish in the pond. What kind of fish did she count?**

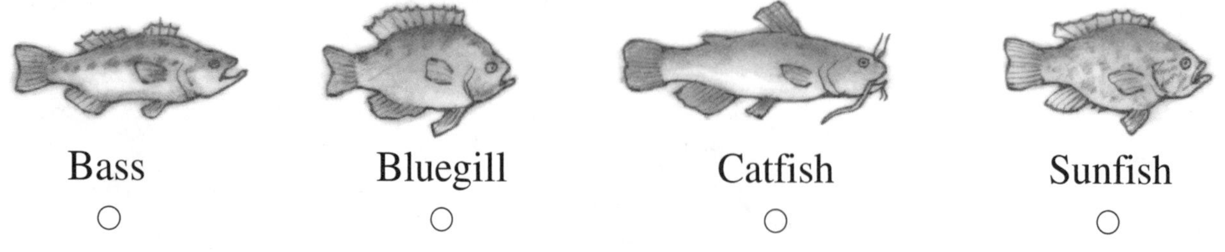

STOP

Reading and Language Arts

Directions: Read the story and answer the questions.

Jawan sat down at the table. He was hungry and the food looked awfully good.

What will Jawan do next?

go outside	read a book	eat dinner
○	○	○

Directions: This is a poem about something we take for granted. Read the poem and then do numbers 1–5.

WHY WHEELS?

Did you ever think
How it would feel
If nobody had
Invented the wheel?

No bikes, no wagons,
No trucks or trains,
No cars to ride,
Not even planes.

Boats we'd have,
And rockets, too.
Sleds would work,
And a pair of shoes.

But life would
Really be a bore,
If wonderful wheels
Were no more.

GO 

Name ____________________

1 **What does it mean to be a bore?**

○ to be exciting

○ to be no fun

○ to be enjoyable

---

2 **Which of these does the writer not mention?**

○ sledding on snow

○ riding a horse

○ riding in cars

---

3 **Which of these is something that can fly but doesn't need wheels?**

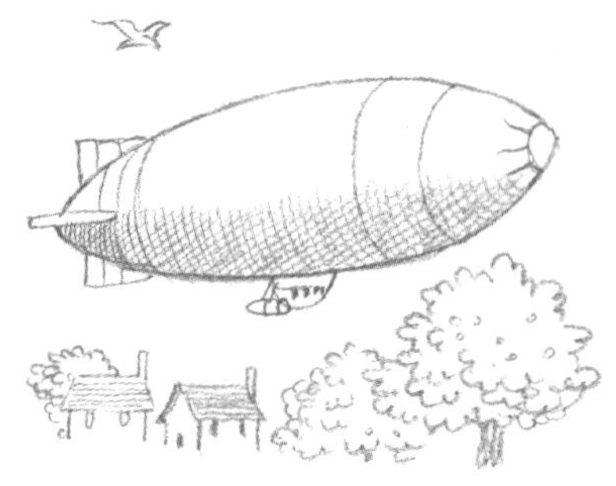

blimp ○

boat ○

bulldozer ○

---

4 **The writer of this poem thinks wheels are**

important. ○

useless. ○

unnecessary. ○

GO

Name ____________________

5 **Why do planes need wheels?**

○ to land and take off

○ to fly high

○ to let people on and off

6 **Find the sentence that completes the story.**

My bike had a flat tire. _____ .
Then we went for a ride.

○ The bike is red and white.

○ I like to ride after school.

○ My sister and I fixed it.

7 **Which one of these is a compound word?**

introduce	describe	overpass
○	○	○

8 **Find another compound word.**

automatic	driveway	repeat
○	○	○

9 **Find another word with the same vowel, or middle, sound as plane.**

stain	than	stand
○	○	○

GO

Directions: Find the words that best complete the sentence.

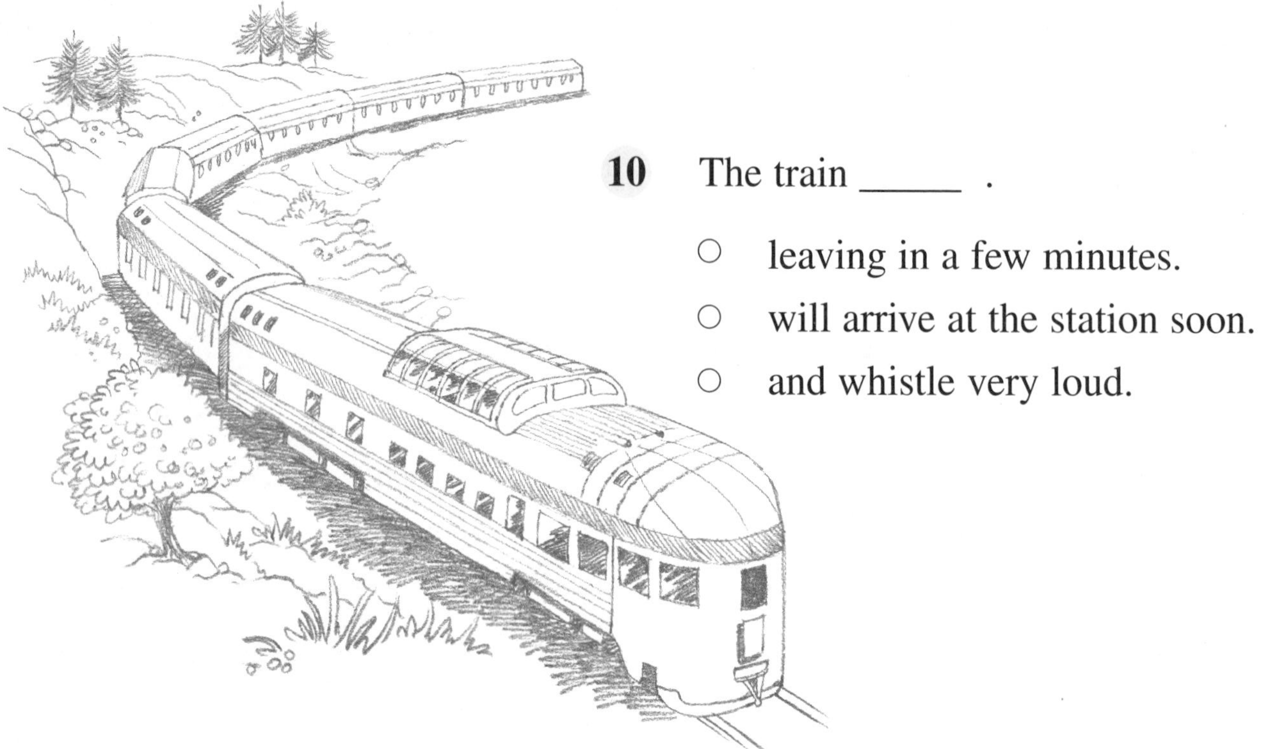

10 The train _____ .

○ leaving in a few minutes.

○ will arrive at the station soon.

○ and whistle very loud.

Directions: For numbers 11 and 12, find and then mark the part of the sentence that needs to be changed. If no part needs to be changed, mark "None."

11 My wagon ○ | is in the garage ○ | None ○

12 Did your brother ○ | go with you? ○ | None ○

STOP

Name ______________________________

Directions: Read the paragraph below that tells how to make a peanut butter sandwich.

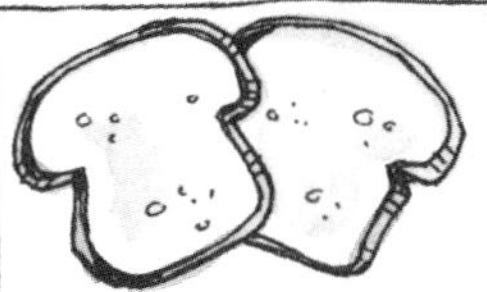

How to Make a Peanut Butter and Jelly Sandwich

JELLY

You will need peanut butter and two pieces of bread. First, spread peanut butter on one piece of bread. Next, spread jelly on the other piece. Then, put the two pieces of bread together. Last, cut the sandwich in half. Eat and enjoy!

PEANUT BUTTER

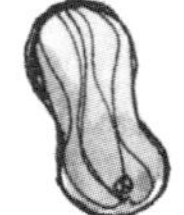

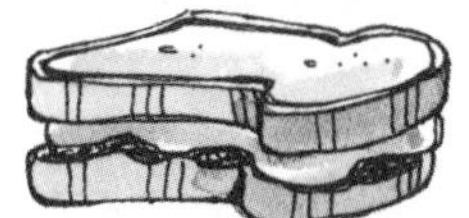

Directions: Think of something you can do or make. Fill in the lines below to write a how-to paragraph.

How to ______________________________

You will need ______________________________

Steps: ______________________________

____

____

____

____

____

____

____

GO

Directions: Read the paragraph that compares.

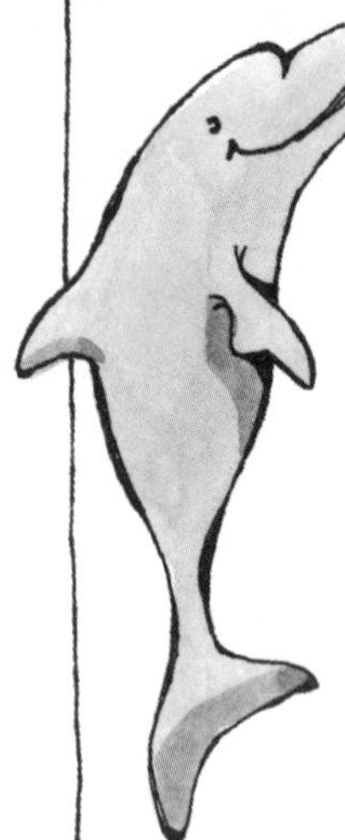

Dolphins and sharks both live in the ocean, but they are very different. Dolphins are mammals, and sharks are fish. Both animals swim underwater. But sharks breathe through gills, and dolphins have lungs and breathe through a blowhole on their heads. Dolphins have smooth, slippery skin, but sharks have scales. Dolphins give birth to live young. Sharks lay eggs. When the eggs hatch, young sharks come out.

Directions: Think of two animals or plants you know a lot about. Write a paragraph that compares them. Answer these questions:

- **What do they look like?**
- **Where do they live?**
- **How are they alike?**
- **How are they different?**

____

____

____

____

____

____

STOP 

Name ____________________

Basic Skills

SAMPLE A **Directions:** Find the word that has the same ending sound as camp.

dump ○ trip ○ dirt ○

SAMPLE B **Directions:** Find the word that is a compound word, a word that is made up of two smaller words.

building ○ darkness ○ plumbing ○ sidewalk ○

1 Find the word that has the same ending sound as best.

loss ○ salt ○ most ○

2 Find the word that has the same vowel sound as same.

ham ○ rain ○ soar ○ sand ○

3 What does the word aren't mean?

are not ○ are late ○ are most ○ are then ○

4 Find the word that is a compound word.

footprint ○ remember ○ narrow ○ explain ○

5 What is the root word of kindness?

in ○ ness ○ kind ○ ind ○

6 What is suffix of careful?

are ○ car ○ reful ○ ful ○

GO

Name ________________________

Directions: Which word means <u>something that lights</u>?

SAMPLE C

- ○ chair
- ○ hose
- ○ door
- ○ bulb

Directions: Which word means nearly the same as <u>grateful</u>?

SAMPLE D

- ○ thankful
- ○ curious
- ○ busy
- ○ finished

7 **Which word means <u>to get better</u>?**

- ○ trace
- ○ sick
- ○ heal
- ○ find

8 **Which word means a <u>note</u>?**

- ○ message
- ○ fashion
- ○ defeat
- ○ container

9 **Which answer means about the same as <u>narrow</u>?**

- ○ not busy
- ○ bumpy
- ○ long
- ○ not wide

10 **Find the word that best completes both sentences.**

Did you _____ your visitor well?
My dog loves to get a _____ from me.

- ○ feed
- ○ enjoy
- ○ snack
- ○ treat

The line for the movie __(11)__ around the corner. This was a film that everyone wanted to see. Cindy __(12)__ there would be seats for them.

11

- ○ stood
- ○ wound
- ○ arose
- ○ lowered

12

- ○ hoped
- ○ bought
- ○ called
- ○ assisted

GO

Name ______________________________

Directions: In Sample E and number 13, decide which punctuation mark, if any, is needed in each sentence. If no punctuation is needed, choose "None."

SAMPLE **E** **Did you forget your hat**

○ .   ○ ?   ○ None

13 **This week it rained every day**

○ .   ○ ?   ○ None

Directions: For numbers 14 and 15, find the sentence that has the correct capitalization and punctuation.

14
- ○ My birthday is in october.
- ○ Last Fall it was awfully warm.
- ○ In June we plant our garden.

15
- ○ The bridge is high.
- ○ the road is new.
- ○ Where is the car
- ○ the keys are on the table

Directions: For numbers 16 and 17, choose the answer that shows the correct capitalization and punctuation for each underlined part. If the underlined part is correct, choose "Best as it is."

(16) We usually take our vacation in July. Mom and Dad rent a house at the beach. (17) Its not as big as our regular house, but everyone has a place to sleep.

16
- ○ vacation in july
- ○ Vacation in July
- ○ Vacation in july
- ○ Best as it is

17
- ○ It's not
- ○ it's not
- ○ Its' not
- ○ Best as it is

GO

Name ____________________

Directions: For Sample F and numbers 18 and 19, choose the correctly spelled word.

SAMPLE F **Be _____ near the pond.**

- ○ carefull
- ○ carful
- ○ cairful
- ○ careful

18 **Dad _____ some corn for dinner.**

- ○ rosted
- ○ rowsted
- ○ roasted
- ○ roastd

19 **Allan felt _____ in his new school.**

- ○ lonley
- ○ lonely
- ○ loanly
- ○ loanley

Directions: For number 20 choose the underlined word that is not spelled correctly.

20
- ○ tasty sandwhich
- ○ huge tiger
- ○ yellow bird
- ○ All correct

Directions: For Sample G and numbers 21–24, solve the problem.

SAMPLE G

$$\begin{array}{r} 10 \\ -\ 9 \\ \hline \end{array}$$

- ○ 0
- ○ 1
- ○ 19
- ○ 90

21 $14 + 21 =$

- ○ 62
- ○ 65
- ○ 36
- ○ 35

22

$$\begin{array}{r} 21 \\ 7 \\ +\ 6 \\ \hline \end{array}$$

- ○ 34
- ○ 24
- ○ 54
- ○ 44

23

$$\begin{array}{r} 874 \\ -\ 172 \\ \hline \end{array}$$

- ○ 1046
- ○ 802
- ○ 706
- ○ 702

24 $2 \times 3 =$

- ○ 1
- ○ 5
- ○ 6
- ○ 23

STOP

Name ______________________________

Mathematics

Directions: If you are counting by ones, beginning with 42, find the empty box where 48 should be.

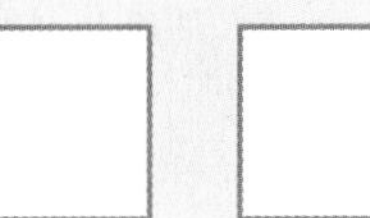

○ ○ ○ ○

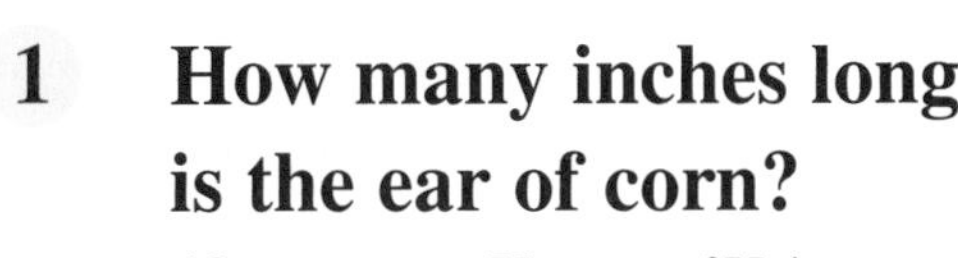

1 **How many inches long is the ear of corn? (from stalk to silk)**

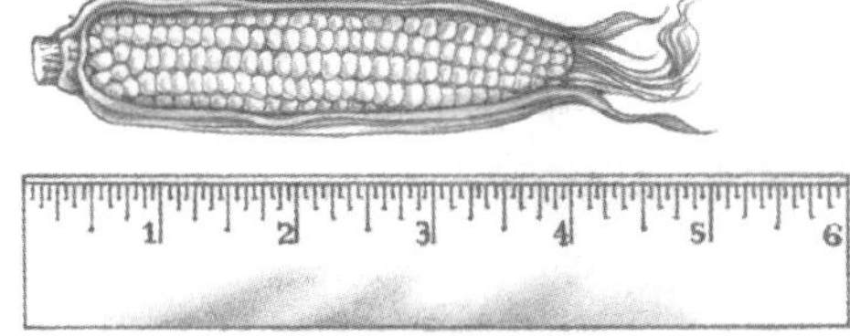

6 inches	5 inches	4 inches	3 inches
○	○	○	○

2 **Find the group of shapes that shows just one rectangle.**

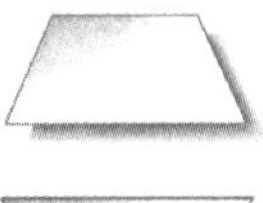

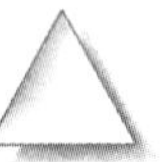

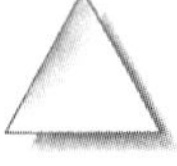

Pair 1	Pair 2	Pair 3	Pair 4
○	○	○	○

3

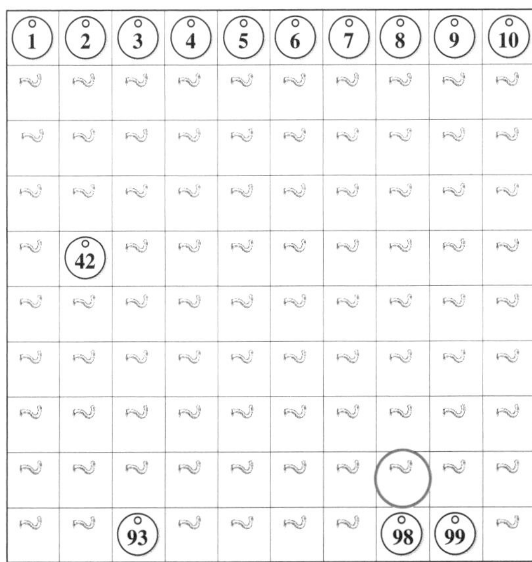

Rudy is hanging numbered keys on a board. Which numbered key should go in the box that is circled?

○ 77

○ 88

○ 89

○ 98

GO

Name ______________________________

4 **Which coin can be removed from the second group so both groups have the same amount of money?**

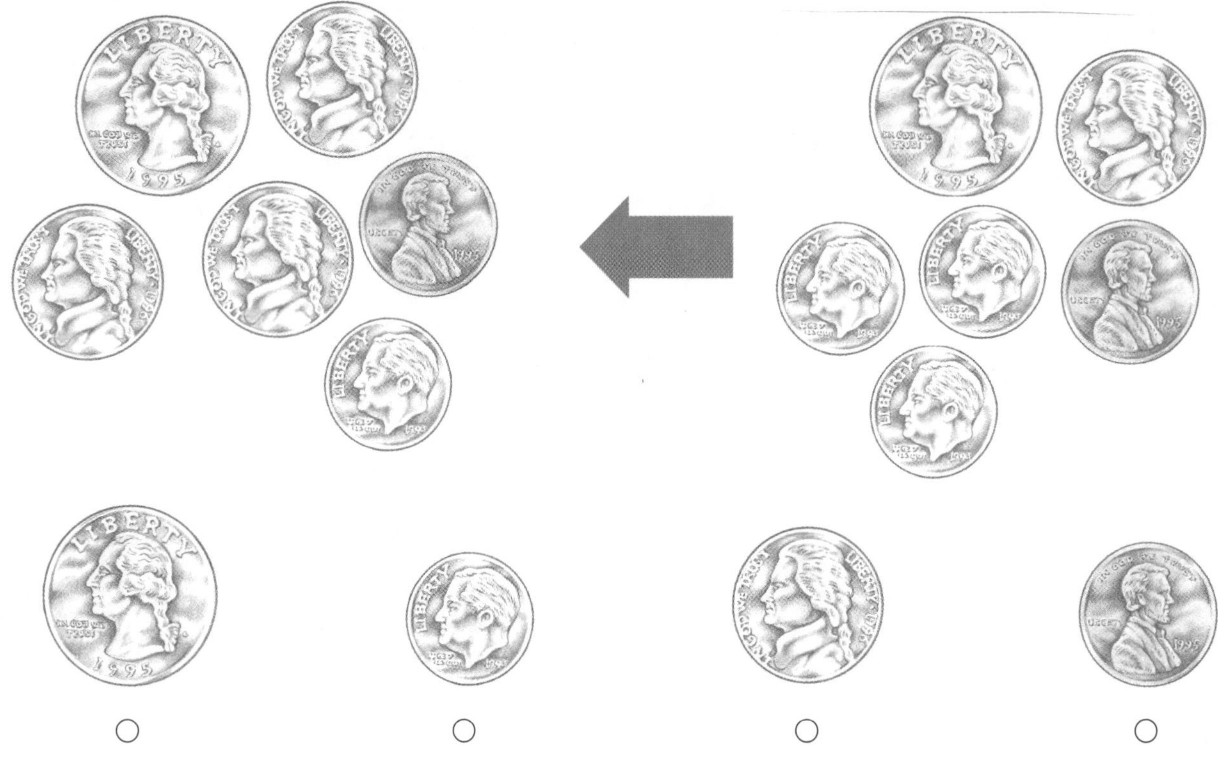

○ ○ ○ ○

---

5 **Find the fraction that tells what part of the set is circles.**

○ $\frac{5}{8}$

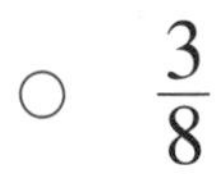

○ $\frac{3}{8}$

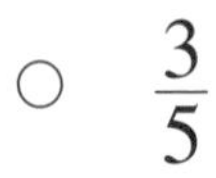

○ $\frac{3}{5}$

○ $\frac{1}{5}$

GO

Name ____________________

6 **Which number should the missing address be?**

427 ○ 421 ○ 437 ○ 434 ○

---

7 **Toshi made a shape on his geoboard. Paula wants to make the same shape. What will her geoboard look like?**

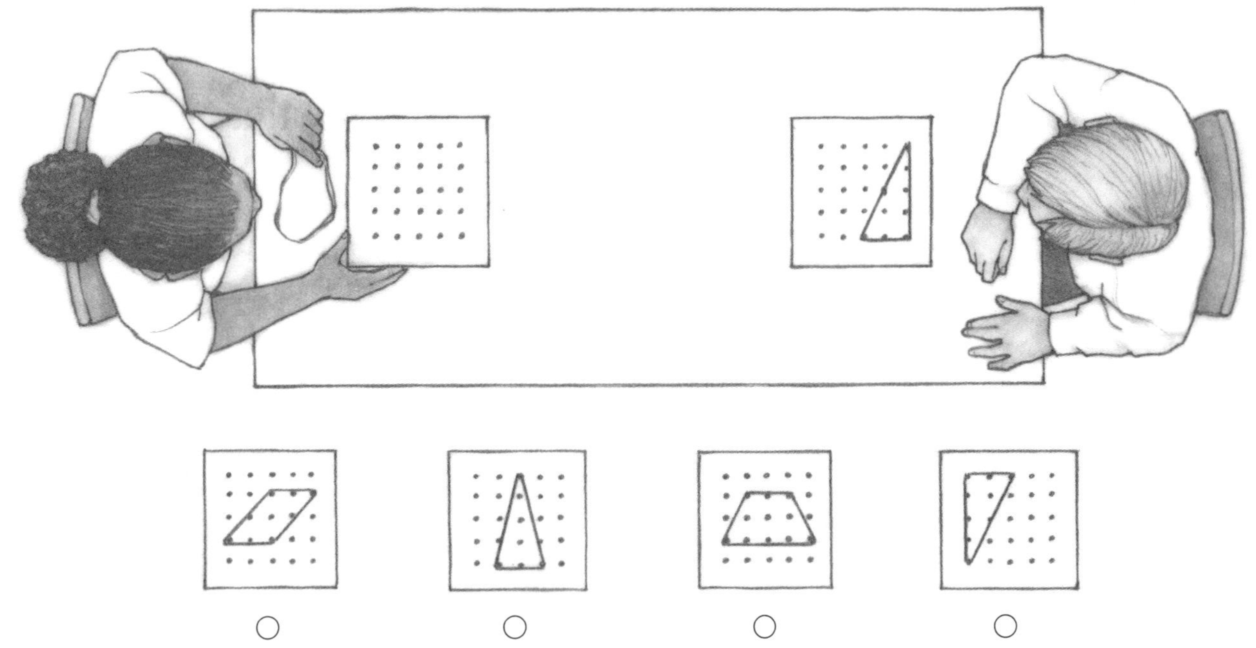

○ ○ ○ ○

GO

SUMMER
LINK

Name ______________________________

8 **Elle saw that some t-shirts on a clothes line formed a pattern. If the pattern continued, which pair of the t-shirts would come next?**

○ ○ ○ ○

9

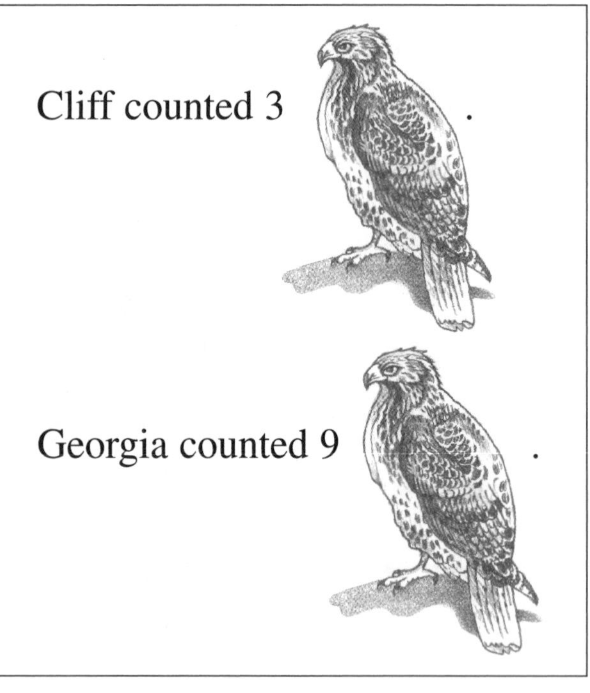
Cliff counted 3 .
Georgia counted 9 .

Cliff counted 3 hawks on bird watch day. Georgia counted 9 hawks. Which number sentence could be used to find how many hawks they counted in all?

$9 - 3 = \square$	$3 + \square = 9$	$3 + 9 = \square$	$9 - \square = 3$
○	○	○	○

STOP

Grade 2 Record Your Scores

After you have completed and checked each test, record your scores below. Do not count your answers for the sample questions or the writing pages.

Practice Test

Unit 1 Reading and Language Arts
Number of Questions: 36 Number Correct ______________

Unit 2 Basic Skills
Number of Questions: 60 Number Correct ______________

Unit 3 Mathematics
Number of Questions: 16 Number Correct ______________

Final Test

Unit 1 Reading and Language Arts
Number of Questions: 12 Number Correct ______________

Unit 2 Basic Skills
Number of Questions: 24 Number Correct ______________

Unit 3 Mathematics
Number of Questions: 9 Number Correct ______________

Grade 2 Answer Key

Page 255

A. in warm clothes
B. big tree

Page 259

1. Jared
2. is lost.
3. first picture

Page 260

4. first picture
5. Then he came home.
6. She feeds the kitten.
7. We
8. she

Page 261

A. depend on

Page 262

1. plane
2. fix belt
3. clouds
4. second picture

Page 263

5. My sister, Pat
6. fly
7. The plane rose quickly.

Page 264

8. plane
9. unfasten
10. They put clothes in a suitcase.
11. Many people come and go.
12. You need a ticket to fly in a plane.
13. This is my seat.

Page 265

Child should write a friendly letter.

Page 266

Child should write a story using a story map.

Page 267

A. gardening

Page 268

1. calm
2. really
3. pleasant.
4. sign "good-bye"
5. know more Sign Language.

Grade 2 Answer Key

Page 269

6. regular
7. makes new friends easily.
8. clown
9. try
10. reach

Page 270

11. Raj was born in India.
12. they
13. May 5, 2001
14. Dear Mom,
15. Your son,

Page 271

The paragraph should describe an animal and use the ideas written in a web.

Page 272

A. dry
1. blink
2. cold
3. hop
4. spoil
5. do not

Page 273

A. alone
B. big
1. decide
2. raise
3. discuss
4. lean
5. dirty
6. usual
7. sack
8. secret

Page 274

C. sink
9. contest
10. guess
D. fine
11. point
12. tire

Page 275

A. on monday.
1. when did
B. period
2. period
C. Nothing is in the bag.
3. She is upstairs.

Grade 2 Answer Key

Page 276

D. Jan Miller
E. Best as it is
4. January 5, 2002
5. Dear Dad,
6. With love,
7. open. When
8. Best as it is

Page 277

A. notice
1. daily
2. window
3. butter
B. All correct
4. fly a plain
5. All correct
6. hot paivment

Page 278

A. 10
1. 50
2. 51 cents
3. 47
B. 4
4. 2
5. 18 cents
6. 6

Page 279

A. crush
B. alone
1. fry
2. meet
3. they are
4. outside
5. fast
6. ed

Page 280

C. fire
7. bird
8. leaf
D. puzzle
9. sure
10. nail
11. neat
12. vegetable

Page 281

E. None
13. on thanksgiving.
14. Wilson, Pennsylvania 18302
15. Labor Day
16. doesn't

Grade 2 Answer Key

Page 282
F. beyond
17. usually
18. cloud
19. nice chare
G. 38
20. 440
21. 64
22. 38 cents
23. 15

Page 283
A. last picture

Page 284
1. 360
2. Shape 4
3. 2 + 2 + 2 + 2 =

Page 285
4. measuring cup
5. 75 cents

Page 286
6. Beth
7. 7 15 10 18
8. box
9. 9

Page 287
10. 12
11. spinner 2

Page 288
A. third picture
1. 6
2. October

Page 290
3. Bass
4. 36 oz.
5. Bluegill

Page 291
A. eat dinner

Page 292
1. to be no fun
2. riding a horse
3. blimp
4. important

Page 293
5. to land and take off
6. My sister and I fixed it.
7. overpass
8. driveway
9. stain

Grade 2 Answer Key

Page 294

10. will arrive at the station soon.
11. is in the garage
12. None

Page 295

The child should write a how-to paragraph telling what is needed and what the steps are.

Page 296

The child should write a paragraph that compares two animals or plants he or she knows a lot about.

Page 297

A. dump
B. sidewalk
1. most
2. rain
3. are not
4. footprint
5. kind
6. ful

Page 298

C. bulb
7. heal
8. message
D. thankful
9. not wide
10. treat
11. wound
12. hoped

Page 299

E. question mark
13. period
14. In June we plant our garden.
15. The bridge is high.
16. Best as it is
17. It's not

Page 300

F. Careful
18. roasted
19. lonely
20. tasty sandwhich
G. 1
21. 35
22. 34
23. 702
24. 6

Grade 2 Answer Key

Page 301

A. last box
1. 5 inches
2. Pair 4
3. 88

Page 302

4. second picture (dime)
5. 5/8

Page 303

6. 427
7. last picture

Page 304

8. first pair
9. 3 + 9 =

This page intentionally left blank.

Test Practice Worksheet

Test Practice Worksheet

Test Practice Worksheet

Test Practice Worksheet

Test Practice Worksheet

Test Practice Worksheet

Test Practice Worksheet

Test Practice Worksheet